Strangers in Many Lands

The Story of a Jewish Family
in Turbulent Times

LEON CHAMEIDES, M.D.

Designed by Dauphin Design, Wethersfield, CT

Manufactured in the United States of America

ISBN 978-0-615-61753-4

I am a part of all that I have met;

Yet all experience is an arch wherethrough

Gleams that untravelled world whose margin fades

For ever and forever when I move.

How dull it is to pause, to make an end,

To rust unburnished, not to shine in use!

— Ulysses by Alfred Lord Tennyson

———•◆•———

The past isn't dead. It isn't even past.

— William Faulkner

———•◆•———

There are stars whose radiance is visible on earth

though they have long been extinct.

There are people whose brilliance continues to light the world

though they are no longer among the living.

These lights are particularly bright when the night is dark.

They light the way for mankind.

— Hannah Senesz

———•◆•———

Life is not what one lived, but what one remembers and how

one remembers it in order to recount it.

— Gabriel Garcia Marquez

CONTENTS

———— • ◆ • ————

אלה אזכרה   *These I Remember and I*
ונפשי עלי אשפכה   *am Overwhelmed With Grief*

Dedicated to the following family members mentioned in this history who are known to have perished during the Shoah. Others, whose fate is unknown to me, were undoubtedly also victims. May their memory be an inspiration and a blessing.

Abraham Abraham
Arthur Abraham
Bruno Altmann
Hannah Königshöfer Altmann
Hermann Altmann
Suzanne Charlotte Altmann
Beno Yitzhak Dov Bamberger
Jonas Moshe Bamberger
Merle Königshöfer Bamberger
Adele Chamajdes
Isaac Chamajdes
Juda Schiff Chamajdes
Sarah Chamajdes
Bela Chameides
Benyomin Chameides
Fayvush Chameides
Freide Roth Chameides
Gertrude Chameides
Izak (Itzie) Chameides
Rabbi Kalman Chameides
Leah Chameides
Mechel Chameides
Milek Chameides
Miriam Luft Chameides
Mundek Chameides
Mundzio Chameides
Rachel Lea Chameides
Reisel Chameides and husband
Salka Chameides
Sheindl Chameides

Szulim (Shulim) Chameides
Tema Chameides
Tzipporah Betersfeld Chameides
Yankele Chameides
Villie Gluck
Benyomin Karl
Elias Karl
Mala Karl
Rivka Chameides Karl
Else Lowenstein Koenigshoefer
Esther Jacobson Koenigshoefer
Flora Koenigshoefer
Helene Tarlowski Koenigshoefer
Jakob Loeb Koenigshoefer
Joseph Heimann Koenigshoefer
Leopold Wolf Königshöfer
Naftali Koenigshoefer
Chana Lustig-Koppel
Jakov Ollech
Moses Schiff
Gustav Thalmann
Kurt Thalmann
Theodor Thalmann
Werner Thalmann
Joseph Wolf
Marianne Koenigshoefer Wolf
Chaya Zwass
Itche Zwass
Joseph Zwass

FOREWORD

———— • ◆ • ————

I never thought that my life was particularly unusual. After all, it is the only life I have known. But as I have grown older, I have come to appreciate that my life was indeed unique at least in one respect: Few children survived the *shoah*, and my generation is probably the last with any personal memory of it. Family and friends who have heard some of my history have urged me to write it down, but I resisted the temptation because I have never had an exaggerated sense of my own importance. All that changed when I started to reconstruct my family's genealogy. Suddenly, I saw myself fitting into a much larger story and how I wished I had memoirs written by my ancestors that told their story. My hope is that one or more of my descendants might someday become interested in their genealogy; this is my gift to them.

I started researching our family history approximately 20 years ago when my cousin, Dov Gilon, showed me my grandmother's birth certificate and my great-grandparents' will. These two items suddenly brought them to life and made me realize that I was a member of a family. As strange as it may seem, I had previously felt myself to be rootless and detached from any family. But here, in front of me, was my maternal grandmother's birth certificate with her date of birth and her parents' names. Despite the distance of time, I could almost feel their excitement and pride at the arrival of this new baby. My great-grandparents' will gave me a glimpse of their accomplishments and their dreams. These were augmented, when Dov's son, Gadi, kindly gave me some *machzorim* (holiday prayer books) that had belonged to my maternal grandmother, Martha. I resolved to find out more. Aunt Lotte, my mother's last surviving sibling, was still alive and when I interviewed her, she was so thrilled that I was interested in our family history that she gave me a beautifully inscribed silver Kiddush cup given to my great-grandparents, the Altmanns, in 1900. Except for my father's handkerchief and my grandmother's *machzorim*, this was the first item that had belonged to a member of my family that I could actually touch; I am most grateful to Aunt Lotte for this gift.

I found writing some parts of my personal story very painful, and I could only write these parts at night when it was dark, quiet, and I was alone. I took the opportunity during a month Jean and I spent in Tucson in February 2005 to rise at 3:00 AM and write until sunrise. Despite the pain, confronting those memories has had benefits. I was forced to revisit incidents buried within the recesses of my memory and organize them in sequential order.

Memory is fickle and deceptive. Mark Twain once said that he had such a good memory that he even remembered things that never happened. I have tried to be scrupulously honest, and, in my personal story, to report only those events I clearly remember. But events and lives do not take place in isolation. As a child, I was of course not aware of the larger geopolitical picture in which my experiences were but a small speck, but I have since remedied some of that deficiency and, in telling my story, I have tried to place my memories and my family history in a historical context. I am not, however, trained as a historian and the references are selective; this is not intended to be a complete historical review.

It is impossible to list everyone to whom I owe a debt of gratitude. First, I am indebted to my parents who gave me life, enveloped me with love in my crucial early years, had the courage to let me go at a tender age in order to save my life, and have been the stars by which I have tried to guide my life. I am indebted to Metropolitan Andrei Sheptytskyi, his brother Klement (now St. Klement), and the Studite brothers who had the courage, under penalty of death, to answer the Biblical question, "Am I my brother's keeper?" in the affirmative.

Words fail me with which to express the debt I owe to Mother Tola for teaching me how to live and for giving me the unconditional love that enabled me to gain self confidence in order to live without rancor or anger. I am deeply indebted to my wife, Jean, who normalized my life, made a loving Jewish home for us, and is my best friend. Finally, I am indebted to our children, Danny, Debbie, and David, their spouses, Rabbi David Small, and Aliza, and our grandchildren, Gabrielle, Sharone, Ilan, Nava, Maia, Tamar, and Noam, who have made it all worthwhile.

I am also indebted to many who kindly shared their family photographs, which appear in this family history. They include: Eva Alberman, Zwi Barnea, Meta and Steven Baruch, Michael Bernet and Sheila Tannenbaum, Meir Chameides, Hannah Cohn, Gabriella Fallscheer, Monica Fazio, Dov and Shirley Gilon, Charlotte Holtzmann, Miriam (Cohn) Nesher, Lily Pohlmann, Jackie Schwarz, and Naphtali Thalmann. Finally, I would like to express my gratitude to our friend, Renana Kadden, who kindly reviewed the manuscript and made many suggestions to improve it.

In October 2007, Jean and I travelled back to Lwów (now Lviv), Szczerzec (now Shchirets), and the monastery in Univ. I didn't want to undertake such a trip until I had finished a draft of my memoirs because I did not want the current reality to influence my memories. I very much wanted my brother, Zwi to join me. His memories would have been invaluable, but he decided that he was not ready to do so. I was thrilled when our youngest son, David, asked if he could come and film the visit. His presence and questions added a dimension I could not otherwise have experienced and I am grateful to him. I have added my impressions of that visit in the appropriate places in italics so they would be clearly separated from my memories.

Place names have changed with the ruling regime. For example, it was Lemberg under the Austrians, Lwów under the Poles, Lemberg under the Germans, Lvov under the Russians, and now Lviv under the Ukrainians. Whenever possible, I have tried to use the geographic name that was current in the appropriate year. Family and place names originally written in the Cyrillic alphabet have been variously transcribed into Latin characters; I have tried to use the English phonetic transliteration. German letters with an umlaut can also be written as _e (e.g. Königshöfer and Koenigshoefer; Fürth and Fuerth; I have used both forms interchangeably.

The appendices contain descendant tables. These are organized as follows: "1" identifies the primary person; the + sign refers to his/her spouse; "2" refers to their children; "3" to their grandchildren; "4" to their great grandchildren, etc. I struggled with these appendices since I wanted them to be informative, but I also wanted to respect the privacy of the living. I tried deleting dates of birth of the living, but found that the remaining information was not in context without them. I hope that the individuals mentioned will appreciate my dilemma and forgive any indiscretions. Following the descendant tables are selective notes. Each individual in every table has a story but, unfortunately, I don't know it. I have included those few facts that I have heard or read. In general, I have not included notes on individuals discussed within the body of the text.

I

THE STUDENT RABBI

———— •◆• ————

The only synagogue in Katowice, a city in Southwestern Poland, was almost filled to capacity on the holiday of *Sukkot* in autumn of 1928. The sanctuary was large and could accommodate 1,184 worshippers, 670 men downstairs and 514 women in the balcony. Chandeliers illuminated the plush red seats and made the marble *bima* and *aron* sparkle. Many of the worshippers held a *lulav* and *etrog*, lending the large and imposing sanctuary a festive and joyous mood. All eyes were on the 26-year-old student-rabbi. He was of medium height, wore spectacles, and was balding despite his youth. His red tinged beard was neatly trimmed. He had made a very favorable impression during the preceding Rosh Hashanah and Yom Kippur services, and was the main topic of conversation after services as clusters of congregants walked home together and then sat in parlors or around dining room tables. They were impressed with his oratorical skills, his command of the German language, and his ability to flawlessly interweave the classical Jewish texts with contemporary literature and issues. They made favorable comments about his well-prepared sermons, his elegant German, and the pace of his delivery,

which focused their attention. German language skills were especially important for this established and well-to-do congregation. After all, until five years ago the city was called Kattowitz and had been part of Prussia for almost 200 years. Since being incorporated into Poland, many native Jews had resettled in Germany and were replaced by poorer Yiddish-speaking Jews from the east seeking better economic opportunities in this capital city of the mining district of Silesia. But they were still considered newcomers, outsiders, not yet part of the establishment. The establishment was still made up of German Jews and the dominant language continued to be German.

The young student-rabbi's name was Kalman Chameides and he would eventually become my father. He must have felt very fortunate to have been given an opportunity at the young age of 26 to lead such a prestigious congregation during the High Holidays and the *sukkot* festival. He was well aware that the position of permanent rabbi was vacant because Rabbi Jecheskel Lewin had unexpectedly given notice just prior to the High Holy Days in order to lead a "progressive" congregation in Lwów. The community

Administration, led by Bruno Altmann, immediately turned to the Jüdisch-Theologisches Seminar (Jewish Theological Seminary) in nearby Breslau (now Wrocław) for help. It was natural for the community leaders to turn to this seminary, located in the capital city of Lower Silesia. The seminary's philosophy coincided with that of the Katowice community, and two of its four previous rabbis had been its graduates.

The young student-rabbi was flattered when his mentors at the Seminary suggested that he lead the High Holiday services for the Katowice community. He was well aware that this was a unique opportunity to become a strong candidate for the permanent position. He had already finished his studies, and he had been informed that he would receive the prestigious Rosin-Preis prize for his research into the *midrash* and Philo[1] at the rabbinical ordination, to take place on January 29, 1929. He had, in fact, already made such a good impression that Bruno Altmann, President of the Community Administration, suggested that he consider taking the position permanently. As the synagogue cantors, Walter Dembitzer and Joseph Wolkowski, led the services, he looked around at the surrounding elegance and his mind must have wandered to his family's humble beginnings and how far he had come.

Two views of the interior of the Synagogue in Katowice.

---

[1] *Bericht des Jüdisch-Theologisches Seminars für das Jahr 1928* (Breslau 1929) 4

Menorah said to be from the Katowice synagogue, currently in Chabad of Beverly Hills, CA. It was said to have been smuggled out of Poland in small pieces and then reassembled.

Stephen Lighton[2] recalled that the incident was immortalized in an amusing poem recited at a meeting of the Katowice B'nai Brith lodge:

"...ich sehe ihn in der synagogue
  am vorstand platz stehen
  und auf die profane masse heruntersehen
  doch meine lieben
  es ist keine frase
  oft verfallt er in tiefe extase
  um das werk des meisters zu loben
  hebt er die augen zum balkon nach oben"

"…Even now I see him in the synagogue
  standing behind the lectern on high
  looking down on the profane masses
    with a sigh
  but, my dear ones,
  I do not exaggerate when I note
  That when he raises his eyes
  to glorify his Master's creations,
    (in deep ecstasy and prayer of course)
  they by chance and temporarily come to
  rest on the ladies' balcony above."

The student-rabbi once again gave a fine sermon in impeccable German and the congregants were again duly impressed. A few of the more alert congregants might have noticed that from time to time the student-rabbi's eyes wondered up to the women's gallery, momentarily resting on Bruno Altmann's niece, Gertrude, or Trude, Königshöfer. She was visiting her uncle and aunt for the holiday of *Sukkot* from her home in Fürth. The student-rabbi couldn't get her out of his mind. Many years later, Dr.

The 26 year-old Kalman Chameides was appointed as Rabbi of the Katowice Jewish Community by its Administration retroactively to September 1, 1928 and a year later, on September 24, 1929, he and the 24 year-old Gertrude Königshöfer from Fürth were married at the home of Bruno Altmann.

---

[2] Dr. Lighton, practiced medicine in Katowice, survived the war and, in September 1984, was on a bus from New York to Hartford to visit his daughter, Terri Cahn, for Rosh Hashana. Our good friends, Andzia and Umek Weinfeld, were on the same bus coming to visit us. They met, found the common connection, and paid us a visit.

Gmina Izraelicka
Katowice G.-Śl.

Telefon Nr. 694

P. K. O. Katowice Nr. 302150

Konto bankowe:
Dresdner Bank, oddział Katowice

L. Dz. Ab/Sa _____ /28

Katowice, dnia 5.września 192 8r.

276

Do

Śląskiego Urzędu Wojewódzkiego

w K a t o w i c a c h.

Niniejszem pozwalamy sobie donieść, iż nasz do-
tychczasowy rabin p.Dr.Jecheskel Lewin opuszcza z dniem
jutrzejszym swe tutejsze stanowisko, przenosząc się do Lwowa.

Ze względu na wzmagający się przyrost ludności
żydowskiej w Katowicach a tem samem niemożność zaspokojenia
wszystkich czynności rabinatu przez jednego duchownego, po-
stanowiły korporacje Gminy przywrócić istniejący tutaj stan
z przed wojny t.j.zaangażować dwóch rabinów. W wykonaniu po-
wyższego postanowienia zaangażowały korporacje Gminy p.rabi-
na Kalmana C h a m e i d e s a z Szczerca koło Lwowa, który
też objął z dniem 1.września br.funkcje rabinackie w tut.
Gminie. Co do drugiego rabina, to toczą się rokowania z kil-
koma rabinami i mamy nadzieję, że już w najbliższym czasie
zostanie to stanowisko obsadzone przez jednego z tych kan-
dydatów.

Prosząc o przyjęcie nominacji p.rabina Chameidesa
do łask.wiadomości, kreślimy się

z poważaniem
Zwierzchność
Gminy Izraelickiej-Katowice.

*Letter from the Jewish community of Katowice to the Silesian Government informing them that, due to an increase in
the Jewish population, they plan to hire two Rabbis and requesting the Silesian Government to approve the first, Rabbi
Kalman Chameides.*

II

THE ALTMANN FAMILY

—•◆•—

At the time of my parents' wedding, fifty-five-year-old Bruno Altmann (1874-1943) was a successful business-man, owner of the firm established by his father, and a highly respected member of the Katowice Jewish community. He learned his business acumen as well as his dedication to serve the community from his parents, Leopold (1841-1917) and Charlotte (1838-1905) Altmann. Leopold (Hebrew name Yehudah) and Charlotte (Hebrew name Sarah) moved to Kattowitz shortly after their marriage in 1865. Leopold was born in nearby Rybnik to parents from Rzuchów*; Charlotte Timmendorfer was born in nearby Sohrau (now Żory).

* There are several towns and villages with this name in Poland. They most likely lived in a village located halfway between Rybnik and Ratibor. Other possibilities include: Rzóchow, a village near Mielec in Rzeszow voivodship; Rzuchowa, a village near Tarnow; a village near Ostrowiec Swietokrzyski; or a village near Kolo in Eastern Wielkopolska.

Ancestors of Leopold Altmann

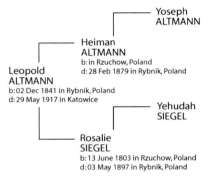

Leopold ALTMANN
b: 02 Dec 1841 in Rybnik, Poland
d: 29 May 1917 in Katowice

Heiman ALTMANN
b: in Rzuchow, Poland
d: 28 Feb 1879 in Rybnik, Poland

Yoseph ALTMANN

Rosalie SIEGEL
b: 13 June 1803 in Rzuchow, Poland
d: 03 May 1897 in Rybnik, Poland

Yehudah SIEGEL

Ancestors of Charlotte Timmendorfer

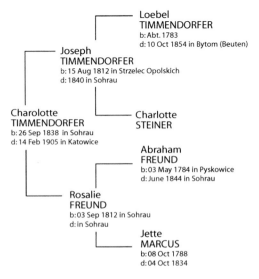

Charolotte TIMMENDORFER
b: 26 Sep 1838 in Sohrau
d: 14 Feb 1905 in Katowice

Joseph TIMMENDORFER
b: 15 Aug 1812 in Strzelec Opolskich
d: 1840 in Sohrau

Loebel TIMMENDORFER
b: Abt. 1783
d: 10 Oct 1854 in Bytom (Beuten)

Charlotte STEINER

Rosalie FREUND
b: 03 Sep 1812 in Sohrau
d: in Sohrau

Abraham FREUND
b: 03 May 1784 in Pyskowice
d: June 1844 in Sohrau

Jette MARCUS
b: 08 Oct 1788
d: 04 Oct 1834

1871 Map of Prussian Silesia. Insert shows the relationship of Fürth (next to Nürnberg) and Kattowitz (arrow) in Silesia. Rybnik, Sohrau, and Kattowitz were in the Oppeln District of Silesia (see next map).

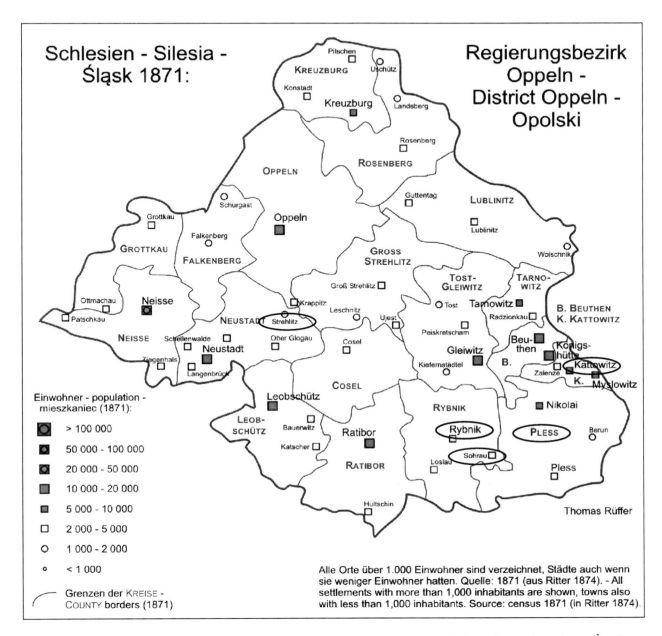

1871 Map of the District of Oppeln in Prussian Silesia. Note the towns of Rybnik in the south, Sohrau (Żory) just below it, and Gross Strehlitz (Strzelce Opolskie) – birthplace of Joseph Timmendorfer, and their proximity to Kattowitz. Note also the towns of Myslowitz (later Mysłowice) about 3 miles to the southeast and Beuthen (later Bytom) about 5 miles northwest of Kattowitz. After the third partition in 1795, when Poland disappeared from the map of Europe, Myslowitz was known as Dreikaisereck (Three Emperors' Corner), the meeting point of the German Empire to the north and west, the Russian Empire to the north and east, and the Austrian Empire to the south. From 1795 to 1918 Kattowitz was therefore a border town. After WW I, when Upper Silesia was divided between Germany and Poland, Kattowitz (Katowice) became part of Poland and Beuthen remained in Germany.

Rybnik, Sohrau, and Kattowitz are all located in Silesia, today the southwestern district of Poland. Slavs and Germans have inhabited Silesia throughout its history and evidence of this can be found in the Silesian dialect, a combination of Polish and German that is still spoken by some village inhabitants. Tension, which had existed between these two culturally and linguistically separate populations throughout Silesian history, erupted into the open after WW I.

Silesia was divided in 1163 into Lower Silesia in the North and Upper Silesia in the South,[3] each ruled by a Polish prince from the Piast dynasty. The Piast rulers encouraged German immigration in order to increase agricultural productivity and develop the mining and textile industries. When Austrian archduke Ferdinand acceded to the Bohemian throne in 1526, Silesia became part of Bohemia and then part of the Austrian Habsburg Empire. Frederick the Great of Prussia conquered most of Silesia during the War of Austrian Succession (1740-1748) in 1742 and it remained part of Prussia, later Germany, until the end of WW I.

The earliest documented evidence of Jewish settlement in Silesia is from the 11th and 12th centuries when Jews fled from persecution by the Crusades and settled in the vicinity of Breslau (Wrocław) in Lower Silesia and in a number of villages in Upper Silesia.[4] Renewed persecu-

tions during the Great Plague of 1349 once again forced Jews to flee the German states to Silesia, where conditions were more favorable. But persecutions, stimulated by economic competition and fanned by the wondering preacher Johannes von Capestrano, known as "the whip of the Hebrews," followed the Jews into Silesia. These culminated in 1582 with a royal decree issued by Rudolph II, expelling Jews from Upper Silesia. By 1600 only 120 Jews remained there, mainly in Glogau and Zülz (now Biała Prudnicka), when the community leaders received special permission for Jews to remain because of their vital role in the community's economic life.[5] After the Thirty Years' War (1618-1648), Jews were allowed to return to Silesia in order to help rebuild that devastated area. Later, Silesia became a haven for Jews fleeing Poland, which, through much of the 17th century, was involved in wars with Cossacks, Swedes, Russians, and Turks, each inflicting heavy casualties and untold suffering on the Jews caught in the middle. Anti-Jewish agitation and persecution reached their peak with the Chmielnicki massacres in 1648. The refugees fleeing these massacres established a number of new Jewish communities in Silesia, including Myslowitz (1628), Neisse (1634), Teschen (1637), Pless (1640), Oppeln (1648), Beuthen (1656), Bielitz (1664), Brankiewitz (1674), Nikolai (1674),

---

3   "Lower" and "upper" refers to the Oder River, which originates in the mountains of the south and flows northward to the Baltic sea.
4   N. Bałaban, *Kiedy i skąd przybyli Żydzi do Polski* (Warsaw 1931) 10.
5   I. Rabin, "Vom Rechtskampf der Juden in Schlesien 1582-1712," in *Wissenschaftliche Beilage zu den Jahresberichten des Jüdisch-Theologischen Seminars fur das Jahr 1926* (Breslau 1927).

Wartenberg (1676), Namslau (1683), and Oberglogau (1694).

When Prussia annexed Silesia in 1742, it was home to about 1000 Jewish families. This number increased with an influx of Jews from nearby Bohemia where the Austrian Empress Maria Theresa, like her father before her, tried to restrict Jewish residence. In 1744 she accused Jews of supporting the Prussians in the Silesian war and sought to expel them. Many of the fleeing Jews probably settled in the border towns, such as Sohrau where some Jews had resided since the 16th century. There were 121 Jews in Sohrau in 1784 and by 1856 that number had increased to 471. It is unclear when the first synagogue was built, but a wooden structure was completely destroyed, along with 150 houses, in a disastrous fire on Shabbat morning, August 15, 1807.[6] A massive new stone synagogue was built in 1830 and dedicated in 1835. Rabbi Abraham Freund (1784-1844), Charlotte Altmann's grandfather, was appointed as the first rabbi of Sohrau in 1828. Charlotte's married name, Timmendorfer, was likely the name of a nearby locality where the family lived when they adopted or were given a surname.[7]

Kattowitz was a conglomeration of villages until 1865 when it received a Royal Charter to become a city. This followed several years of tension between German and Jewish residents who were united in favor of such a charter and Polish peasants, the "Gromada," who opposed them. The first Jewish family settled in the area in 1825 and by the time the Altmann newlyweds arrived, Kattowitz had a Jewish population of 624. Despite their small number, the Jewish contribution proved critical as Kattowitz progressed from village to city to regional capital. Evidence of their importance, despite their small number (12% of the population) can be seen from the fact that in the first municipal elections (March and April, 1866), Jews won half the seats (9 of 18) on the Municipal Council.

Its economic potential made a move to Kattowitz desirable, but it was Dr. Richard Holtze, one of the city's early and dynamic leaders, who made the young married couple's move to Kattowitz possible. In contrast to most in his position, Dr. Holtze nurtured a relationship with anyone who might be of benefit to the city without national or religious prejudice. He was successful in repealing the restrictive anti-Jewish laws of 1597 (Privilegium de non tolerandis Judaeis) and the royal decree of August 3, 1781 both of which limited the number of Jewish merchants and artisans, laws still being enforced in other Prussian cities.

The economic potential of Kattowitz was due to the discovery of lead, zinc, and especially coal in its vicinity. During much of the 19th century, coal provided the

---

[6] Jan Delowicz, *Gmina Wyznania Mojzeszowego w Żorach 1511-1940* (Towarzystwo Miłośników Miasta Żory 2002).

[7] "Dorf" means village in German and "dorfer" is the suffix for someone from a village. Timmendorfer would therefore suggest the name for a family who moved from Timmendorf. Timmendorf is a village (now known as Szeroka) and now part of Jastrzębie Zdrój just south of Rybnik almost on the Czech border.

energy that heated homes and the power that moved engines. Coal fueled the industrial revolution. It provided the power to mass-produce goods, and to move them efficiently by land and sea. The coal mines of Upper Silesia supplied much of the coal for energy-starved Europe, and provided an incentive for the rapid growth of the region. The first steam railroad in Prussia started operating in 1835 between Nürnberg and Fürth, and by 1847 the first train arrived in Kattowitz, which would eventually become a major east-west railroad junction. It should be remembered that during the 19th and the beginning of the 20th century (1795-1918), Kattowitz bordered two powerful empires, Austria to the south, and Russia to the east just beyond Myslowitz.

Leopold Altmann opened a hardware and engineering supplies store in 1865 at Rynek 11 (now ul. Warszawska) in the center of Kattowitz. The official name/description of the store was: "L. Altmann, en gros – en detail: Werkzeuge und Bedarfsartikel für Gruben, Hütten, Maschinenwerkstätten und elektrische Anlagen. Gas-, Wasserleitungs- und Kanalisationsgegenstände, Eisen, Bleche, Träger, sämtliche Baubedarfsartikel, Spezialgeschäft für Baubeschläge, Magazin für Haus – und Küchengeräte. Kattowitz O.S."[8] [L. Altmann, wholesale and retail: Tools and essential supplies for mines, foundries, machine shops, and electric installations. Gas, water, and drainage pipes. Iron, sheet metal, carriers, complete line of building materials; specialty store for metal fittings

Leopold and Charlotte Altmann, my great-grandparents. The photo of Charlotte on the right was taken in 1887 when she was 49 years of age.

---

[8]   F. Weiß, *Wirtschaftlicher Heimatführer für Schlesien* (Breslau 1920) 55.

for construction; storehouse for home and kitchen appliances. Kattowitz, Upper Silesia]. He came to the right place at the right time and the business flourished along with the town. Judging from tax records, by 1928 the Altmanns were among the 1.6% richest families in Kattowitz.[9]

Postcard of Warszawska Street in the 1940s. Note the Altmann sign on the storefront.

Its strategic location between east and west, excellent accessibility via railroad, and abundant hotel space, made Kattowitz a site for important international conferences. Leo Pinsker founded the Chovvei Zion, forerunner of the Zionist Organization, there in 1884. The Agudath Yisrael party was established there in 1912, and, in March 1933, the World Council of Zionist Revisionists had their fateful meeting in Katowice at which a split occurred and Zeev Jabotinsky took his faction out of the World Zionist Organization.

Leopold and Charlotte Altmann established a traditional Jewish home in a spacious apartment above their store.

Their home became a well-known stop for Orthodox Jews. Here, they would be assured warm hospitality and food whose *kashrut* was unquestioned. There were many such guests because, as a major east-west rail junction, all travelers going westward from Russia and Poland had to pass through Kattowitz. When the number became a flood as a result of the Czar's pogroms in the 1880s, the Jewish community organized a committee of women who met each train and helped the many transients with food and encouragement. The Altmanns had a proud middle class German home. German was the spoken language, German literature was read to the children, and the Altmann daughters (my grandmother Martha and her sister Getrud) were taught piano and an appreciation for the arts. Like many Jewish families in German-speaking lands, the Altmanns were culturally, but not religiously, assimilated and they strictly adhered to their Orthodox Jewish values and practice.

The Prussian law of July 23 1847 granted Jews theoretical equality with Christians except in certain professions. For example, Jews could not become deputies in the Diets or serve as judges or administrative officers. In the universities, Jews were allowed to teach languages, mathematics, and natural sciences but could not become members of the university senate or serve as deans. This law also required Jews to be organized in each town as a religious community (Synagongemeinde) and gave Jews

---

[9] Wojciech Jaworski, *Ludność żydowska w wojewodzie śląskim w latach 1928-1939* (Śląsk 1997) 60.

the right to elect their own representatives and officers. Each community had to be financially independent, subject to governmental control. The government pledged itself not to interfere in the communities' internal affairs and in religious matters. Fifty-five such synagogue communities were created in Silesia (10 in the administrative area of Breslau, 7 in the Liegnitz area, and 38 in the district of Oppeln.) The synagogue communities in Upper Silesia merged in 1888, and those in Lower Silesia in 1897. Interestingly, the 1847 law continued to be the basis of Jewish organizational life even after the area was annexed to Poland in 1918.

The Prussian regional district seat in Oppeln recognized Kattowitz as a separate Synagogengemeinde on April 4, 1862 although it did not become self-governing with its own elected representative organization until 1866, when the government approved its by-laws. Through these by-laws, the Jewish community obligated itself to pay for the establishment of institutions for its social and religious needs (Article 58). These included care of the poor and sick (Article 59), religious education of the young (Articles 60-67), and for burial of the dead (Article 58). To cover expenses, the community was authorized to levy and collect taxes, a function enforced, if necessary, by the civil authorities. These by-laws also called for a representative form of government with an elected (by men only) Assembly of Representatives, and an Administration elected by these represen-

tatives. Leopold Altmann became an elected representative in 1872.[10] At first, a Jew could only leave the community Synagogengemeinde through baptism and by joining another recognized community, but the Law of July 28, 1876 made it legal to leave one community without necessarily joining another.

The Kattowitz community dedicated its first synagogue on September 4, 1862, a *mikvah* (ritual bath) in 1867, and a cemetery in 1869. Until these facilities were functional, the Kattowitz community used the religious facilities of the nearby Synagogengemeinde of Myslowitz. For example, Leopold and Charlotte Altmann's first-born son, Albert, died in infancy before 1869 and was therefore buried in the Myslowitz Jewish cemetery. The community's first social organization, founded in December 1863, was a Chevrath Nashim (Women's Organization) whose purpose was to perform acts of charity. In 1891, its listed activities included: Support for poor women, girls, widows, and orphans; support for poor pregnant women; dowries for poor brides; and sewing shrouds and performing Taharah (ritual washing and shrouding) for deceased women. Charlotte Altmann became one of the early leaders of this organization. Another important community organization of which Leopold Altmann was a proud leader and driving force was the Chevra Kadisha and Bikur Cholim (Society for Burial and Aid to the Sick). It was founded in October 1868 to "visit the

---

[10]   Jacob Cohn, *Geschichte der Synagogen-Gemeinde Kattowitz* (O.S. 1900).

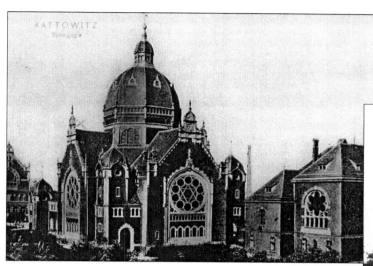

Katowice Synagogue (above), dedicated in 1900 and destroyed (right) by the Germans on September 4, 1939.

sick, provide medications and nursing care for the poor, not to abandon the dying in their last hours; and if death comes, to perform the necessary Jewish ceremonials and burial." The community was especially proud of its burial practices, whose cost was part of the community budget and was not borne by the individual families. This avoided the unseemly haggling that often took place in other communities where burials were an important budgetary source. The society hired a nurse and eventually also a physician. It cared for poor transients, who became especially numerous in the 1880s with the westward flight of Jews from the pogroms of Tsarist Russia, during WW I (1914-1918), the economic depression of the 1920s and 1930s, and in the years preceding WW II, with the flight and the expulsion of formerly Polish Jews from Germany.

The Jewish community of Kattowitz grew rapidly but always remained a small proportion of the general population. The latter grew from 14,000 in 1888 to 130,645 in 1930 while the growth of the Jewish population can be seen in the following chart.[11]

In 1939 Katowice had a Jewish population of 8,327, which constituted 6.2% of the total.[12]

The synagogue, built in 1862, was enlarged in 1883, but the growth of the community forced it to draw up plans for a new facility. The gov-

Year	No. of Jews
1840	12
1844	17
1855	105
1867	624
1870	812
1895	1600
1899	2126
1910	2979
1932	9000

[11] Adapted from Cohn.
[12] Jaworski 35.

ernment approved the project on July 14, 1897. It included a synagogue, an adjoining administrative building with a slaughter house for fowl, a kosher butcher shop, study rooms, apartments for the sexton and janitor, a sausage factory, and a matzo bakery. Land was purchased from the city, and a sum of 400,000 marks was budgeted for the project (the cost eventually exceeded 500,000 marks.) Built by the architectural firm of Ignatz Grünfeld in a Renaissance style with echoes of late gothic, the dome of the synagogue dominated the Kattowitz skyline. It was a short walk from the Altmann residence. One crossed the street (now Warszawska) at the beautiful Greek revival theater, crossed the many lanes of the Rynek, and headed into one of its main thoroughfares, August-

Photo of the Altmann children probably taken in 1886-7. Left-to-right: Gertrude (b 1872), Bruno (b 1874), Martha (b 1876), and Gottfried (b 1878).

Schneider-Strasse (now ulica Kościuszko.) The beautiful new synagogue, in which the young student-rabbi Kalman Chameides would lead High Holiday services in 1928, was dedicated on September 12, 1900. On September 4, 1939 the Germans would pack it with dynamite and destroy it.

After settling in Kattowitz, the Altmann family grew in prosperity, community influence, and number. In addition to Albert, who died in early infancy, Charlotte and Leopold had nine children:

- Josef Georg (circa 1868 – 1934), {App. 1}
- Ismar Max (circa 1869 - 1945), {App. 2}
- Hermann (circa 1870 - 1934), {App. 3}
- Artur (1871 - 1938), {App. 4}
- Gertrud (1871 - 1938), {App. 5}
- Bruno (1874 - circa 1943), {App. 6}
- Martha (1876 - 1950), {App. 7}
- Gottfried (1878 - 1938), {App. 8}
- Robert (circa 1878 - 1937), {App. 9}

In November 1898, Leopold and Charlotte wrote a will, which gave evidence of their material well-being and their philosophy of life. It divided their considerable estate very exactly among the children. It also provides for the care of a number of surviving elderly relatives, for charitable annuities to the Kattowitz synagogue "as long as it remains orthodox," to the Society for Burial and Aid to the Sick, to the Women's Organization, and to the synagogues of Sohrau, Rybnik, Myslowitz, and Ratibor. Money was also

My grandmother's birth certificate.

wish that their son, Robert, who at the time was studying in Frankfurt/Main, should consider becoming an orthodox Rabbi, "if he has the talent," or choose an academic profession, which would allow him to properly observe the Sabbath and religious holiday laws.

Tragedy befell the Altmann family in 1905 (Adar 9, 5665), when Charlotte died of intestinal cancer. She was buried in the Kattowitz cemetery. In the course of the next few years, many grandchildren were named in her memory. The story is told that the town clerk suggested a stop to this practice when two baby girls were named Charlotte on the same day.[13] After his wife's death, Leopold wrote to his daughter, Martha, my grandmother in Fürth, and advised her that if she did not move to Kattowitz with her family to take care of him, he would remarry;[14] apparently, he did not wish to live with his daughters-in-law. Since grandmother did not move, Leopold married Fanny Glueckstadt. He died in 1917 (Sivan 4, 5677) at the age of 76 and was buried next to his first wife in the Katowice Jewish cemetery.

World War I ended on November 11, 1918 with Germany's defeat. One result of the Treaty of Versailles was the re-creation, after 130 years, of an independent Polish state. Lower Silesia was given to Germany, but the Allies could not agree on what to do with Upper Silesia, especially with its industrial triangle, so rich in natural resources. The compromise

left to the Kattowitz municipality to be used for care of the needy, and a sum was to be distributed among all the employees of the business on the day of the funeral. It stipulates that as long as the business bears the Altmann name, it must adhere to a strict moral and ethical code, and must be closed on Sabbaths and all Jewish holidays. The will also expressed their

13 Charlotte Holtzmann, Personal communication.
14 Charlotte Holtzmann, Personal communication.

Tombstones of Charlotte and Leopold Altmann in the Katowice Jewish cemetery.

was to hold a plebiscite under the auspices of a special commission and, in the meantime, to place it under the jurisdiction of the League of Nations. The plebiscite campaign divided the population into propaganda war camps ("Abstimmungskampf") and the rivalry between the two groups was nasty and often violent. Poles accused Germans of importing voters, and Germans accused French troops of not controlling Polish rabble rousers. Most Jewish residents supported Germany, and therefore incurred a double wrath of the Poles, as Jews and as German sympathizers. A Polish uprising in August 1919 had to be militarily suppressed. A second Polish uprising took place in August 1920. The plebiscite, held on March 20, 1921 showed that a narrow majority of the population (50.4%) wished to remain part of Germany. A third Polish uprising in August 1921, however, convinced the Allies to have the League of Nations deal with the problem. The League of Nations decided to divide Upper Silesia, giving about 70% of the land to Germany, but rewarding Poland with practically all the coal mines, ore reserves, and industrial sectors including Kattowitz, which was renamed Katowice. The treaty, with which neither the Poles nor the Germans were happy, was signed on May 15, 1922. Most Germanophiles, including many Jews, promptly left and resettled in Germany. Out of a Silesian Jewish population of approximately 10,000 about 8,000 left during the years 1922-1924.[15] By 1927, the number of Jews in the Polish section of Upper Silesia had declined by 50%.[16] The Altmann family was no exception and only two of Leopold and Charlotte's children, Bruno and Hermann, remained in Katowice. Over the ensuing decade the Jewish community grew once again as Jews from Eastern

---

[15] Jaworski 147.
[16] S. Reis, "Die Juden in Oberschlesien," in *Die Provinz Oberschlesien* 3, 1928 578.

Poland, especially from Galicia and Posen migrated to Silesia seeking better opportunities during the economic crisis of the late 1920s and 1930s.

BRUNO ALTMANN

Bruno Altmann lived at Rynek (now Warszawska) 11 in apartment #3 and his brother Hermann lived in apartment #4 of the house previously owned by their father, Leopold. Bruno took over the mantle of leadership from his father in both business and community affairs. He became a member of the community's Administration in 1919 and President of the Administration in 1921, a position he held until the outbreak of WW II in 1939. It took a great deal of skill and diplomacy to keep the community together as it changed with the influx of Polish Jews who spoke a different language and maintained different customs. He was considered a fair and wise administrator who was able to rise above party

squabbles and personality issues and always tried to do what was in the best interests of the community.[17] He also had the confidence of the Polish authorities who wanted to "Polonize" the area as rapidly as possible and were suspicious of "Germanophiles." An example of this occurred in the Jewish community elections of 1932. Election results had to be approved by the Governor (Wojewoda) of Silesia before they could become official. On this occasion, the Governor apparently felt that the elected Administration was too "German." The election was therefore nullified and the Governor appointed a new administration headed by Bruno Altmann.[18] The latter, in turn, dissolved the Assembly and appointed new members.

Bruno Altmann married Jette (Jettchen) Königshöfer in 1906 when he was 32 years of age and his bride was 24. They had two children, Jonas and Charlotte (see Appendix 6). Tragically, Jette died on their sixth wedding anniversary (12 Jan 1912 - 22 Teveth 5672) and is buried in the Katowice Jewish cemetery. The cause of death is not certain but likely occurred during childbirth, a not uncommon event in those days. A little over three months after her death, Bruno married Jette's younger sister, Hannah Königshöfer with whom he had three children, Norbert, Leopold, and Manfred. These two marriages were not the only bond between the Altmann and the Königshöfer families. In 1899, Bruno's

Altmann family gathering, probably around 1919.

---

[17] *Urzędowa Gazeta Gminy Izraelickiej w Katowicach* (GGGIK) #57 1934 1.
[18] Jaworski 111.

sister, Martha, my grandmother, had married Izak, brother of Jette and Hanna, and it was their daughter, Gertrude, who visited her uncle, Bruno, for the Sukkoth holiday in 1928, met the young Rabbi Kalman Chameides, and eventually became my mother.

The last we know of Bruno and Hannah Altmann is that they were in the Warsaw ghetto and, according to a Red Cross report, were killed during the 1943 ghetto uprising.

Leopold Altmann (extreme right) with his second wife, Fannie Gluckstadt in 1913. Others are unidentified but the three gentlemen in the center are undoubtedly his sons.

Wedding of Lotte Altmann (Bruno's daughter) to Adolph Felsenstein – 1927 or 1928. Sitting on floor are Lotte's half brothers Manfred (right) and either Norbert or Leopold (left). To the left of bride are Bruno and Hannah Altmann, Fannie Gluckstadt, and unknown. To the right of the groom are his parents, Rosa and Hermann Felsenstein, Rosa Altmann, and Hermann Altmann. Second row right-to-left are: Gottfried Altmann (with pointy beard), Trude Koenigshoefer (later Chameides), Frieda Altmann (wife of Gottfried), Jonas Altmann (Bruno's son), Meta Altmann (later Baruch – Artur's daughter), unknown, Herbert Altmann (son of Robert), Lisl Lotte Altmann (daughter of Joseph Georg), unknown, unknown, Martha Koenigshoefer, Izak Koenigshoefer, Joseph Georg Altmann, Max Heinemann (with beard), Gertrud Altmann Heinemann. Therese Altmann is in 3rd row behind Joseph Georg Altmann.

III

THE KÖNIGSHÖFER FAMILY

The name Königshöfer suggests that the family originated in a town called Königshof (the king's courtyard). In fact, three such towns exist in Germany (Bad Königshöfen, Gau Königshöfen, and Lauda-Königshöfen) but I have been unable, thus far, to trace the family to these locations. The name became infamous for a brief period when Menachem Begin, former head of the Irgun and later Prime Minister of Israel, hid under the alias of Yonah Koenigshoefer[19] to avoid arrest by the British in Mandatory Palestine. A passport belonging to one of the grandsons of Jonas K. {Appendix 13} was said to have been found by chance in a library, although I cannot imagine that a scion of such a "yekke" family misplaced his passport.[20]

Emanuel Loeb (also known as Menachem Ari Mendel) appears to have been the first to bear the name Königshöfer,[21] which was either chosen by him or given to him in 1826 as part of the enforcement of the Bavarian "Judenedikt" of 1813, which required Jews to adopt last names.

EMANUEL LÖB KÖNIGSHÖFER (1806-1878)

Emanuel Löb Königshöfer also known as Menachem Ari Mendel.

Emanuel Loeb's parents were Jette (1785-1854) and Jonas Maennlein from Ermreuth. Maennlein was probably a "kinnui" or common name for Menachem rather than a last name since last names were not yet required.

There is evidence that Jonas Maennlein was the son of Menachem Mendel Maennlein and Frumet who lived in the early part of the 18th century. Jonas died on December 2, 1815 and Emanuel Loeb (also known as Menachem Ari Mendel) was adopted by his stepfather, Jonas Loeb Obendorfer (1776-1885)[22] when he married Jette. Jonas was a merchant and, in his later years, also a cantor ("vorbeter"). Marrying Jette provided Jonas Loeb

---

19 Menachem Begin, *The Revolt* (Steimatzky Tel Aviv 1977) 128.
20 The term "yekke" was applied to refugees to Palestine from Germany because of their formality and organization. They reputedly wore a jacket (hence "yekke") and tie even in the hot Mediterranean climate.
21 Records of the Church of Latter Day Saints (film #1334620 entry 2051).
22 Central Archives for Jewish History Jerusalem.

Obendorfer with a protection document (Schutzjude), which his new wife appears to have inherited.

Emanuel Loeb was born in Ermreuth, a small town in Upper Franconia between Erlangen and Schnaittach. For a time he probably attended the yeshiva in Fürth[23], which was closed in 1830, and he became a protégé, and later a close friend, of Rabbi Yitzhak Seligman-Baer Bamberger, the "Würzburger Rav." Around 1833, he became religious teacher for the Jewish communities of Welbhausen and Uffenheim in Middle Franconia for which he received a salary of 150 fl and an additional 22 fl for housing in the synagogue building #15.[24] A Synagogue had been established in Welbhausen in 1768.[25] Before 1838 and again after 1880, Welbhausen was part of the Ansbach Jewish community. Until late in the 19th century the number of Jews permitted to live in cities was limited and Jews were therefore forced to settle in such small, isolated communities. When the restrictive laws were relaxed, Jews migrated from these scattered communities to the larger cities. Welbhausen was no exception. In 1808 Welbhausen had 68 full legal citizen residents (Buerger) and 36 Jewish families (181 people) who were considered partial citizens. The number of Jews in Welbhausen gradually declined until 1900 when, after 400 years, the Jewish community ceased to exist.

Ancestors of Emanuel Mendel Loeb Koenigshoefer

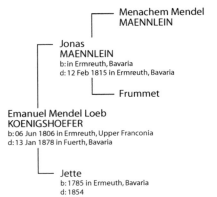

Menachem Mendel MAENNLEIN

Jonas MAENNLEIN
b: in Ermreuth, Bavaria
d: 12 Feb 1815 in Ermreuth, Bavaria

Frummet

Emanuel Mendel Loeb KOENIGSHOEFER
b: 06 Jun 1806 in Ermreuth, Upper Franconia
d: 13 Jan 1878 in Fuerth, Bavaria

Jette
b: 1785 in Ermeuth, Bavaria
d: 1854

Tombstone of Jonas Maennlein. The central inscription: Ish Tam veYashar (an upright and honest man) keMar Jonah bar Menachem meErmreuth (like Mr. Jonas son of Menachem from Ermreuth). Around the perimeter: "Died on the holy Sabbath, and was buried on 2 Adar I, 575."

---

23 According to the 1815 Ermreuth Judenmatrikel, he was pursuing language studies in Fuerth ("treibt Sprachenstudium in Fuerth") a code for Yeshiva studies.

24 Karl Ernst Stimpfig, *Die Juden in Ermetzhofen, Welbhausen, Gnostadt, und Uffenheim* (Druckeriei Sigfried Klein).

25 The huppah stone (cornerstone) is dated 1763; it is likely that the synagogue was a "house of worship" between 1763 and 1768 since the Judenedikt required a minimum of 50 Jews for the establishment of a synagogue.

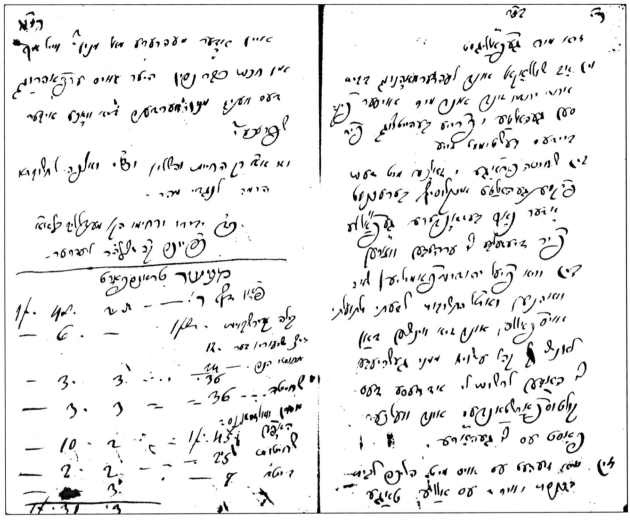

Pages 101-102 of the diary. The lower part of the left page is labeled "Tithes" and appears to be a list of contributions.

Emanuel Mendel K. married Merle Miriam Suggenheimer from Theilheim, Bavaria {Appendix 10} with whom he had five children: Babette (Bella) (b 1836), Fratel (1939-1940), Moses Jonas (1840-1894), Samuel (1843-1915) {Appendix 16}, and Jette (1847-1928). After his wife's death on July 25, 1847, Emanuel Mendel married Jeanette Mork (1811-1905) from Euerbach. They had no children.

Emanuel K. started keeping a diary about 1858. It is in German/Yiddish written in difficult-to-read Hebrew letters and appears to consist of appointments and insights rather than events. The 354 page dairy was last in the possession of Mordechai Kohn in Germany. To my knowledge, it has not been transcribed, studied, or translated.

The restrictive Judenedikt of 1813 required Jews to register with the government and limited the number of Jews allowed to live in Bavarian communities to a predetermined number. Each Jew had to obtain a "metrikel" number, which could be transferred only to the first-born son after the "metrikel" holder's death. A "metrikel" number was also required in order to be allowed to marry, so first-born sons had to wait until their father's death in order to get married. Younger sons were not allowed to settle in the community at all, accounting in part, for the large emigration of Bavarian Jews to the United States in the early part of the 19th century. In keeping with government plans, the Jewish population of Bavaria declined from its peak of 60,000 in 1848 to 54,000 in 1857. The "metrikel" system was liberalized in 1861, which allowed Emanuel Mendel K. and his wife to move to Fürth in 1875 to be closer to their son, Moses Jonas. Emanuel K. died there two years later, on January 13, 1878 (3 Heshvan); his wife died on May 19, 1905 (Iyar 10).

Emanuel Menachem Loeb must have been a remarkable personality because the following obituary appeared in a German-Jewish newspaper shortly after his death:

Permit me, dear esteemed editor, to share in your valued pages an emotional expression of deep pain felt by many Jewish hearts. Our Jewish community mourns the death of one of its most noble leaders. The venerable Rabbi Mendel Königshöfer departed this life after a seven-week illness. The departed was a צדיק גמור [a completely righteous individual] in the truest meaning of the term. His entire life was dedicated to the support of those majestic pillars of the world: תורה, ועבדה, וגמילות חסדים [Torah, Prayer, and Good deeds]. Everything he did carried the imprint of his honest, sincere reverence for God. He understood that conceit is man's most dangerous enemy and he neutralized that mortal weapon by making the words of our sages: שעושים לשמה ולא שעושים לא לשמה [everything should be performed for the sake of God and nothing should be performed that is not for the sake of God] into an unshakable principle of his life. Based on this principle, which directs the heart heavenward, he became a self-sacrificing human being, not at all conscious of his virtues, whose friendship, even in old age, did not lose spontaneity. Since he followed the path of God's truth and His holy word, he dedicated himself to God.

Material wealth was never a goal of his life on earth, and he never possessed them. His ardent love of God made him cognizant that what he was unable to distribute as צדקה, [charity] he could make up by תענית שהוא יותר מן הצדקה [fasting, which is even greater than charity]. It was not unusual for him to fast for two or three consecutive days and still learn half the night; indeed he once fasted ששה ימים רצופים בין כסא לעשור [Six consecutive days during the 10 Days of Penitence between Rosh Hashana and Yom Kippur].[26] Since God was always his only refuge, the house

---

[26]   A literary reference to the 10 days of penitence between Rosh Hashana and Yom Kippur.

of God was his sanctuary until his final illness. Despite a weakened body, with trembling limbs, he always sought to מתפלל עם הציבור [to pray with a minyan]. On the last day of his life, when all strength was drained from his body, he asked that the תפילין be placed on him in order to allow his last תפילה [prayer] to ascend heaven-ward from this crown of Israel. How fitting are the words of the Torah: ויהי ידיו אמונה עד בא השמש [his hands were faithful until sunset], which Targum Onkelos interprets as referring to a prayer for those who pass away with God!

A soul, so inebriated with God's love, shares its fragrance with the people among whom it lives. כל ישראל בני מלכים הם Rabbi Shimon teaches that all Israel, all those who carry on the battle on behalf of God and His holy Torah are royal princes. The deceased was a prime example of this truth. He showed us that even in poverty one can be as generous as the son of a King. During the difficult economic times, when he barely had enough bread for himself, he borrowed bread from a baker and distributed it among the poor who had absolutely nothing! And as husband and father? My dear esteemed reader, in this too, the deceased can serve as an ideal model. He understood well that one endowed by Heaven has to transmit his many splendid qualities to his children. Neither poverty nor the enticement of the modern destructive culture could keep this noble human being from directing his sons to Torah studies. He understood well that without knowledge of Torah, there can be no true Judaism; no genuine Jewish community, no Jewish family life. He was convinced of the truth that the ultimate value of children for parents is when children become a נחלת ה' namely that the parents live on in their children. And how magnificently this gentleman achieved this! Faithful to this principle, he had the pleasure of seeing one of his sons become a teacher and a dedicated father to orphans in the local orphanage. He lived to see his own spirit in his son as he selflessly and tirelessly labors for the welfare of humanity and the dissemination of the holy Torah and support of its institutions.

אלו צדיקים שבמיתתן נקראו חיים [those are righteous who in death are called the living] - our Sages explain: החיים יודעים שימותו. [the living know that they will die]. With sorrow, we see these words faithfully fulfilled with the departure of this צדיק from our midst. His mortal remains lie in the cold grave but his pious life continues in his children. That is how a pious human being dies. He enjoys the interest on his labors, his heavenly reward, already in this world; but the principle remains for him to enjoy in the world to come."[27]

---

[27] "Rabbi Mendel Königshöfer," *Der Israelit* #5 January 1878 102-03.

As can be surmised from the obituary, Emanuel Loeb K. was an extraordinarily pious and generous person, and the pages of the newspaper, Der Israelit, are filled with notices of the money he raised for a variety of charitable causes. One family story attests to his pious and generous character. Every Thursday evening after dark, he would take his children to the homes of families even more impoverished than he and leave food for the coming Shabbat on their doorstep. The children would be instructed to leave the food very quietly and then run away so the family would not know who left it and possibly be embarrassed.

MOSES JONAS KÖNIGSHÖFER (1840-1894)

Momentous changes in the lives of the Jews of the German states took place during the lifetime of Moses Jonas Königshöfer (in Hebrew, Moshe Yona). Emancipation and the end of the detested "metrikel" system brought some measure of freedom to the community. But it came with a price – disruption and change. Until 1847, the Jewish community was autonomous, a state within a state, and all Jews were legally under the community's jurisdiction. The Prussian Law of 1847 recognized the community as a political entity. All Jews had to belong to it and pay taxes in return for communal services, but the community ceded civil jurisdiction to the State. This deprived the organized Jewish community of much of its power and

allowed the Reform movement to develop. With the development of the Reform movement during the early part of the 19th century, first the nascent Reformers when they were the minority, and then the Orthodox, when they became the minority, petitioned to be allowed to resign from the recognized community and form their own separate community. This was finally allowed by the Austrittsgesetz or Law of Separation of July 28, 1876. The Orthodox community was split whether to take advantage of this law. Rabbi Shimshon R. Hirsch (Therese Altmann's grandfather) advocated it and insisted that Jewish law demanded a withdrawal from a community dominated by the Reform movement, while Rabbi Bamberger, the "Würzburger Rav", was of the opinion that Jewish unity was more important, and that withdrawal from the community was not mandated by Jewish law. Approximately one third of the Jewish community in Frankfurt, including Samuel Königshöfer (brother of Moses Jonas) followed Rabbi Hirsch's advice and seceded from the Jewish community.[28] The new reality forced Jews, for the first time, to struggle to reconcile their faith with their nationality and their newly acquired Prussian culture. This struggle gave birth to the Reform as well as to the Modern Orthodox movements. Hirsch summarized his philosophy in the phrase "Torah im Derech eretz" (Torah with the ways of the land), a fusion of traditional Judaism with the prevailing culture.

---

[28] Eliyahu M. Klugman, *Rabbi Samson Raphael Hirsch* (Mesorah Publications Ltd. 1996) 357.

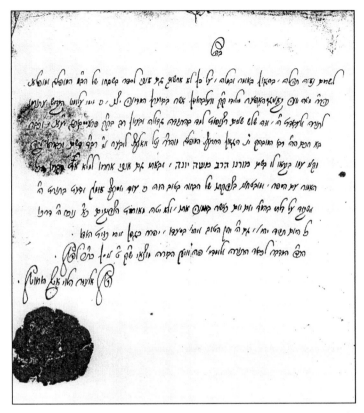

Attestation of Semicha by Rabbi Eleazar Horowitz in Vienna on the 9th of Nissan '620 (1860). It was written and signed on motzaei Shabbat *probably because Moshe Jonas was on his way home from Pressburg for Pesach (5 days hence) and stopped in Vienna for Shabbat. Rabbi Horowitz attests that Moshe Yona studied for three years in Pressburg. He quotes Rabbi Nettel Wolf Lieber the* Av Beth Din *of Pressburg who called Moshe Yona "our master" and agrees with him about the young man's qualities and scholarship. He adds "we are confident in this young man's righteousness; that he will add strength and knowledge of God's Torah by learning daily, as he has until now, and that he will not deviate from its holy ways." The latter phrase would be unusual for such a document and was probably a reaction to the Reform movement in Germany.*

Within one generation, both Reform and Orthodox Jews of Prussia, in contrast to those living in Hungary or Poland, became thoroughly integrated into German culture. Jews prided themselves on their German language and culture and, even in the Orthodox Rabbinical seminaries, students were expected to pursue a higher general education and obtain a university degree.[29] Jewish life in the United States owes much to the pattern of Jewish life in Prussia and the German States. In contrast, in Eastern Europe, there continued to be a strict separation between the Jewish and non-Jewish worlds.

Moses Jonas was born on April 14, 1840 in Welbhausen. His father was his first teacher[30] and he was taught both Jewish and general subjects privately. From 1856 to 1860, he studied at the Yeshiva in Pressburg (now Bratislava) with Rabbi Wolf Sofer (also known as the Ketav Sofer, son of the Hatam Sofer[31]) and with Dayan Netl Wolf Lieber, a native of Franconia,[32] from whom he received the first of a number of *semichot* (Rabbinical ordinations). He continued his secondary school studies privately while in Pressburg, and passed the matriculation examination in 1860. He enrolled for the winter semester of

29 David Ellenson, *Rabbi Esriel Hildesheimer and the Creation of a Modern Jewish Orthodoxy* (University of Alabama Press 1990).

30 The dossier on the Koenigshoefer family in the Municipal Archives of Fürth contains an early Jonas report card signed by his father.

31 The Hatam Sofer (Moses Sofer 1762-1839), originally from Frankfurt-am-Main, was a leading rabbinic authority and Rosh Yeshiva in Pressburg.

32 Much of the information on Moses Jonas' life was derived from Michael Brocke and Julius Carlebach, *Die Rabbiner der Emanzipatzionszeit in den deutschen, böhmischen und grosspolnischen Ländern 1781-1871. Teil 1. Band 2* (K.G. Saur Mänchen 2004) 546 entry # 0964.

1860/61 in the Würzburg Yeshiva where he studied with the Würzbürger Rav, Seligmann Bamberger from whom he also received a *semicha* certificate. In addition, he received a certificate from Rabbi Eleazar Halevi Horowitz from Vienna.[33] In the summer of 1861, he started studying in Munich and received another *semicha* from Rabbi Asher Aub in 1864. Simultaneously, he attended the University of Jena from which he received a PhD degree on June 22, 1864. His prize-winning dissertation was entitled, "Reconciling Plato's polemic against poetry with his many poetic quotations." It is interesting that even though he picked a thoroughly secular topic for his dissertation, his analysis is so Talmudic – an attempt to reconcile the seemingly contradictory. His University of Jena dossier[34] contains his handwritten thesis, an autobiographical sketch written in Latin, and a letter of recommendation from a local Priest with whom he studied Latin who considered him a prodigy.

In order to be recognized as a Rabbi ("Rabbiner") by the state, Moses Jonas had to take a qualifying examination, which he passed on August 14, 1853. Thereafter, he was appointed as a Rabbi for the district of Hagenbach in Upper Franconia with a seat in Ermreuth (incidentally his father's birthplace) where he was also a teacher. He resigned in 1866, either because he was

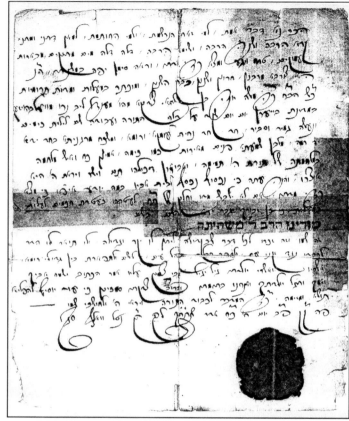

Semicha given to Moshe Yona Königshöfer by Rabbi Netl Wolf Lieber of Pressburg who calls his father a Tzaddik. The document praises Moshe Yonas' personal traits and scholarship. The certificate testifies that he has been awarded the highest rabbinical degree of Yoreh yoreh, Yodin Yodin.

troubled about deriving his livelihood from the Torah, thus contravening the advice in Pirke Avoth 4:7[35] (the family story) or because of community discord and a salary insufficient for his needs (the official story).[36] He was then appointed as Director of the Jewish Orphanage of Bavaria in Fürth.

---

[33]   Rabbi Horowitz (1803-1868) from Floss, Bavaria, studied with Moses Sofer (1762-1839) - the Hatam Sofer, and was invited to lead the Vienna community in 1828.

[34]   Kindly transmitted to me electronically by the Archive Department of the University of Jena.

[35]   Pirkei Avoth (Chapters of the Fathers) 4:7 states: "Don't make a crown of it [the Torah] with which to aggrandize yourself, nor an axe with which to strike." [Namely, don't derive worldly benefit from the Torah].

[36]   Brocke and Carlebach 546.

Top: Jewish Orphanage building in Fürth built while Moses Jonas Königshöfer was its Director. Below: Plaque inside the building memorializes its last Director and 33 children who were deported to their deaths on March 22, 1942.

The Jewish Orphanage in Fürth, established in 1763, was the first Jewish orphanage in the German lands and was modeled after similar orphanages in Prague and Amsterdam. Its goal was to bring up and educate Jewish orphans (children without a father or without both parents). Eventually, educational opportunities were also provided for children from poor families, even if both parents were alive. The imposing orphanage building, which still stands on what was once Julienstrasse (renamed Hallenmannstarsse after its last Director) was built under Moses Jonas K.'s leadership in 1868. Originally, only boys were admitted, but after renovations and an expansion completed in 1884, girls were also admitted. The renovations and expansion were made possible by the fruits of the industrial revolution (a generous donation of 100,000 Marks by Lazarus and Bertha Schwartz from Nuernberg),[37] and money sent back by expatriates forced by the Metrikel laws to leave for the United States. The new building contained its own synagogue, which would be the only synagogue in Fürth not destroyed during *kristallnacht* in 1938. The last inhabitants of the orphanage, 33 children and their Director, Dr. Isaak Hallermann were sent to their deaths by the Nazis on March 22, 1942. Today the building serves as the community synagogue and as an assisted living facility for Jewish elderly.

At the beginning of Moses Jonas Königshöfer's leadership the orphanage

[37] *Der Israelit #87 1884 1429-30.*

was home to only 7 children, but by the 1890s their number had increased tenfold. His appointment as Director of the Jewish Orphanage, also made him the acknowledged leader of the Orthodox community of Fürth, since the official head of the community, Rabbi, Isaac Löw, was a Reform Rabbi. In addition to Jewish religious education, taught by Moses Jonas K., the orphanage children received instruction in arithmetic, German language, penmanship, geography, natural science, business, art, singing, and French. The orphanage employed some of the teachers, while others came from the public schools.

Fürth, which was incorporated into the newly formed Kingdom of Bavaria in 1806, was one of the great centers of Jewish life in Germany. Despite being home to the fifth largest concentration of Jews in German speaking lands (surpassed only by Prague, Hamburg, Berlin, and Frankfurt), its total Jewish population in 1800 numbered only 2,400. Jews had lived in the town since at least the 15th century. The Jewish community dedicated a cemetery in 1607, a synagogue in 1616, a Jewish hospital in 1653, and a yeshiva towards the end of the 17th century. Chaim Zwi Hirsch built the first Hebrew publishing house there in 1737 and, under the leadership of his successor, Isaak David Zirndorfer, Fürth became famous as a Hebrew publishing center. A Jewish elementary school was opened in 1869. It was enlarged and renamed Israelitische Realschule in 1883, and was subsequently recognized by the State as a secondary school. The Fürth Jewish community became so well established that it developed a unique prayer tradition, known as "nusach Fürth." The main synagogue was rebuilt during the 19th century in a gothic style to serve the growing liberal or reform group, while the orthodox prayed in three smaller synagogues in the "shulhof."

I have not been able to locate a photograph of Moses Jonas K. but he must have been an imposing figure. His military exemption certificate[38] describes him as being a little over 6 feet tall, with black hair, high forehead, black eyebrows, gray eyes, and a black beard. He married Rebecca Ottenheimer[39] (1844-1868) in

JEWISH POPULATION OF FÜRTH

Year	No. of Jews (% of total)
1720	1,500
1816	2,434 (19)
1880	3,336
1933	2,000 (2.6)
1939	785

Leah Königshöfer

[38] Fürth archives Koenigshoefer file.
[39] In one reference the name is listed as Rebeka Ettenheimer.

Kleinerdlingen on March 15, 1865. She came from a religiously observant family; her father, Moses, was a merchant as well as a Talmudic scholar. Tragically, two years later she and her newborn baby died four days after delivery.[40]

In 1877, Moses Jonas K. married Leah Feuchtwanger (1850-1919) from Schwabach, south of Fürth. The family originally came from Feuchtawangen, hence the family name. Leah was one of 12 children of Nathan and Gelch (Bechhofer) Feuchtwanger (see Appendix 11). Nathan was a pillar of the Orthodox Jewish community of Schwabach with a title of *parnas* (Community Leader) for 48 years (1848-

Exterior (right) and interior views (below) of the Schwabach synagogue.

Right: Obituary of Nathan Feuchtwanger as it appeared in the Schwabach Israelit of May 2, 1889.

Schwabach. Die verehrten Leser Ihres sehr geschätzten Blattes sind seit Jahren gewöhnt, wenn des hiesigen Platzes Erwähnung geschieht, daß es sich um Schilderung unserer תורה-Schule handelt, die es sich zur Aufgabe macht מרבץ תורה בישראל zu sein, und diese ihre Aufgabe in anerkennenswerter Weise löst, umsomehr bedaure ich, gezwungen zu sein, heute eine traurige Botschaft bringen zu müssen, die bei der großen Bekanntschaft, die der Mann, dessen ich hier gedenken will, in weiten Kreisen hatte, gewiß allgemeine, aber ebenso berechtigte Trauer hervorrufen wird. Wir haben nämlich am 6. ניסן מורינו רב ר' Nathan Feuchtwanger ז"ל, wenn auch im hohen Alter von 80 Jahren, plötzlich rasch aus unserer Mitte verloren und mit uns das orthodoxe Judenthum einen seiner treuesten Kämpfer und Kämpen. Der Verlebte war einer jener Säulen des wahren Judenthums, wie sie leider heute nur noch selten zu finden sind; obzwar Geschäftsmann, der für eine große Familie zu sorgen hatte, war jede freie Minute seiner Zeit, seit seiner frühesten Jugend dem Studium תורתינו הק' gewidmet und konnte man ihn bis vor einigen Jahren bei strengster Kälte morgens 4 Uhr an der גמרא treffen, man konnte ruhig auf ihn sagen לא פסק גירסא מפומיה, nie wich die תורה aus seinem Munde. Er bekleidete 48 Jahre das Amt des פרנס in der hiesigen Gemeinde und kannte nur ein Motto: שלום, selbst unter den schwierigsten Verhältnissen gelang es ihm aber auch stets und mit שלום alle Stellen so zu besetzen und alle Gemeindeinstitutionen so zu erhalten, wie es הק' תורתינו vorschreibt. Es braucht wohl gar nicht erwähnt zu werden, daß er als Familienvater ein rein patriarchalisches Haus führte und daß die Familie in erster Linie den herben Verlust mit uns allen fühlt und mit uns in den Klageruf stimmt מי יעמד לנו בפרץ denn mit sein Leben war nur dem Gutesthun und der Fürsorge für seine Familie, seiner Gemeinde und dem Judenthume gewidmet. Dabei war er die Bescheidenheit selbst und was er an Armen und Reichen that, es geschah im größten Geheimnisse. Bei seinem Leichenbegängnisse war, obzwar das בית הקברות mehrere Stunden entfernt von hier ist (in Georgensgmünd), die hiesige Gemeinde vollständig vertreten, aber auch Deputationen von allen Nachbargemeinden waren anwesend, da er lange Jahre das Amt des Kreisvorstehers für den Bezirk des Begräbnißplatzes versah. Des חרום ניס halber, konnte unser hochverehrter Herr Rabbiner Wißmann נ"י nur einige Skizzen aus dem thatenreichen Leben seines dahingegangenen Freundes verflochten mit einigen מדרש-Stellen Erwähnung thun und schließe auch ich mich der Bitte des verehrten Herrn Rabbiner an: möge die Familie des edlen Dahingegangenen und unsere Gemeinde das Leben dieses Großen sich zum Vorbild nehmen und durch Nachahmung seiner guten Handlungen, diese große Lücke nach Möglichkeit ausfüllen, damit Schwabach seinen Namen auch weiter als Heimstätte der תורה עבודה וג"ח erhalte. —ר—

---

[40] The official cause of death was peritonitis undoubtedly caused by puerperal sepsis.

1889). He earned his livelihood as a merchant but was learned in Talmud, had Rabbinical ordination and, on the death of Rabbi Abraham Wechsler, he filled the position of Rabbi in Schwabach for a year (1850-1851). He apparently did this because the community had promised Rabbi Wechsler's widow financial support for a year. During that year Nathan Feuchtwanger performed the duties of Rabbi without a salary, so the community could fulfill its obligation to Mrs. Wechsler.[41]

Leah and Moses Jonas Königshöfer had 16 children, 12 of whom survived infancy:

- Isaak (1870-1951)
- Meir Loeb (1872-1962) {App. 12}
- Samuel Gedalia 1873-?) {App. 13}
- Merle Miriam (1875-1942) {App. 14}
- Fannie (1876 - ?) {App. 15}
- Bella (1878-1968) {App. 19}
- Emanuel Loeb (1879-1905)[42]
- Jette (1882-1912) {App. 6}
- Betty (1883-?)[43]
- Leopold Wolf (1886-194?) {App. 17}
- Joseph (1888-1916)[44]
- Hanna (1890-194?) {App. 6}

In addition, two infants died at birth and Gelche Karoline died at 17 months of age.

Leah Königshöfer was initially in charge of the girl's division at the orphanage, but as the number of her own children increased, an additional supervisor was hired. Leah and Moses Jonas' children

Document issued in 1939 attesting that "this community's Jewish register of births #660 includes the entry that on August 3, 1870 a son named Isaak Königshöfer was born in Fürth to orphanage teacher Dr. (phil) Moses Königshöfer and his wife Lea born Feuchtwanger."

lived in the orphanage with the other children and their parents treated them exactly as they treated the orphans. Leah would always admonish her own children, "if you squabble with the other children, never complain because you will always be at fault; the other children are orphans."[45] We are fortunate to have a memoir written by Meier Königshöfer when he was in his 90s, which is the source of much of the information about the orphanage. He describes his mother as a patient, cheerful,

---

[41] *Allgemeinen Zeitung des Judentums* 10 November, 1851.
[42] Emanuel Loeb was a physician. He never married and died of strep sepsis which he caught from a patient he was treating for erysipelas. He lived in Berlin and is buried in the Alte Friedhof in Fuerth.
[43] Betty Koenigshoefer married Heinrich Siechel in 1911. They lived in Breslau where she died.
[44] Joseph was killed while fighting for Germany in 1917. His name is listed in Fuerth on a tablet in the courtyard of what used to be the Realschule and is now the Jewish community Center.
[45] Meier Königshöfer, *My Recollections* (unpublished memoir; the Leo Beck Institute, New York 1962).

warm, and highly educated woman who loved to read, delighted in telling stories, and recited poetry to her children in the Nürnberg dialect.

As leader of the Fürth Orthodox Jewish community, Moses Jonas K. was confronted by many questions of Jewish Law. One of these has been preserved in the writings of Rabbi Shimshon Raphael Hirsch (1808-1888),[46] founder of Modern Orthodoxy. The question concerns the practice of *metzitzah b'peh*, part of the circumcision ceremony during which the traditional *mohel* sucks a drop of the baby's blood with his mouth. This practice became particularly controversial towards the end of the 19th century.

On the evening of March 24, 1882 Robert Koch (1843-1910) delivered an address to the Berlin Physiologic Society in which he incontrovertibly demonstrated that the tubercle bacillus was the causative agent of tuberculosis. This generated a great deal of excitement and was a major topic of conversation. Over the next 20 years, bacteria causing a whole host of human diseases were identified in rapid succession, and the public became aware of contagion as a mechanism for the spread of disease.

In January 1885, Rabbi Jonas Königshöfer wrote Rabbi Hirsch that he had a congregant who wanted a circumcision for his son on condition that *metzitzah b'peh* not be performed. Rabbi Hirsch answered that in his opinion this was an essential and mandatory part of circumcision. He went on to state that

"the knowledge our sages gained from one year's experience is a thousand times greater than that which modern doctors will gain in their entire professional lives." He recommends that a *mohel* should refuse to perform a circumcision without *metzitzah*. To his credit, Rabbi Hirsch wrote an addendum dated 28 Kislev 5649 (December 2, 1888) in which he bemoans the increasingly widespread disregard of *metzitzah* because of fear of infection. He again reiterates that it is essential, but states that the recently described method of *metzitzah* using a sterile thin glass tube is an acceptable alternative to *metzitzah b'peh*. Almost 120 years later, in 2005, this again became controversial when several babies in the ultra-Orthodox community were infected, and one died, from herpes simplex infection after *metzitzah b'peh*. It is discouraging that the issue is still debated and that the clear-cut evidence for the transmission of disease is disregarded in some circles to the peril of our children.

Moses Jonas K. also carried on a correspondence with Rabbi Esriel Hildesheimer, one of the leaders of German orthodoxy and Director of a Yeshiva in Berlin. These questions, in 1881 and 1883, deal primarily with Halachic problems relating to the newly formed stock exchange.

A great tragedy befell the family and the Jewish community of Fürth when Moses Jonas Königshöfer died suddenly on June 28, 1894 (24 Sivan) at the young age of 54 years. His tombstone had the following inscriptions: (In Hebrew) "This honorable, dear, and great man. He always

---

[46] Rabbi Shimshon Rafael Hirsch, *Shemesh Merape: sheelot utshuvot* (Mesorah Publications, NY 1992) 69.

occupied himself with holy work. The ways of the Torah were entrusted to him and he is worthy of all the crowns of the next world. We will remember his name together with all the righteous. We mourn the loss of this man who has left us forever. Our teacher and Rabbi, Moshe Jona Königshöfer, ז"ל, he was born on 1 Nisan 600[47] and rose to heaven on Thursday 24 Sivan 654." In German, the tombstone read: "There his soul will be rewarded for his deeds. There he deserves to acquire the Light of Life because he led his sons and daughters into the circle of righteousness and the fear of God. He drew and drank from the well of Torah, was a righteous teacher to his community, and many sought his counsel and saw through his eyes. Like an angel from heaven, he stretched out his hand to the poor and powerless orphans. Great and small found carefree peace as if enveloped by the wings of a dove. He supported them with truth, planted faith in them, and transmitted morality into their hearts. He stood on their right side as a protector, taking the place of their parents. His religious faith and righteousness will accompany him to the heavens above. This stone will enlighten future generations about his activities. May his soul be bound with the bonds of life."

The cemetery in which Moses Jonas K was buried was vandalized on kristallnacht (9 November, 1938). In 1942, a portion of the cemetery, including the Königshöfer graves, were dug up and

New tombstones for Leah and Jonas Koenigshoefer were erected in the new Jewish cemetery since the original tombstones were destroyed by the Nazis.

flooded to make a water reservoir for the fire department. After the war, scattered bones were reburied in no particular order, and parts of the tombstones were returned to the cemetery. The family has honored his memory by naming many male descendants with some variation of his name. The Jewish community of Fuerth devoted an issue of its bulletin in 1994 to the 100th anniversary of his death, and described a communal service during which the *kaddish* was recited.

---

[47] The 5000 is understood so this is in reality 5,600-5,654.

Plaque hanging in what used to be the Realschule and now serves as a community center in Fürth commemorating members of the Jewish community who fell during WW I fighting for Germany, including the name of Josef Koenigshoefer (3rd from bottom, left side).

Moses Jonas' death left his widow with 12 children, nine of whom still lived at home, the youngest barely four years old. She was now also without a home since a successor was soon found to direct the orphanage. The family moved into an apartment on the corner of Friedrich-strasse and Weinstrasse.

Another tragedy struck the family when Joseph (1888–1916) was killed in battle in Kirlibaba while fighting in the German army on the Romanian front. In a letter of sympathy to his grieving mother, the mayor of Fürth wrote: "May I offer you this consolation of gratitude, that he who dies prematurely in battle for a great cause has achieved a heroic death that will be inscribed forever on the fatherland's and the city of Fürth's honor roll." On March 13, 1917 Leah received a letter awarding Joseph a posthumous King Ludwig Cross with an expression of gratitude and a promise that the family's ultimate sacrifice would always be remembered by a grateful nation. Germany's gratitude was soon forgotten. Joseph's name still appears on a tablet in what used to be the Israelitische Realschule on Blumenstrasse 31, now a Jewish Community Center. Leah died on 13 Adar *sheni* 5679 (1919).

Joseph Koenigshoefer in German uniform. The message reads: 'The photo was taken in Rolki in Russia near Styr'.

Der
Bürgermeister
der Stadt Fürth.

Fürth, 27. September 1916.

Werte Frau Königshöfer!

Wie ich zu meinem herzlichen Bedauern er-
fahre, ist Ihr Herr Sohn Joseph Königshöfer,
Offiziersstellvertreter, auf dem Felde der Ehre
geblieben.

Ich kann den tiefen Schmerz empfinden, der
das Herz seiner Lieben bei dieser schweren Heim-
suchung durchbebt.

Wie ich sind weite Kreise der hiesigen Bevölkerung von herzlicher Anteilnahme ergriffen.
Ich bitte Sie, werte Frau Königshöfer, den Ausdruck meines innigen Beileides hiedurch entgegen-
nehmen und auch den übrigen Angehörigen zur Kennt-
nis bringen zu wollen.

Möge Ihnen der Gedanke Trost bieten, daß
der früh Heimgegangene im Kampfe für die große
Sache den Heldentod erlitten hat und daß sein
Name auf der Ehrentafel des Vaterlandes wie der
Stadt Fürth allezeit prangen wird.

Hochachtungsvoll!

Dr Wild.

I. Bürgermeister.

Office of the Mayor
Town Of Fuerth
27 Sept. 1916

Worthy Mrs. Königshöfer,

To my great sorrow I have learned that your son, Mr. Josef Königshoefer, active officer, has been killed on the field of honor.

I can feel the deep pain which vibrates through the hearts of his loved ones over this terrible news.

Like I, the wider circle of inhabitants of this community are deeply moved with heartfelt sympathy. I beg you, worthy Mrs. Königshöfer, to accept the expression of my deepest sympathy and to be so kind as to transmit them also to his next of kin.

My I offer you this consolation of gratitude, that he who dies prematurely in battle for a great cause dies a heroic death and his name shall shine forever on the honor roll of the father-land and the city of Fürth.

With highest esteem,

The Mayor

Letter sent to Mrs. Leah Königshöfer notifying her of the death of her son, Josef, fighting for Germany during WW I.

Der
Oberbürgermeister
der Stadt Fürth.

Fürth, den 13. März 1917.

Euer Hochwohlgeboren!

Zur Allerhöchsten Auszeichnung mit dem
König Ludwig-Kreuz beehre ich mich meine besten
Glückwünsche auszusprechen.

Mit dem Ausdruck vorzüglichster
Hochachtung!

Wild

Oberbürgermeister.

Left: Letter from the Mayor of Fürth expressing his "fondest best wishes to the most highly distinguished recipients of the King Ludwig Cross award." It was given as "a sign of esteemed and grateful recognition of unusual service to the homeland." Above: The Ludwig Cross was a medal established by the King of Bavaria, Ludwig III, in 1916.

Berliner Tageblatt No. 460
Freitag, den 3. September 1916

Auf dem Felde der Ehre ist unser Herr

Josef Koenigshoefer

Offizierstellvertreter im 3. Grenadierregiment,
Inhaber des Eisernen Kreuzes,
gefallen.

Das Ende dieses von uns besonders geschätzten Mitarbeiters
bedauern wir aufrichtig und werden seiner stets in Treue gedenken.
Berlin, den 6. September 1916.

Hirsch, Kupfer- und Messing-Werke, Akt.-Ges.

An advertisement in a Berlin newspaper, placed by his co-workers, announcing that Josef Koenigshoefer had fallen on the "field of honor," and that they will forever remember his extraordinary sacrifice.

IZAK KÖNIGSHÖFER (1870-1951)

Izak, who was to become my grandfather, was the oldest, but not the first born (*behor*) of Moses Jonas and Leah's children. We were always reminded of this when he did not fast on the eve of Passover, as required of the firstborn. As mentioned above, Moses Jonas' first wife, Rebecca and her newborn died four days after delivery. The first child born to his second wife, Leah, also died shortly after birth. This so frightened Moses Jonas that when Leah became pregnant again (with Izak) he "sold" the baby to Rabbi Esriel Hildesheimer[48, 49] in order to "fool" the angel of death.

Izak K. lived in the orphanage together with his siblings, and received his elementary school education (from six to 10 years of age) there. His father taught Chumash, Mishna, and prayers. A teacher, hired by the orphanage, taught most of the secular subjects, and teachers brought in from public school taught specialty subjects, such as science. After an elementary education at the orphanage, Izak, along with his siblings, attended the Israelitische Realschule in Fürth for the next four years. Its director, Dr. Desau, was a highly educated and religious man. The basic child rearing and educational philosophy in the German lands was, at that time, one of absolute and unquestioned obedience to parents and teachers. The slightest infraction was cause for corporal punishment. Izak's brother, Meir K. recalls a special form of punishment administered with a "Spanish stick" by a teacher when he could not recite, in their correct order, the names of the mountains in the Bavarian sub-alpine range. After finishing the Realschule, Izak probably continued his religious education with his father, who gave several *shiurim* (classes) a week in Dinim and Talmud, but he was never considered to be a scholar.

Today, we take the existence of a Jewish day school, such as the Israelitische Realschule for granted but the first such school, in which general and religious subjects were taught, was established in Frankfurt only in 1853 by Rabbi Shimshon Raphael Hirsch, who resigned the prestigious position of Chief Rabbi of Moravia in 1851 in order to lead a tiny Orthodox congregation in Frankfurt. When he arrived, the congregants wanted to build a synagogue building, but he insisted that the priority was to build a school. His school model spread rapidly throughout Germany, and the Fürth school, established in 1862 and recognized by the State in 1880,[50] was undoubtedly patterned after it. Most of the teachers in the Realschule were Jewish but Christian teachers from the Fürth school system or from nearby Nürnberg taught specialized subjects, such as physics,

---

[48]   Esriel Hildesheimer (1820-1899), founder of the Berlin Orthodox Rabbiner Seminar (Rabbinical Seminary), was one of the founders of Modern Orthodoxy in Germany.
[49]   Charlotte Holtzmann, Personal communication.
[50]   Moshe N. Rosenfeld, "Talmudschule und jüdische Erziehung in Fürth" in Werner J. Heymann (Ed) *Kleebatt und Davidstern* (Verlag Maria Mümmler 1990) 91.

chemistry and mathematics. The cost of the school for 150 students was borne almost exclusively by the small Orthodox community whose members sacrificed for it. The city's organized Jewish community, dominated by the liberal wing, did not begin to support the school until many years later. The liberal members of the Jewish community preferred to send their children to public school, and only when their children did not do well there did the Jewish Realschule become an acceptable alternative.

On May 18, 1899 Izak married Martha (Miriam) Altmann from Kattowitz. The marriage, like most in those days, was almost certainly arranged. Marriage was not viewed as a union of two people, but rather as a union of two families. It was therefore important that the families thus joined shared similar values, traditions, and, if possible, economic circumstances. The wedding took place in Fürth. Rabbi Shlomo Halevi Bamberger, the son of the Würzbürger Rav who was married to Izak's sister, Merle, gave grandmother an inscribed book, צאינה וראינה as an engagement present[51] and spoke at the wedding. The Altmann and Königshöfer families were united once again on January 12, 1906 when Jette K. married Bruno Altmann, and again after Jette's tragic death in 1912, when Bruno married her sister, Hanna, in 1913.

After their father's death, the three oldest sons, Izak, Meir, and Samuel formed a business partnership called "Bro. Königshöfer, Fürth." The company, established in 1894, imported raw leather and wool, but soon limited itself to importing only raw wool for the textile industries. It became quite successful and continued until 1933, when it declared bankruptcy, owing 1,000,000 marks. According to Aunt Lotte, Uncle Ulu on hearing about such a large debt said, "kol hakavod, I couldn't have been so successful!" My Grandfather then started a cheese factory that,

My maternal grandparents, Martha and Izak Königshöfer, in 1924 (top) and around 1950 (below).

---

[51] The צאינה וראינה is a Yiddish retelling of the Bible stories, usually read by women, and was first published in the 16th century by Rabbi Jacob ben Isaac Ashkenazi of Janow and was popular well into the 20th century.

Left: Copy of marriage certificate of Isaak Königshöfer and Martha Altmann.

Right: Speech given by Rabbi Solomon Bamberger (Izak Koenigshoefer's brother-in-law) at my grandparets' wedding on 14th Sivan 5659 or May 29, 1899. As his text, he uses the phrase, "we are grateful for the past and pleading for the future." He reminds those assembled that all blessings emanate from God and wishes happiness and obedience to the Law for the happy young couple embarking on their married life.

Children of Martha and Izak Koenigshoefer

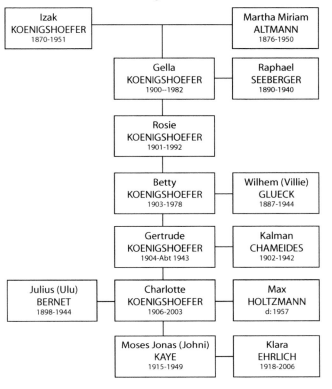

Izak KOENIGSHOEFER 1870-1951	Martha Miriam ALTMANN 1876-1950
Gella KOENIGSHOEFER 1900--1982	Raphael SEEBERGER 1890-1940
Rosie KOENIGSHOEFER 1901-1992	
Betty KOENIGSHOEFER 1903-1978	Wilhem (Villie) GLUECK 1887-1944
Gertrude KOENIGSHOEFER 1904-Abt 1943	Kalman CHAMEIDES 1902-1942
Julius (Ulu) BERNET 1898-1944 / Charlotte KOENIGSHOEFER 1906-2003	Max HOLTZMANN d:1957
Moses Jonas (Johni) KAYE 1915-1949	Klara EHRLICH 1918-2006

according to Aunt Lotte was quite successful. Martha and Izak had five daughters:

- Gella (1900-1982) {App. 18}
- Rosie (1901-1992)
- Betty (1903-1978) {App. 20}
- Gertrude (1904-circa 1943) {App. 22}
- Charlotte (1906-2003). {App. 21}

They prayed for a son, and finally their wish was granted with the birth of Moses Jonas (Johni) (1915-1949) {Appendix 23}. To express their profound joy, Martha and Izak named their son in memory of his grandfather and had a special *sefer Torah* written for the occasion. In accordance with the German custom, it was wrapped in a *wimpel* describing their joy, Johnis' milestones, and their hope for his future. The *sefer torah* is now in an old age home in Tel Aviv.

Grandfather Izak was proud of his ability to arrange marriages and must have looked forward to doing so for his four daughters. Aunt Rosie (1901-1992) was unfortunately born with mild mental

Left-to-right: Rosie, Gertrude, Betty, and Gella Koenigshoefer circa 1905-06.

Left-to-right: Charlotte, Rosie, Gella, Betty and Gertrude Koenigshoefer circa 1913.

retardation, made worse by her parents' overprotection. I remember that she had a phenomenal memory, but she received little education. She was not allowed to blossom until well into old age, after her parents' death, when she entered a nursing home in Tel Aviv.

Aunt Gella (1900-1982) was the first to be married. The story is that my grandfather heard about a good potential match for her in Raphael Seeberger (1890-1940) from the village of Gunzenhausen. Grandfather took Aunt Gella to meet Raphael with a pre-arranged sign that if Gella approved, she would tell a joke she had just heard. Gella really disliked him but, to break the tension, she told the joke anyhow and my grandfather immediately announced their engagement.[52] Apocryphal or not, their marriage was not a happy one. They fled Germany in 1936 and their son, Rudolph (1923-1996), celebrated his Bar Mitzvah on board the ship bound for Palestine. Aunt Gella worked as a nurse in Haifa until her death.

Next was Aunt Betty's (1903-1978) turn. My grandparents used to go to Marienbad for vacations and on one such occasion met a couple who told them about their eligible son, Villie (1887-1944) who was back home in Hungary. Villie (Wilhelm) was extremely pious, studied at the famous Pressburg Yeshiva, and was the son of a wealthy kosher wine merchant. The wedding took place in 1922 and the newlyweds moved to Fürth and joined my grandfather in his business.

Left-to-right: Charlotte, Rosie, Johni, Gertrude, and Betty in the 1920s (Gella is absent).

My mother's marriage was, as already mentioned, arranged through my grandmother's brother, Bruno, with the eligible and newly appointed Rabbi of Katowice, Kalman Chameides.

Aunt Charlotte or Lotte (1906-2003) was the only one who arranged her own destiny by secretly getting engaged to Julius (Ulu) Bernet (1898-1944) from Nürnberg. They fled Germany to England in 1939 with their two children, Erna (1929-1995) and Manfred (Michael) (1930-2010).

Grandfather Izak had a reputation for being extremely stern and self centered while my grandmother was loving, warm and soft. In her ninth decade Aunt Lotte remembered how unfair her father had been, and that his major concern was "what will others say?" Appearance seemed to have been most important for him. Aunt Lotte recalled that her son Manfred was born in 1930 shortly before her father's 60th birthday. Grandfather insisted on having a party to celebrate his

52   Dov Gilon, *Tomorrow Came* (Tel Aviv 2000) 17.

My mother, Gertrude Königshöfer in photo probably in early 1920s.

birthday even though his daughter could not attend. She also told me of her anger at getting a second hand watch for her wedding. Her bitterness transcended the years.

Shortly after the Nazis came to power in 1933, SS party members visited my grandparents in their Fürth home and suggested that, as "foreigners" in Germany, they should contribute to Hitler's election campaign. They protested that they were not foreigners, but loyal Germans who had lived in Germany for many generations and, as proof, produced a black velvet box with a display of the medals the family received when Josef was killed fighting for Germany during WW I and the message assuring the family that "a grateful nation

would never forget their great sacrifice." The SS threw the box out the window shattering the glass. Grandfather was arrested and sent to a concentration camp, and released only after a ransom was paid. The family decided that Bavaria, the birthplace of Nazism, was now too dangerous and moved to the small town of Bensheim in the Bergstrasse district in southern Hesse, which they thought might be safer. Interestingly, their street address there was Adolph-Hitler Strasse 69. When this too proved not to be safe, they moved to their summer home in Marienbad in 1937. Marienbad was a famous resort town located in the part of Czechoslovakia known as Sudetenland, which was given to Germany the following year by Chamberlain in exchange for a piece of paper guaranteeing "peace in our time." Aunt Rosie and Aunt Betty (Glueck) with her children, Felix and Bernd, lived there with my grandparents. The Gluecks were eventually forced to leave Germany because the Germans considered the family Hungarian since Villie was a Hungarian citizen. The Hungarians, on the other hand, were willing to admit Uncle Villie, but not the rest of the family, whom they considered to be German. The family was stuck in no man's land until the proper bribes could be paid and the family moved to Hungary. In 1939, my grandfather was once again arrested and charged with being in Marienbad without permission. Uncle Villie managed to smuggle money from Hungary and bailed him out on condition that the family leave Germany. With Uncle Johni's help, my grandparents and Rosie were given permission to enter England just before the outbreak of the war.

My grandmother, Martha Koenigshoefer (left) and my mother, Trude Chameides on a Katowice street around 1932.

IV

THE CHAMEIDES FAMILY

———— •◆• ————

The origins of the Chameides family are buried in the mists of history. We don't know when the first ancestor arrived in Galicia, the southeastern part of interwar Poland, and now partly in western Ukraine. The surname "Chameides" is found in many Galician towns around Lwów but I have so far been unable to connect most of them.[53] Even though the exact family origins are not known, one can sometimes get hints from last and first names, especially if they are unusual. It is tempting to ascribe the family name's origin to "חמדות" or "the charming one" a name given to Daniel in the Bible, but the name is more likely a patronymic. The ending "ides," or variant "idis" (the "son of" in Greek) was a well-known ancient patronymic said to originate in Pontus on the Black Sea and in Greek Asia Minor.[54] Its use was revived in later centuries (e.g., Maimonides and Nachmanides in Spain and Gershonides along the Rhine). Chama was not an uncommon name in Talmudic times. Thus, the name 'Chameides' probably meant 'the son of Chama.'

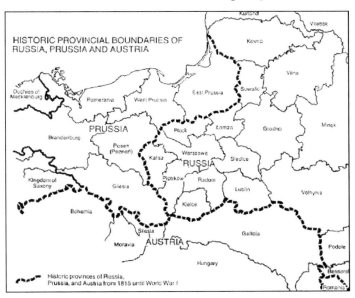

Map showing the division of Poland with the three Empires meeting at the Kaiserecke *(the Emperors' Corner) in Myslowitz, Silesia. Galicia became an Austrian province.*

[53] A search on www.jri-poland.org accessed on August 28, 2006 revealed families with the name of Chameides in the following adjoining localities: 134 in the Lwów region (in the towns of Borysław, Drohobycz, Gródek, Komarno, Lviv, Mosciska, Przemyśl, Sokal, Szczerzec, Wynniki); 60 in the Stanisławów region (in the towns of Bursztyn, Kolomya, Obertyn, Rohatyn, Rozdol, Stanisławów, Stryj, Zurawno; and 4 in the Tarnopol region (in the towns of Gliniany, Sasów, Złoczów). There were 2 entries for Kraków. Families with the same name were also present in Tysmenica and Buczacz and a number of immigrants with the same name came to the US during the 19th century.

[54] The ending "ides" first appears in Homer's *Iliad* as Atreides and then in Homer's "The Odyssey" as Halitherses Mastroides. Homer probably lived in the 8th or 9th century BCE. In Greek mythology, Zeus, the son of Cronus and Rhea, is also known as Cronides.

First names recurred in Jewish families since children were usually named after a deceased (among Ashkenazim) or a living (among Sephardim) close relative. The first name "Kalman-Kalonymus," which is common among families with the last name of Chameides in Galicia, is the Greek equivalent of שם טוב (beautiful name),[55] a composite of *kalos (beautiful)* and *onoma (name)*. Beider,[56] in an extensive study of Jewish first names, claims that families with this first name can be traced to Lucca in Northern Italy. The name Kalonymus appears quite commonly in medieval times among the Jews of Puglia in southern Italy, and the families bearing that name appear to have migrated north to Lucca around the year 1000.[57] Jews lived in Rome even before Pompey transplanted an entire community from Judea in 63-70 CE[58] and the Jewish population of ancient Rome reached an estimated 50,000 or 10% of the total population. Greek language and culture, including Greek names, predominated among the intellectual classes in Rome even before the Roman Empire split into western and eastern

Map of Galicia. Szczerzec is just south of Lwów. Note also the location of Bóbrka, southeast of Lwów, and Jaworów, northwest of Lwów.

[55] In addition to 'beautiful name' Kalonymus also referred to a 'miracle worker' who knew how to use God's name for miraculous deeds as in its Ashkenazi equivalent, 'baal shem tov', or 'master of the good name'.

[56] Alexander Beider, *The Origins, Structure, Pronounciation of Ashkenazic Given Names* (Avotaynu, Inc. Bergenfield, New Jersey 2001).

[57] Nardo Bonomi, Personal communication AIJGS conference 8-15-2006.

[58] Paul Kriwaczek, *Yiddish Civilization* (Alfred A. Knopf, New York 2005) 29.

parts in the fourth century. After the split, many Jews migrated to the eastern half of the empire and its capital, Constantinople. From there, some eventually migrated across the Black Sea into Crimea,[59] and then westward with the massive population migration of nomads (Bulgars, Goths, Magyars, etc.) The first record of Jews in the Lwów region of Galicia dates from the 3rd century,[60] long before the great Ashkenazi migration from the west, and there is evidence of an even earlier presence of Jews in what became the Galician province of Poland.

Another possibility is that the Chameides ancestors remained in the western part of the Roman Empire, and migrated to Europe (the Rhine, Frankish Lands, or Spain) after Rome fell to the invading Visigoths in the fifth century. They then migrated to the Polish lands with the great migration starting in the 11th century. For non-Jews, the motivation for this migration was primarily economic; for Jews it was also spurred by persecutions during the time of the Crusades. One example of such a family migration is that of the famous rabbinic family, Kalonymus, which had migrated from Lucca to the Rhine and, in the thirteenth century, eastward to Poland.

In the latter part of the 16th century, Poland was one of the largest countries in Europe whose borders extended well into what is now Ukraine, to the outskirts of Kiev, and included all of Lithuania. Polish society was feudal and highly stratified. Most of the land was controlled by a few noble families and about half the population were serfs. The Jewish community was self governing (1553-1764) under a *kehilla* system run by the *Vaad Arba Arzot* (Council of Four Lands), which had ultimate authority to enforce Jewish religious law, arbitrate conflicts between Jews, and collect taxes for the government.

Economically, Jews were part of the small middle class of merchants, and later also became professionals. Many worked for the nobles as tax collectors, and in the production and sale of alcohol, grain, and lumber in which the nobles had a monopoly. The Jewish employees and their families lived in concentrated clusters on land owned by the nobles; these eventually coalesced into small villages (*shtetlach*). Their involvement with the production and sale of alcohol led Jews to establish inns, and inn keeping became a uniquely Jewish occupation. Their role as tax collectors and involvement in the manufacture and sale of alcohol won them the enmity of both the local population and of the Church, which accused Jews of leading the peasants to sin.

[59] Yaroslaw Hrystak, "Lviv: A Multicultural History through the Centuries," in John Czaplicka (Ed) *Lviv A City in the Crosscurrents of Culture* (Harvard University Ukrainian Research Institute, Boston 2005) 48.

[60] Wacław Wierzbieniec, "The Processes of Emancipation and Assimilation in the Multiethnic City of Lviv during the Nineteenth and Twentieth Centuries," in Czaplicka (Ed), *Lviv A City in the Crosscurrents of Culture* (Harvard Ukrainian Studies, 24 (1/4) 2000) 223-250.

The class frictions that resulted from this economic and social system, and the inability of the country to enact changes (laws proposed in the nation's parliament could be vetoed by a single negative vote by a noble) led to a loss of Polish independence when Prussia, Austria, and Russia, Poland's neighbors to the west, south, and east, divided the country (in 1772, 1793, and 1795). Poland ceased to exist as an independent country for almost 130 years.

Galicia and its neighboring area to the northeast, Volhynia (in Latin – Lodomeria), were originally individual principalities of Kievan Rus and, for a time, separate kingdoms, but were eventually united. Galicia was named after the town of Halych, an ancient provincial capital city important for its salt mines in the era before refrigeration[61] and was located on a trading route with the west. What would become the largest city in Galicia, Lwów in Polish, Lvov in Russian, Lemberg in German and Yiddish, and Lviv in Ukrainian, was founded by King Danylo in 1256, and named for his son and successor Lev Danylovych who made it the capital of the Galician-Volhynian kingdom in 1272.

Austria annexed Galicia in the 1772 partition of Poland. Restrictive laws discouraged Jews from settling in Austria proper, which not only excluded them from the professions and land ownership but even dictated where they could settle and how many of their children (only the first born) could marry. As a result, Austria had few Jews of its own. With Poland's partition, Austria acquired 18% of its land, 32% of its desperately poor population, and a large Jewish population (the census of 1800 showed that there were 250,000 Jews in Galicia) second only to that acquired by Russia. Empress Maria Theresa immediately imposed Austrian laws relating to Jews on the newly acquired province. Jews were now allowed to own real estate and acquire a general education, but they could no longer have their own law courts and they were subject to much higher taxes than their Christian neighbors. The additional and discriminatory taxes included a protection tax, a property and occupation tax, marriage tax, kosher meat tax, and Sabbath candle tax. Failure to pay the taxes was punishable by expulsion from the province.

The newly acquired Austrian territory became officially known as "Galicia and Ludomiria," but was generally referred to simply as Galicia. Empress Maria Theresa designated the city of Lwów as the capital, renamed it Lemberg, and set the stage for its architectural and bureaucratic development as an Austrian city. At that time, Jews constituted about 10% of the city's population (to become 30% immediately before WW II); the remainder of the population included Poles, Ukrainians (previously known as Ruthenians from the German name for Rus), and Germans.

---

[61] P. R. Magocsi, *Ukraine* (University of Toronto Press, Inc. 2007) 51-56. Magosci points out that Halych comes from the Indo-European word Hal, which means salt.

Maria Theresa (died in 1780) was succeeded by her relatively enlightened son, Joseph II. But Jews had only a short breathing spell since Joseph died in 1790 and his successors, Leopold II and his son, Franz Leopold I, followed the example set by Maria Theresa and reversed all of Joseph's reforms. The previous harsh rules including marriage restrictions, high taxes, occupational and residence restrictions, etc., were re-imposed, and new taxes on candles and kosher meat were introduced. These lasted until 1848 when the relatively benevolent and highly popular long reign of Franz Joseph (1848-1916), affectionately known among Jews as Froim Yossel, started. Galician Jews, theoretically emancipated in 1869, were now freed from most economic and educational restrictions, and the government formally cancelled the discriminatory high taxes. Serfdom was abolished, the economy gradually improved, and the middle class grew. The improved economic conditions led to a dramatic rise in the Jewish birth rate so that, despite a large emigration to the United States and a number of European countries, by 1880 the Austrian Jewish population reached 1 million, the majority of whom resided in Galicia. Part of Franz Joseph's "benevolence" (forced by uprisings in Hungary) was to grant regional local autonomy (1867). In Galicia, local autonomy led to Polish rule and to local anti-Jewish discrimination, that included pogroms and economic boycotts. Jews were increasingly caught between Poles and Ukrainians, each fighting for cultural and political dominance.

The Edict of Tolerance of Emperor Joseph II (1787) required all Jews residing in the Austrian Empire (including Galicia) to acquire last names, but the law was not enforced until the beginning of the 19th century. Since the ruling authorities wanted to "Germanize" the Jews in order to counterbalance Polish and Ukrainian nationalism in their newly acquired lands, they required the new names to be German. As a result, German names predominate among the Jews of Galicia and in time became known as "Jewish" names. The surname "Chameides" does not fit into this pattern, and is further evidence that the name probably antedated the 19th century Austrian requirement. In fact, we know that Hersch had the last name "Chameides," even though his birth almost certainly antedated the law that required Jews to have last names. Ashkenazim did not have surnames until the law required them to, but Sephardim did, and they undoubtedly influenced others in the former Byzantine Empire. The likelihood is therefore great that the family was named "Chameides" before they migrated to Galicia.

Ancestors of
Kalman Chameides

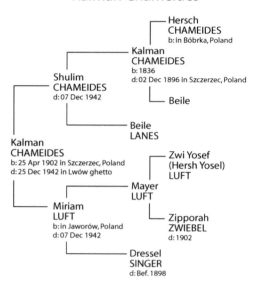

Hirsh (or Hersch) Chameides and his wife Beile are the earliest direct Chameides ancestors I have been able to identify. They lived in Bóbrka (known in Yiddish as Boiberek), were probably born towards the end of the 18th century, and therefore lived most of their adult lives during the harsh rule of Franz Leopold I.

Hirsh and Beile's son, Kalman Chameides (1836-1896) {Appendix 24} was born towards the end of Franz Leopold's reign, lived in Szczerzec with his wife, Beile, and died there at the age of 60 of "pneumonia."

Several years before Kalman's birth, a terrifying cholera epidemic struck Galicia. The epidemic had started in the slums of Calcutta, sowed a path of death and destruction across Asia and Russia, and, in 1830, came to Galicia. It continued westward and devastated most of Europe in the ensuing years. The frightening part was the suddenness with which it struck.

An apparently healthy individual would suddenly become violently ill with cramps and breathing difficulty. Within as short a time as two hours the victim would suffer a horrible convulsive death. Thousands of people died during this epidemic, which left a trail of fear that would last for generations. The word "cholera" entered the Polish language as a terrible curse and, since its cause was unknown, fear of the disease gave rise to many superstitious practices, which I still remember. For example, children were forbidden to drink water after eating certain foods, such as cucumbers.

It was during Kalman's lifetime that the government began enforcing the law that made last names mandatory, and (in 1877) required each Jewish community to maintain registers of life events (birth, marriage, and death). Prior to 1877, registers were kept by the Catholic Church, and the paucity of information before then, is undoubtedly due to the reluctance of Jews to register their life cycle events with the Church. After 1877, rabbis recognized by the state, were permitted to perform "civil marriages," and only these marriages were officially registered. Most Jewish marriages, however, were not performed by these rabbis, especially in the early years of the system, and were therefore not registered. Children resulting from only religious unions were regarded as "illegitimate" by the state, and were given the mother's surname. One has to be cognizant of this as one traces a family history. For example, Wunder[62] lists a rabbinic family by the name of Chameides who were Levites. Our family was not Levite. This discrepancy is probably due to the fact that the last name may have been the mother's, if the children were registered as "illegitimate," while the Levite status is passed down through the father.

There were a number of important developments in Galician Jewish life during Kalman Chameides' lifetime. Hasidism made significant inroads into Galicia and found a large number of adherents in the smallest of hamlets. Beginning about 1836, the year of Kalman Chameides' birth, a secular movement (Haskalah) came to Galicia and, as it gained strength, frictions developed between these movements.[63] An increasing number of Jews became interested in literature, the arts, and university studies. Some pursued these interests in Polish, others in German, and a small group of authors began writing in Yiddish, the spoken language of the majority, but looked down on even by its early authors as a "jargon." In addition, the Zionist movement (or its antecedent, the Chovvei Zion) fired the imagination of many and gained adherents. Unfortunately, we don't know how the early Chameides family was affected by these crosscurrents.

SHULIM CHAMEIDES

My grandparents, Miriam (left) and Shulim Chameides.

Kalman and Beile's son, Shulim (or Szulim, in the Polish spelling),[64] my paternal grandfather, was born in Szczerzec around 1870 and married Miriam Luft from the nearby town of Jaworów {Appendix 25}. Their first two children, Dressel Chane (born June 13, 1898 in Szczerzec) and Chaje (born June 29, 1899 in Szczerzec) died shortly after birth. These deaths were tragic, but not surprising, considering the high infant and child mortality. For example, in 1903 there were 71 births and 111 deaths recorded for the Jewish community of Szczerzec.[65] Of the 111 deaths, 66 (>50%) were in children <10 years of age.

The small town of Szczerzec (known in Yiddish and Ukrainian as Shchirits) is located approximately 30 km south of Lwów (Lviv in Ukrainian, Lvov in Russian, Lemberg in German and Yiddish). Jews are first recorded in the

---

[62] Meir Wunder, *Encyclopedia le'chachmei Galicia* (Jerusalem, 2005) volume 6 722.

[63] Marcin Wodziński, *Haskalah and Hasidism in the Kingdom of Poland. A History of Conflict* (The Littman Library of Jewish Civilization. Portland, OR 2005).

[64] I have not found proof that my grandfather Shulim was the son of Kalman Chameides, but the fact that the latter lived in Szczerzec, that Grandfather Shulim named his first born Kalman, and another son Hirsh, the name of Kalman's father, is very strong circumstantial evidence.

[65] JRI Poland.

town in 1629 and reached their highest number of 1,385 in 1880, when they constituted 80% of the total population. Beginning about 1878 most of the members of the Municipal Council and the mayors (including one of my grandmother's relatives) were Jews. In 1900, it was home to 1,324 Jews out of a total population of 1,730. Most Jews were very poor and many were unemployed or worked in petty trades. After WW I, most would have starved to death if it were not for help from the Joint Distribution Organization. Grandfather Shulim made a meager living as the town's *shohet* and cantor. According to the 1935 Community Budget[66] he earned an annual salary of 2,310 zł (60 zł for being a cantor; 2142 zł for being a shohet; and 108 zł for maintaining a slaughtering facility for chickens in back of his house.) To put this in perspective, my father's annual salary as Rabbi in Katowice was 14,900 zł in 1927 and 15,600 zł in 1928.[67]

Galicia was one of the battlegrounds on which the Russians, Austrians, and Germans slaughtered each other during WW I. The Russians conquered part of Galicia in September, 1914, shortly after the outbreak of war, only to lose the territory to the Austrians in 1915. Jews suffered terrible hardships as the front shifted back and forth. Fear of the Russians caused many Jews to flee westward so that by the end of the war

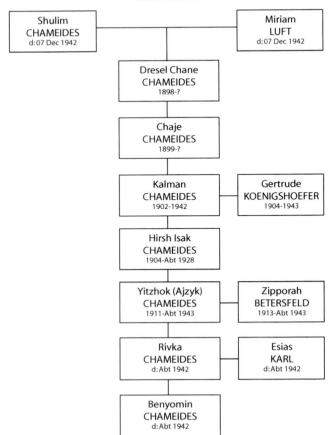

Children of Miriam and Shulim Chameides

Shulim CHAMEIDES d:07 Dec 1942 — Miriam LUFT d:07 Dec 1942

Dresel Chane CHAMEIDES 1898-?

Chaje CHAMEIDES 1899-?

Kalman CHAMEIDES 1902-1942 — Gertrude KOENIGSHOEFER 1904-1943

Hirsh Isak CHAMEIDES 1904-Abt 1928

Yitzhok (Ajzyk) CHAMEIDES 1911-Abt 1943 — Zipporah BETERSFELD 1913-Abt 1943

Rivka CHAMEIDES d:Abt 1942 — Esias KARL d:Abt 1942

Benyomin CHAMEIDES d:Abt 1942

there were half a million Jewish refugees in Bohemia, Austria, and Hungary, but our immediate family was not among them. In addition to the usual companions of war —hunger and disease— the Russians accused the Yiddish speaking Jews of being German spies and encouraged pogroms against them. Looting, murder, destruction of property, and kidnapping became a daily reality. The Russians instituted a policy of mass deportations. Many houses were

---

[66] Archives of the History of the Jewish People, Jerusalem HM2/8902 and HM 7106.
[67] Wojciech Jaworski 114.

destroyed and the population of Szczerzec declined for the first time, from a Jewish population of 1,264 in 1910 to 712 in 1921. Immediately after the Russian invasion, the Russian Governor-General, Count Bobrinski, enacted edicts to degrade Jews and bring them down to the level of the Jews of Russia. He confiscated land from Jewish landowners, and forbade Jews to own, lease, or rent land. In order to prevent "spying" by Jews, Grand Duke Nicholas gave an order on February 13, 1915 that Jews not be allowed to enter Galicia or travel between its districts. Any Jew disobeying this rule was fined 3000 rubles ($1,500) or faced a three months mandatory jail sentence. As an example of Russian cruelty, a Jew by the name of Jacob Mischel, a Szczerzec town councilor, was accused by the Russians of disobeying the law. He was doused with oil and set on fire in the town square.[68]

The end of World War I and the establishment of the independent state of Poland in 1918 did not end Jewish suffering. Since the Treaty of Versailles following WW I did not clarify Poland's eastern border, Ukrainians led an uprising in 1918 and declared their independence. The resulting war did not end until July 1919 at which time Russia joined in an attempt to invade Lithuania. Jews were once again caught in the middle of heavy fighting. Poles accused Jews of siding with the Ukrainians in the conflict. They encouraged anti-Jewish pogroms in Lwów in 1919, which resulted in 150 deaths. The conflict ended in 1921 with the Treaty of Riga, which gave Poland sovereignty over Galicia, although this was not recognized by the international community until 1923. The 1929 census showed that Szczerzec was home to 136 Poles, 174 Rusinows (Ukrainians), 668 Jews, and 75 Germans.

JEWISH AND TOTAL POPULATION OF SZCZERZEC

Year	No. of Jews	Total Population
1880	1,385	1,731
1900	1,324	1,730
1910	1,264	NA
1921	712	NA
1929	668	1,053

KALMAN CHAMEIDES

My father, Kalman (named after his grandfather), was born in Szczerzec in 1902. Grandfather Shulim and the town Rabbi, Dr. Abel Schönblum, were probably his first religious teachers. My father may also have attended a Zionist supplementary Hebrew school, which was established in Szczerzec in 1911. The hardships of WW I forced my father to leave public school at the end of the 5th grade.[69] He undoubtedly continued his religious education through these perilous times because a number of stories were told about his perseverance and brilliance.

---

[68] *The Jews In The Eastern War Zone* (The American Jewish Committee New York 1916).
[69] From an autobiographical sketch located in the Katowice library that my father had to write for the Government when he applied for the Rabbinical position in Katowice.

One was about his losing track of time and spending an entire night, during which he derived both heat and light from a single flickering candle, trying to understand a difficult Talmudic text. Another was about a visit with his father to a friend in a neighboring town. On the way back his horrified father discovered that his son had "borrowed" a volume of the Talmud and hidden it under the straw in the cart. They had to turn around to return the "borrowed" volume.

With financial help from relatives, the 18-year old Kalman went to Vienna in 1920 to further his education. War always changes the status quo. It saps the energy of the old, but it introduces new ideas to the young. Szczerzec must have seemed very confining to a bright teenager with a thirst for knowledge and dreams for the future. Vienna was the capital of the former empire that had ruled this region for some 130 years. It was an intellectual and cultural center of Europe and, for a young boy from a hamlet in the provinces, a portal into a wider world. His desire to go to Vienna must have filled his parents with anxiety and foreboding. They were undoubtedly concerned about his physical safety, but their greater concern must have been for his religious well-being. There were many stories of Yeshiva boys who could not withstand the temptations of the big cities. Some became involved in the

Haskalah movement, others joined the growing Reform movement, and some even became apostates, abandoning their people and faith completely. There are hints of friction between father and son in essays written by my father many years later. In an essay about the Rabbis of the Haggada, my father wrote about a schism between Rabbi Eliezer and his father. When, after many years they met again, "I [Rabbi Eliezer] was never able to find a way into his heart. Years of discord and separation that cast a shadow over my life to this day stood between us. Wounds opened in youth, never seem to heal. Ruts, created by suffering and anguish in the dawn of our lives, are not easily smoothed over later in life. An absence of love and understanding from parents leaves an indelible imprint on the rest of our lives."[70] One can't help but wonder whether he was speaking from personal experience.

Life in Vienna was extremely difficult for a poor boy from a *shtetl* whose primary language was Yiddish and whose last formal general education was in the 5th grade. He had to perfect his German[71] and teach himself literature, mathematics, science, philosophy, and other subjects that would allow him to pass the demanding state matriculation examination. He passed that examination in 1923 after three years of study "under the most trying living conditions."[72]

[70] Kalman Chameides, "A Seder in Bnei Brak," *UGGIK* #29 April 1933 4. Original in Polish.
[71] I thought that he didn't know German when he came to Vienna, but Mr. Moshe Escott from NJ kindly sent me a copy of a poem that my father wrote in German to Moshe's great grandfather when the latter left Szczerzec for the USA in 1920.
[72] From his brief autobiographic sketch referenced above.

Above: Application to the University of Vienna.

versity of Vienna. It is true that he had to "fib" a little to be admitted to the University. His application shows that he gave his father's name as "Max" (line 8), his father's occupation as "merchant" (line 8), and his native language as "German."(line 5).[74]

The Beit Midrash LeRabanim in Vienna (Israelisch-Theologisches Lehranstalt) was founded in 1893, and followed the philosophy and curriculum of the Breslau Seminary (see below). Its first and only Director, the Talmudic scholar Adolph Arye Schwartz, was a graduate of the Breslau seminary. My father's enrollment in the Bet Midrash LeRabanim, and later in the Breslau seminary, represented a clear religious and intellectual break with his past and must have confirmed his parents' worst fears.

After two years of study in Vienna and with encouragement and help from Rabbi Chajes, my father won a Hamelitz scholarship that enabled him to study Hebrew language and literature at the newly opened Hebrew University in Jerusalem (1925). This was an unusual step for a young rabbinical student from Poland and is evidence of his strong Zionist convictions and love for the Hebrew language, then in its infancy as a modern, resurrected means of daily communication and creativity.

My father drew on this year in Eretz Yisrael in later years when he wrote about his love for the land and the Hebrew

During this time he also attended the Hebrew Pedagogium, a seminary for the training of Hebrew teachers under the direction of Rabbi Hirsch Zvi Peretz Chajes, Chief Rabbi of Vienna. Rabbi Chajes had a magnetic personality, was a great orator, a fervent Zionist, and tended toward liberal orthodox religious views. He appears to have been one of my father's mentors and role models. After he passed the matriculation examination, my father was admitted to the Beit Midrash LeRabanim (Israelisch-Theologisches Lehranstalt)[73] and to the Philosophy Department of the Uni-

---

[73] Reuven Mas (Editor), *Sefer Zikaron Lebet Midrash leRabanim beVina* (Jerusalem 1946).
[74] From a copy of his application obtained from the University of Vienna.

language. He tirelessly sang the praises of the rebirth of the Jewish people on their native soil. He saw this as the only ray of sunshine and hope for the Jewish people on an otherwise gloomy horizon. "And indeed have we not ourselves survived to see the miracle of the splinters coming together and becoming whole again? Have we not witnessed parts, torn asunder come together into a new community? Haven't we defied all satanic powers and, in spite of universal derision, haven't we accomplished, or more correctly haven't we begun, something that should fill us with a feeling of pride and satisfaction?"[75] He described the salvation and continuity of our nation as a miracle dependent on seemingly insignificant things—a small crucible of oil overlooked by the anti-Hasmoneans, a coffin containing Rabbi Yohanan ben Zakkai smuggled out of Jerusalem during its siege by the Romans, and he wonders what is going to save us now: "The Jewish nation is pressed by boundless burdens of suffering: Hatred from the outside and poverty from the inside. Our youth is wasting away. Hope for a better future is melting away. Our only joy is blooming in the East. A silent, deep joy. A new Jewish reality is being established in the Holy Land. A new generation is growing up on the old land. The eyes of millions of believers are turned toward it—a land of eternal longing. The cradle and source of religion. The fire of faith. Our only

harbor for the future! Our only small vial. Will the miracle of Hanukkah repeat itself? Will there be enough oil? Let us believe and work for it. Let us work and believe!"[76]

But he also expressed concern about party factionalism and unwillingness of opposing groups to compromise their points of view. He especially bemoaned the split between religious and secular communities. On the occasion of the 25th Anniversary of the founding of Tel Aviv he wrote: "When mother Rachel arises from her tomb near Jerusalem each night to watch over her children, she sees before her a curious picture. On the one hand there are the somewhat too noisy, boisterous children of Tel Aviv and on the other, the white-bearded solemn men of Jerusalem whose faces radiate the brilliance of Kabalistic secrets; the worldly tumult of the new city and the majestic stillness of the old town. Confused, she turns her glance heavenward to God, who in the Holy Land is so close to human beings, and her lips bring forth a fervent prayer: 'Let, Oh God, the spirit of Tel Aviv and the soul of Jerusalem become one. Let there be a union between the cleverness of Tel Aviv and the radiant wisdom of Jerusalem; the zest for life with the solemnity, the thirst for enterprise with the dream, the worldly with the holy. Build O God, an arc of fire from the old to the new'...Only when Jerusalem and Tel Aviv no longer vie with each other; only when the heart of Jerusalem and the

---

[75] Kalman Chameides, "The Broken Tablets," *UGGIK* #56 May 1934 5-6. Original in German.
[76] Kalman Chameides, "Small Vessels," *UGGIK* #22 December 1932 1. Original in Polish.

head of Tel Aviv have both found a home within the Jewish people will the broken Jewish tablets once again become whole, and only then will Israel once again become the messenger bearing God's tidings at Sinai."[77] On the occasion of the anniversary of Theodore Herzl's death he wrote, "it will take a long time for the crust of the *galut*, formed around our hearts over a period of a thousand years of exile, to peel off. We no longer have to use Herzl's words, 'if you will it, it is no dream.'" For it is no longer only a dream; a generation is growing up in Eretz Yisrael that no longer knows the *galut*. The rivulet started by Herzl has long ago left its banks of party narrowness, and today flows powerfully around the entire people. Herzl's dream has become a reality. Herzl's dream has become deed."[78]

My father returned from Palestine in 1926 and enrolled in the Jüdisch-Theologisches Seminar in Breslau and in the University of Breslau, where he studied ancient philology. The Seminary did not charge tuition, and each student received a stipend, regardless of means so as not to embarrass those students who needed financial aid.[79] He received his rabbinical ordination from the Seminary in January 1929,

The Jüdisch-Theologisches Seminar was established in 1854 as an answer to the changes in liturgy and theology introduced by the Reform Movement. Zechariah Frankel, the founder of the Positive Historical movement, became its first Director. The Seminary's educational model was the university rather than the yeshiva, but it promoted traditional practice of Judaism and adherence to *Halacha*. Its philosophy, that social and historical forces influenced the development of the oral law, encouraged an open examination of the forces that shaped those practices. The Seminary emphasized modern tools of scholarship, encouraged its faculty and students to pursue and publish their research, and, in contrast to the traditional *yeshivot*, placed a high value on secular education. It boasted a superb library, and published a Jewish scholarly journal (Monatschrift für Geschichte und Wissenschaft des Judentums). The Breslau Seminary was the forerunner of the Conservative movement in Judaism and a model for the Jewish Theological Seminaries in Vienna and New York.[80]

Frankel and his philosophy met with stiff opposition from many Orthodox leaders. When Zechariah Frankel published his *magnum opus, Darchei Hamishna* (1859), he was severely attacked by the leader of Orthodox Judaism in Germany, Shimshon Raphael Hirsch. The latter argued that Frankel's thesis, that Mishnaic law was influenced

---

[77] Kalman Chameides, "Small Vessels," *UGGIK* #22 December 1932. Original in Polish.

[78] Kalman Chameides, "Herzl's Dream," *UGGIK* #58 June 1934 5-6. Original in German.

[79] Bernard Drachman, "Activities, Contacts, and Experiences in Breslau," in Guido Kisch, *The Breslau Seminary Memorial Volume 1963* (J.C.B. Mohr (Paul Siebeck) Tuebingen) 319.

[80] The terms "Reform" and "Conservative" are used in their 19th century meaning. The reform movement has since become much more traditional, while the Conservative movement has moved in the opposite direction.

Main building of the Jewish Theological Seminary of Breslau.

by social factors and folk custom was tantamount to a denial that both the Oral and Written Laws were given by God at Sinai. Frankel was, however, vigorously defended by other Orthodox luminaries, such as Rabbi Shelomo Yehudah Rapoport, but Frankel never answered Hirsch's charge or commented on it. As a result, both leaders of Modern Orthodoxy in Germany, Rabbis Hirsch and Esriel Hildesheimer, counseled Orthodox communities against appointing graduates of the Breslau seminary as Rabbis.[81] The Katowice Jewish community did not adhere to this counsel since three of its Rabbis, including my father, were graduates of the Breslau seminary.

GERTRUDE AND KALMAN CHAMEIDES

Following their wedding at the Altmann home in Katowice on September 29, 1929 and a honeymoon trip to Switzerland (I remember my mother telling me that they once stood on top of a mountain with their heads in the clouds), they settled into a spacious apartment at 10 Dyrekcyjna Street. This was around the corner from the Altmann's on a prestigious street near the central railroad station, so named because it was home to the Directors of the Railroad. The apartment was located in an elegant building designed by the famous architectural firm of Grünfeld (who also designed the synagogue). The buildings at #10 and #8 were built for Leopold Altmann in 1906. For many years, a flower shop and a fashionable clothing store were located on the ground floor.[82] The building originally had a cupola that was apparently removed when a 4th floor was added to the original three-story building. The façade of the building contains a coat-of-arms of the city with the date of its founding.

The coat of arms of Katowice is embedded in the building façade.

My father busied himself with community affairs while my mother became involved with the ladies' benevolent and educational organizations. This was a dif-

---

[81] David Ellenson, *After Emancipation* (Hebrew Union College Press 2004) 173.

[82] Jadwiga Lipońska-Sajdak and Zofia Szota, *Gruss aus Kattowitz* (Katowice 2008) 108.

An old postcard depicting Dyrekcyjna Street from Warszawska Street. We lived in the corner building on right.

Engagement photo of Gertrude Königshöfer and Rabbi Kalman Chameides in 1929.

Gertrude and Kalman Chameides on their wedding day, September 29, 1929.

ficult time for the community. The world economic downturn hit the Jewish community, much of it already impoverished, especially hard. The void left by the German Jews who left when Katowice became part of Poland in 1923, was being rapidly filled with Yiddish speaking immigrants from eastern Poland. Friction between the two communities was inevitable and for the first time a city, which boasted a single large synagogue, became home to *shtiblach* (small prayer halls), many of them belonging to various Hasidic sects. The Radomskyje Hasidim were especially strong, but Gerer Hasidim also had strong presence. My father tried to bridge these various worlds and to pacify the inevitable frictions. His sermons were often trilingual. He would start in German, then switch to Yiddish, and finish in Polish. He would also attend services from time to time in the Hasidic *shtiblach*. Many years later, when I met individuals who had prayed there, I was always impressed with the universal respect they had for his knowledge and personality. A newspaper article described

Wedding of Gertrude Königshöfer and Kalman Chameides. Left-to-right sitting: Adelheid Altmann, Artur Altmann, Freida Altmann, Gottfried Altmann, Klaire Thallmann, Cantor Walter Dembitzer. Standing: Bruno Altmann, Izak Königshöfer, unknown, Rosa Altmann, Herman Altmann, Hannah Altmann (Bruno's wife), Valerie Altmann (Robert's wife), Gertrude Chameides, Jonas Altmann (Bruno's son), Kalman Chameides, Willie Gluck, Heinrich Siechel (husband of Betty Königshöfer), Felix Gluck, Betty Gluck, Gustav Thallmann, Kurt Thallmann, Cantor Wolkowski.

Left-to-right sitting: Felix Gluck, unknown, Bella Vogelmann, Rabbi Vogelmann, Left-to-right standing: Bruno Altmann, Hannah Altmann, unknown, unknown, unknown, Miriam Chameides, ?Ajzyk Chameides, Shulim Chameides, Gertrude and Kalman Chameides, Heinrich Siechel (husband of Betty Königshofer), Hermann Altmann, (sitting) Martha Königshöfer (in front of Heinrich Siechel).

him as "an impressive presence. He does not give up the 'spiritual' in his every day behavior, bearing, or speech; his speech is refined and his tone is lofty. An excellent orator, he knows how to mold the rules of the various languages. He speaks German with conviction and Polish with feeling. He knows his heterogeneous community quite accurately and wields a strong influence on them."[83]

In order to better communicate with his community, my father founded and edited a community newspaper, *Urzędowa Gazeta Gminy Izraelickiej w Katowicach* (Official Newsletter of the Katowice Jewish Community), in 1932. Fortunately, 118 issues (1932-1937) of this newspaper have survived and we can get a glimpse into his philosophy from the many articles he wrote in German and Polish. Each essay is carefully crafted. His language is soaring, at times almost poetic, and the ideas are always well grounded in Jewish classical texts. His attention to the details of orthodox Jewish practice and laws are evident from his elaboration of the Laws of Passover[84] and the involved and detailed question that he poses to a Talmudic authority,[85] but his essays deal mainly with behavior, ethical conduct, national and Jewish existential issues, the gathering storm of anti-Semitism, and words of encouragement and hope. Each of these issues is carefully woven into a tapestry of Jewish tradition and sources. He tends to use the Aggadic literature, consisting of stories and parables, much more than strictly legal sources. His broad education is evident from quotes of Polish poets, German authors, English writers, and quotations in Hebrew, Aramaic, Latin, English, and French. It is impossible to summarize their content because of their diversity but it is worthwhile to give some examples, which will be limited here to observations on the Jewish predicament as viewed by him in the 1930s.

My father was much concerned with discord and division within the Jewish community: "Since time immemorial, we Jews have suffered from a malady, a disease that seems almost to be incurable: disunity, factionalism, and discord. Our tragedy is not only that we are tossed around the whole world; that we are constantly confronted by hatred and contempt; ...our misfortune and oppressor is an absence of internal unity and unanimity; an almost unbridgeable cleft that is opening between brother and brother."[86] He emphasized the universal application of the prophetic teachings,[87] and the value of each human being: "The work of a sage and that of a manual laborer, of a philosopher, or a field hand has an equal value from an ethical standpoint. Each of us has been endowed by God

---

83 *Jüdische Wochenpost mit Wirtschaftsblatt 3* (1936) #1 2.
84 Kalman Chameides, "The Laws of Passover," *UGGIK* #28 March 1933 3. Original in German.
85 Arieh Zwi Fromer, *Sheeloth Utshuvoth Eretz Zwi* (Lublin, 1939 # 81) 180.
86 Kalman Chameides, "Unity," *UGGIK* #27 March 1933 8. Original in German.
87 Kalman Chameides, "Jewish Ethics," *UGGIK* #4 March 1932 3. Original in Polish.
88 Kalman Chameides, "Jewish Ethics," *UGGIK* #9 May 1932 3. Original in Polish.

with certain strengths and abilities."[88] He emphasized the importance of mutual support, especially in times of distress: "Misfortune is the test of a community. When misfortune strikes a community, no one may say: 'I will go home, satisfy my hunger and thirst and not allow distress to disturb my soul' .....Instead everyone's obligation is to participate in the misfortune of the community and to suffer together with others [Taanit IIa]."[89]

The essays show that their author was a realist who clearly understood the temper of the times and the mortal danger that awaited the Jews individually. In November 1933, on the occasion of the 15th anniversary of Polish independence he stated: "...we have not yet come to terms with the idea that in the enlightened 20th century, the middle ages could arise for us—a dark era of anguish and suffering. But are we going to be the only sacrifices to that dangerous rage? Doesn't that megalomania contain within itself the spark of a new world war, a spark of *bellum omnium contra omnes?* ...We [Poland and the Jews] have a common enemy who lies in wait for our destruction and, if given the opportunity, will not hesitate to remove the crown of freedom from Poland's head with his sword; the freedom for which the nation has suffered so much and fought so hard."[90] In 1935,

he prophesied what awaited our Jewish people: "They want to defame and degrade us. They first pronounce a sentence of death on our spirit, in order then, with a clear conscience, to bury our physical existence."[91] "A threatening reality has overtaken us and is demanding the greatest sacrifices from us. Accordingly, let each of us understand the first verse of our daily prayer '*Shema*': 'Love your eternal God with all your heart, with all your soul, and with all your might'. With all your soul - even if you have to pay for loving the God of your ancestors with your life. However, Jewish martyrology must not weaken our resolve for self-preservation. For after this dark night, the dawn of freedom will shine at last and the words of our prophet will be fulfilled: 'The nation that walked in darkness will see a great light; a great light will shine on those who walk in the shadow of death.'"[92] "Here, we have been and, unfortunately, continue for the time being to be martyrs. Here, we must be prepared to suffer for our Judaism. Our surrounding world demands this sacrifice of us. Here, we must often pay with our happiness and the happiness of our children for our Jewish existence."[93] "It is becoming ever darker in the Jewish street. Previously, we had to deal with individual enemies of the Jews. Today, states and nations have

---

[89] Kalman Chameides, "Jewish Ethics: The Individual and Society," *UGGIK* #13 August 1932 4. Original in Polish.

[90] Kalman Chameides, "Anniversary of the Resurrection of the Polish State," *UGGIK* #44 November 1933 5. Original in Polish.

[91] Kalman Chameides, "Haman's Arguments," *UGGIK* (#75 March 1935) 7-8. Original in German.

[92] Kalman Chameides, "A Seder in Bnei Brak," *UGGIK* #29 April 1933 9. Original in German.

[93] Kalman Chameides, "Hero and Martyr," *UGGIK* #46 December 1933 9. Original in German.

conspired against us. For many, Jew-hating has become a philosophy of life, the essence of life, a creed and, yes, even a religion. It is proclaimed and preached like a holy sermon from the highest positions. It is fomented, disseminated, and incited by false apostles and prophets. It penetrates like a poison into the souls of the deluded masses and disturbs the harmony of human society."[94]

He wrote the following about the Hebrew language: "Knowledge of Hebrew vocabulary derived directly from the original ancient literary sources is necessary for another reason. Just as personal relationships are influenced by the circumstances of the first meeting, every Hebrew word maintains the color and character of the literary creation from which it stems and where it was first encountered. For a Jew, whose first encounter with the word "heaven" is in a dictionary rather than in the first sentence of the Bible where it is placed in the context of creation of the world, the word will never have a deeper meaning than its Polish equivalent, "niebo" or the German equivalent, "Himmel." In contrast, a Jew who receives a traditional education will subconsciously have a different reaction to this word. Emotional and conceptual associations surround the word "hashamaim" in the poetic words of the author of the book of Psalms, 'the heavens relate the glory of God' or in the majesty of the sentence 'in the beginning God created the heavens and the earth.' A prosaic word like "ladder" conceals within it some of the enchantment of the dream of Jacob if it is engraved into our memory for the first time as a component of the beautiful picture of this dream in the Bible ("and he dreamed, and behold a ladder is standing on the ground and its top reaches heaven and behold angels of the Lord are ascending and descending, etc.") It is clear from this, that studious reading of the Bible and of our ancient religious texts in general, lead to a deeper understanding and appreciation of the Hebrew language, not only in terms of its linguistic and etymological richness but, above all, the artistic and emotional flavor of each word."[95]

My father was the head of the local *Beth Din* (Jewish Court) and was very involved with the religious education of the community's children. He was responsible for religious instruction in the pubic schools, in the local Jewish elementary school named after Berek Joselewicz, a Jewish hero of the 19th century Polish uprising against Russia, and in the supplementary Hebrew school (Talmud Torah) maintained by the community. In addition, he founded a Beis Yaakov school and recruited Mrs. Taube, who lived with us, as its first teacher. My wife, Jean, and I had the great pleasure to meet her at her home in the Meah Shearim home section of Jerusalem.

[94] Kalman Chameides, "Herzl and Bialik," *UGGIK* #84 July 1935 6-7. Original in German.
[95] Yosef Chrust and Yosef Frankel (eds), *Katowitz Perihatah ushkiata shel hakehilah hayehudit. Sefer Zikaron* (Tel Aviv 1996 (Hebrew) 20; 22.

Rabbi Kalman Chameides (on left with top hat) with other Rabbinic dignitaries at the opening of Yeshivath Chachmei Lublin on June 24-25, 1930.

1936 meeting of Western Galicia Zionist Congress in Katowice. Rabbi Kalman and Gertrude Chameides are seated 2nd and 3rd from right; Rabbi and Mrs. Vogelmann are seated 2nd and 3rd from left.

Rabbi Kalman Chameides standing in the rear (with hat) of the Katowice Talmud Torah School probably in the early 1930s.

Rabbi Kalman and Gertrude Chameides in the late 1930s.

HERBERT AND LEON CHAMEIDES

My brother was born on September 16, 1932. He was named Herbert (Hershl in Yiddish and Zwi in Hebrew) in memory of my father's younger brother who died at a young age approximately six years before, probably of tuberculosis. Shortly after Herbert's birth, my father published an essay[96] full of joy, hope, and pride in which he emphasizes the role of innocent children in Jewish legend and their ability, through their innocence, to influence God's actions.

The mood was very different by the time I was born, on June 24, 1935. Hitler had become Chancellor of Germany, not far from Katowice, on January 30, 1933 and moved rapidly to establish his dictatorship and anti-Jewish policies. The first major campaign of terror including beating of Jews in the streets of Berlin took place on March 9, 1933, which also marked the opening of the Dachau concentration camp used at first for "opponents" of the regime, including many Jews. Closer to home, all

Jewish judges and lawyers were dismissed from the courts in Breslau. On April 1, storm troopers enforced a boycott of all Jewish owned businesses in Germany. By April 7, all Jewish civil servants were dismissed. Cities vied with each other in their zeal and banned Jewish actors, artists, teachers, and professors from practicing their professions. On May 10, the Nazis organized a massive bonfire and burned thousands of so called Jewish books in front of Berlin University. Jews tried to flee from Germany to England, the United States, and Palestine. By the end of 1934, more than 50,000 Jews had left Germany, but about 450,000 remained. The Nuremberg Laws, which totally isolated the Jews of Germany and deprived them of all civil rights and the means of earning a livelihood, took effect on September 15, 1935.

The hatred of Jews spilled over the border into Poland. There were calls for boycotts of Jewish businesses and the Nazi party became active, especially in Upper Silesia. In January 1934, Germany and Poland signed a non-aggression pact and, ominously, in September 1934 Poland renounced the Minorities Treaty of 1919 under which Poland had obligated itself to protect minority rights. To add to Jewish anxieties, Marshal Józef Piłsudski, the beloved benevolent autocrat who had ruled Poland from 1926, died in May 1935. He had kept the right wing, anti-Jewish Endecja party under control and now he was gone. The mood at the time of my birth was therefore one of

---

[96] Kalman Chameides, "Jewish Ethics IX: The Child," *UGGIK* #15 September 1932 5. Original in German.

foreboding, gloom, and fear.

Like my brother's birth, my father also celebrated my birth with an essay, but what a different essay! It was based on a speech he delivered at the cemetery in Katowice on the saddest day of the Jewish calendar, the 9th of Av, which commemorates so many calamities in Jewish history including the destruction of both Temples and the loss of Jewish independence. The essay shows that he clearly understood the danger ahead. One can almost hear his anguished cry, "how could I have brought a child into this world at this time?" Here is my translation of the essay in its entirety:[97]

Jewish Children as Martyrs: On the 9th of Av

In every age, the voice of children is drowned out by the energetic, pompous voices of grown-ups. Grown-ups make war. Grown-ups make history. Grown-ups write history. It is of course their interpretation, from their point of view. *They* fought. *They* made peace. *They* suffered. But no historian knows how to describe the suffering of children. They bloom like flowers and decorate our path of thorns. And, just like flowers, they are often trampled underfoot by the relentless march of ruthless events. Quietly and without a sound. They fade rapidly because they need much sunshine and don't receive it. Everywhere there is only haze, shade, and a sorrowful darkness...Created by adults and brought into the world through their transgressions! Their souls shatter easily because they need so much joy and have none. Everywhere, there is only sorrow, anxiety, and distress...Conceived by adults; their presence is their fault. They age early because they need so much freedom and have none. Everywhere, - only oppression, bondage, and persecution...Pushed by grown-ups and camouflaged under a veneer of their degenerate morality! Born into a cold, joyless, and subjugated world, they carry the burdens that we impose on them. But their voice, that thin voice of children, is not heard. For grown-ups have no time. Their heroism remains unacknowledged. For, after all, no weapon glitters in their tiny hands. Grown-ups can be so easily deceived. They are certain that heroism resides only in the mouths of cannons and on the sharp edge of polished knives. "Children cannot be heroes" say the grown-ups who make and write history. "Children can be heroes if they are taught heroism," answers an echo from bygone days...

On this 9th of Av, we want to visit the grave of the unknown Jewish child-hero. Shh..., quiet, we are entering the ancient Jewish children's cemetery...

---

[97] Kalman Chameides, "Jewish Children as Martyrs," *UGGIK* #85 August 1935 4-5. Original in German.

I

"When you pass through water, I will be with you" (Isaiah 43:2)

A ship is on the high seas with 400 Jewish children, boys and girls who are being sent by a heartless tyrant into the unknown. Behind them is a destroyed homeland and ahead of them, an ignominious future. In distant lands, across the sea, they are to fall prey to dishonor and prostitution. Now, they are still pure and untouched by carnal, sensual pleasures. But they have already been half awakened from their youthful innocence. The disgrace into whose arms they are being led is beginning to dawn on them immaturely but darkly. Where could they flee? The waves of the ocean are motioning that they are their only escape and shelter. Therein lies a solution and freedom...Their childish eyes are fixated on the alluring ocean floor. They are filled with an indescribable fear. Fear of death? No! They are acquainted with death. They are no longer afraid of it. They met death on the streets of Jerusalem when it robbed them of their fathers and mothers and subdued the young warriors. No, they are afraid of God's punishment. Jewish law prohibits suicide. The following passage was impressed on them in school: "One who commits suicide, loses his portion of the world to come." Should they dash their hope of resurrection into the depths, together with their lives? Doesn't this suddenly-noticed means of escape from the disgrace in store for them, mean eternal annihilation and condemnation? Helpless, they look to the oldest and wisest among them. And this one frees their afflicted souls. Relying on a verse in Psalms, he predicts happiness and a reward for his companions in misfortune: "I will drag you out of the lion's jaws" says God, "and from the bottom of the sea." Doubt and fear are immediately abolished. A supernatural radiance lights their faces. Quietly, the girls plunge into the sea. They are followed by the boys. The following scriptural words are applicable: "For your sake, O Lord, we have daily surrendered our life; we are like a lamb, led to the slaughterhouse."

Bloody red, the sun sets in the west. Trembling, its last rays fall momentarily on the body of the youngest before he too is swallowed by the waves. Four hundred children's souls hang suspended against the red evening heavens. The empty ship continues into the night...(Gittin 56).

II

"Strength arises out of the mouths of children" (Psalms 8:3).

The Roman Imperator sits on his throne in a large, expansive hall. Rome's generals and famous commanders surround him. The walls are brimming with gold and war booty. The campaign against Judea has come to a successful conclusion. Jerusalem has been reduced to rubble. The Temple has been burned. Jackals howl at night where once the holy altar stood. The spoils of this war were rich.

But why does a barely perceptible shadow cross Caesar's face? Why is there a wrinkle of dissatisfaction around his lips? Doesn't he have every reason to be completely happy?

The great conqueror, hailed by all, feels that he has been beaten. His pride and vanity have been offended. It is impossible to vanquish this tiny Judean people. Hasn't he leveled their homes, plundered their belongings, and desecrated their holy places? Nevertheless, they continue to maintain the same stubbornness and tenacity. They cannot be dissuaded from worshipping their invisible God, who has obviously deserted them. No power has been able to force them to worship the powerful Caesar. He knows that they respect him, but, despite being beaten and confined in shackles and chains, they remain proud and self-confident. They recognize no man as their master; their prayers are directed only to God. It would have satisfied him if, at least superficially, they showed him the same divine reverence as all the other subjugated nations. But they refuse any form of obeisance. Even their children are unbending and fight for their faith like lions. He wants to try one more time. Shouldn't he, who has conquered and held dominion over lands and seas, be able to bring the mother and her seven children, whom he has captured, to their knees? He will deal with them gently, yet cruelly. He will infatuate them and terrify them with threats. They will whimper and worship him as a god. "Bring them in, one at a time," he orders his servant.

The children stand huddled around their mother in front of the palace. The mother's face is rigid and unemotional. Will her children be able to endure the test; will they be able to withstand the temptation? Had she planted the faith in the God of their ancestors deep enough in their hearts? Would the religious upbringing that she gave them be strong enough to withstand the seductive attractions of Caesar's court? Soon, the king's courier approaches to take them. She lifts her maternal hands and quietly blesses her children: "May the Lord bless you and protect you"...

A Jewish child stands at the foot of the throne, facing the king. The child's dazzling beauty momentarily forces Caesar to lower his eyes. What an uncanny power radiates from the child's flaming eyes! The eyes of the Minister and the servants are fixed expectantly on this child who stands totally unaffected. Caesar collects himself. He must not become sentimental. He has to remain stern. "Convert to our faith," Caesar's voice is both harsh and inviting. "Our Torah states: 'I am the Eternal One, your God!' We are not allowed to worship other gods," the child answers, firmly and without fear. The constable immediately seizes the child and leads him out. He will pay for his steadfastness and faith with his life.

Six are prepared to die a martyr's death. The last one now comes before Caesar. Outside, the mother stands alone. "Renounce your faith!" The voice from the throne is almost gentle and imploring. If only this last child could be convinced..."We have promised our God that we will never exchange Him for another!" answers the last of the seven children. As he is led to the place of execution, his mother sees him and kisses him. "Go, tell father Abraham that whereas he was prepared to offer one son to God, I have brought Him seven children!" When the mother follows her children in death, a heavenly voice rings out: אם בנים שמחה – Mother and children are united in joy" (Gittin 56).

III

"Better off were those slain by the sword that those who died by famine"
(Lamentations 4:9).

Whenever suffering becomes most severe and the Jewish people plead in vain for help, the prophet Elijah appears as a comforter and holy messenger. He mingles with the starving masses that fill the streets of Jerusalem but even he can no longer ward off the disaster since the destiny of his people has been sealed. Years of exile and suffering must follow the misspent hundreds of years of freedom. Idolatry and immorality have led the people to become degenerate. The holy places have been defiled. On every hill there are images of strange gods, against which he fought so relentlessly when he wondered the earth as a zealous prophet and seer of the true religion. But today, he is here neither to threaten and agitate, nor to battle against false prophets, as he once did on Mt. Carmel. He has come to the ruins and remnants of the holy city in order to help and to comfort...

Suddenly, a shrill cry of a child reaches his ears. He turns and sees before him a half starved boy, lying on a dung heap, wrestling with the Angel of Death. Full of pity, the prophet bends over the languishing lad. "What is your name, my child?" The name of an esteemed family, once among the aristocracy of Jerusalem, is poised on the pale lips of the exhausted boy. "Would you like to learn a declaration that will restore your life and your strength?" "Yes", the child, barely audibly, whispers. "Then, from now on, say this declaration of faith every day: "Shema Yisrael - Hear, O Israel. The Eternal One, our God is one." The child is startled at the sound of these words. He jerks and with his last ounce of strength says: "Keep quiet! Don't mention that name! I don't know this God! My parents never told me about Him."

With these words, the boy pulls an idol from his bosom, embraces and kisses it. As his eyes close, his soul departs. He continues to hold the idol firmly in his stiff hands, whitened by death. (Sanhedrin 63)

That is how strong-willed and determined Jewish children are even in sin. That is how persistent and uncompromising they are, even when they go astray as a result of crimes committed by adults. They die worshipping the ideals taught them by their parents.

What a terrible disgrace it is for parents, to have their children die holding onto an image of a false idol because their parents never taught them about the true God.

What a disgrace it is for a generation, to have their youth, in their very last moments of life, refuse to accept the truth from the mouths of prophets!

The prophet's words ring out like a last warning: A reminder to return and to repent; to contemplate and to atone: "Hear, O Israel. The Eternal One, our God is one!"

The child discards this declaration. He dies with an illusion and a delusion.

"My father and mother told me nothing about this God"....

The portals of the children's cemetery are closing. Deeply moved, we take our leave of the graves of Jewish children - heroes of a bygone day. We find ourselves once again in the heart of Europe, in the first half of the 20th century. Today, a Jewish child sees a world of enemies confronting him like once little David faced the giant, Goliath. His martyrdom begins in his earliest school days, where the first principles of racial prejudice are taught. He knows nothing of golden childish dreams since the childhood of a Jewish child is filled with great anxiety about the future.

Jewish children have hardly become conscious of life and joy, when they realize that they are surrounded by enemies; encircled by hatred and distrust and, like those 400 children on the ship, are to be handed over to shame. In which port will that ship anchor? Will they ever be allowed to feel firm land underfoot or will they be irrevocably condemned to perish in the wildly surging waves?

The mother stands outside, frightened and worried, like that mother of the small martyrs, and waits for her child. Will the tyrant on the throne have pity? Today, the Caesar is no longer trying to win over Jewish children's hearts. He no longer tries to convert them to his own faith. He wants to annihilate them. He knows no pity. Sympathy is a stranger to him.

And because of this, Jewish children must once again become heroes. Teach your children the affirmation of one God early, so that in their hour of distress, they won't worship false gods and say: "My father and mother told me nothing about a Jewish God." Teach them to bear humiliation with pride; to accept degradation in peace; and teach them, in suffering, never to deny; in an assault from hostile forces, never to lose hope. Hope in the enlightenment of humanity. Hope in the deliverance of the Jewish people."

That is the world I was born into, but of course, I did not know it then. I was named in memory of my mother's grandfather, Leopold (Altmann), and given three Hebrew names, an unusually large number: Yehudah, my great-grandfather's name (Leopold Altmann), Chaim, and Jehonathan. I am reasonably certain that "Chaim" was in memory of my mother's uncle, Herman (Hebrew name Chaim) Altmann, who died unexpectedly in December 1934. I suspect that "Jehonathan" was in memory of my maternal great-grandfather, Moses Jonas (Yona) Königshöfer. My world consisted of loving parents, my brother, Herbert, our Polish cook, Anna, and her niece, Agnes, our nanny. My first language was German since my mother knew no Polish, but I learned Polish from Agnes on our many outings to the park when I invariably asked for "iglu" ice cream.

My wife, Jean, and I returned to Katowice for the first time in June 1989 to participate in the dedication of a monument on the grounds of our former synagogue. I was privileged to sing the *kel*

male rahamim prayer and the entire event was extensively covered by the local press. As I was standing in line to check out of the hotel, an elderly lady dressed completely in black shyly approached me and addressed me in Polish. "Pan Chameides?" she asked. "Yes," I replied. "Happy birthday to you – your birthday will be on the 24th of this month and your brother's birthday will be on September 16th." I looked at her, dumbfounded. "Only Agnes could know that," to which she nodded and we had a wonderful 50-year reunion.

We left Katowice when I was four years old and my memories of our apartment are therefore somewhat vague. I do remember the dining room with a brass "Shabbat lamp" and a glass cabinet containing tiny silver furniture with which I was allowed to play on special occasions, especially at the *seder* on Pesach. My brother, Herbert, and I shared a room, which was long and narrow and, much to mother's disgust, the wall on my side was covered with a collection of treasures I managed to withdraw from my nose. I also remember my father's book-lined study especially when the *huppah* was set up for a wedding. I would hide in the corner to watch the proceedings and admire the *huppah* poles made of shiny and smooth turned twisted wood.

During the summer we used to go to a resort in Ustroń where we rowed a boat on the lake. We were surrounded by family. The Altmanns lived around the corner and Bruno's teenaged son, Fred (Manfred) often came to see us. The Thallmans lived in the apartment above ours with their children Kurt (12 years old) and Werner (6 years old). They were grandchildren of Getrud, Bruno's and my grandmother's sister. My father's younger brothers, Ajzyk and Beniu visited frequently. Uncle Ajzyk was a fine Talmudic scholar and I have been told that my father and he would compete on their vast knowledge of the text and commentaries, and invariably wound up in the study to verify some fine point of Jewish law. For a time, before my birth, Uncle Ajzyk lived in our home. On November 28, 1931 he became part-time rabbi to the nearby community of Mikołów. Since the community was too small for a full time rabbi, Uncle Ajzyk lived with us and traveled to Mikołów for the Sabbath and Jewish holidays. In July 1935, the Silesian government offered Uncle Ajzyk a position to serve a number of small communities in the vicinity (Bierun Stary, Mikolów, Pszczyna,

My mother (right), Agnes (left), Herbert and I, probably in the summer of 1938 in Ustroń.

Siemanowice Śląskie, and Żory)[98] but Uncle Ajzyk declined the offer.[99] My father desperately tried to get him out of the country and I found two letters written by him to Rabbi R. Piekarski in Geneva seeking help for his younger brother who had gone to the Montreux Yeshiva (Etz Haim founded in 1927) as a teacher. The letters are written in the flowing Hebrew style which Rabbis used to address each other, almost like royalty. The following are my translations of the two letters:

[98] http//kirkuty.xip.pl/pszczyna_historia.pdf accessed 5-19-2009.
[99] Wojciech Jaworski 115.

Kalonymus Kalman Chameides
Head of the Beth Din of the Katowice Community

Thursday, Parshat Korach
2nd day of Rosh Hodesh
Tammuz 5697
[June 10, 1937]

To my honored friend, Rabbi, Gaon,
Sharp and well versed, a garden bed of spices,
our noble teacher, Rabbi Yisarel Yizhok Piekarski,
may he live a long life, The Av Beth din of the Community
of Geneva, may God protect and preserve him.

After inquiring about your well being I, respectfully and with great love, would like to inform you that my brother, may his light shine, whom the honorable Rabbi met while in my home, traveled this week to Yeshivath Etz Chaim in Montreux to spend some time there as a teacher. He was recently offered several positions as a community Rabbi and he remains a top candidate for the position in Gdynia. However, after becoming acquainted with the chaos and controversy that reigns at the present time in Poland, my brother, may his light shine, searched for an opportunity to leave this land, which, as you well know and heaven forefend, devours its inhabitants. One of his acquaintances proposed that he go to the above named Yeshiva in Switzerland, made efforts on his behalf, and after Rabbi Boczko, may his light shine, invited him, he decided to follow this route. I have already received a letter that he arrived there safely and that his situation is, thank God, good.

However, as you know, this position is not one that provides a living wage on the basis of which one could establish a home. My aim for him is that he strike roots overseas where he can spread his tent because the situation here is bad from every respect. In view of the fact that you have had an opportunity to assess my brother's (may his light shine) qualities and also are acquainted with my household, I am turning to you with a sincere and urgent request. Perhaps you would find him an appropriate position which would provide him with a grasp on life [livelihood]. I am sure that within a short time he will acclimate himself to Switzerland and will easily acquire knowledge of the language. He already speaks good German and is learning French. I pray that he does not need to return here.

Please let me know that you are well and I thank you in advance for your effort and kindness to my brother (may his light shine).

I hereby send best regards with great affection, esteem and respect.
[Signed] Kalonymus Chameides Av Beth Din

The second letter thanks Rabbi Piekarski for his efforts.

Thursday, 15 Tammuz 5697
[June 24, 1937]

To my honored friend, Rabbi, Gaon,
Sharp and well versed, a garden bed of spices,
our noble teacher, Rabbi Yisarel Yizhok Piekarski,
may he live a long life, The Av Beth din of the Community
of Geneva, may God protect and preserve him.

After inquiring about your well being, respectfully and with great love, I would like to express my gratitude for his honor's assistance by visiting my brother (may his light shine) in Montreux. If the Lord wills it, I will happily reciprocate the favor. I have a friend, Rabbi Taubes (may his light shine) in Zurich, we studied together in our youth, and I shall, please God, also write to him. I am overwhelmed with work until it is almost unbearable, and my soul is very weary from the many communal burdens I must bear. How sad it is to see time pass and I, who have always, day and night, been accustomed to performing spiritual functions, must now devote so much time to rabbinical business and the day-to-day problems, which come to me in a multitude. In the meantime I have also been honored with the official rabbinical position in Bedzin occasioned by the insipient dispute there [the community was split between the hasidic and non-hasidic factions and could not agree on a rabbi to succeed one who died]. I travel there three times a week to deal with all the matters which fall to the duties of the office of rabbi. If at least the times were peaceful! But what can we do? Things are getting more difficult from day to day and I avoid leaving my home in the evening for fear of the night and of the mischief makers who gather in the streets. May the Lord guard and save us from evil afflictions.

If possible, I intend to visit Switzerland on my holidays. I have so far not made a decision because of the many impediments but I hope, with the help of God, to carry out my intention and then, with God's help, we will see each other.

And now I once again want to express my feelings gratitude to your honor for his efforts on behalf of my brother (may his light shine). We hope that your labor bears fruit, that he finds his path in life, and may that merit accrue to your honor. Good deeds are done by good people.

Devoted to you with heart and soul, I wish you all the best

[Signed] Kalonymus Kalman Chameides

Letter from Rabbi Kalman Chameides on behalf of his brother, Ajzyk, to Rabbi Piekarski in Geneva, Switzerland.

Unfortunately, Uncle Ajzyk could not find a position abroad and he was forced to return to Poland sometime in 1938. I remember his return because he brought me back a green felt *kippah* with a small red tassel.

One of my earliest memories is from 1938 when I was three years old and we took a train to Marienbad in Czechoslovakia to visit my maternal grandparents. The train ride is especially vivid in my memory because we slept on the overnight train, and I insisted that I sleep in the upper berth. Much to Herbert's chagrin, since he slept on the lower berth, I wet the bed that night. I don't remember anything else from this trip but Aunt Betty's son, Dov with whom I became very close in later years, remembers my coming to the window of his room. We were not allowed to be together because he was ill with polio at the time and was confined to his room. Fortunately, it left him with no ill effects.

Nineteen-thirty-eight was a tragic year for Jews in general and for our family in particular. During that year the Germans annexed Austria, which went on to set an example of anti-Jewish brutality. On the night of the 27th of October, thousands of Polish Jews who resided in Germany were rounded up by the Gestapo. All their belongings and money were

My father, my mother, Herbert, and I on a visit to our maternal grandparents in Marienbad in 1938.

confiscated and they were taken to the Polish border and ordered to walk into Poland. Poland refused to admit them and so, under inhuman conditions they were stuck in border towns, the most crowded of which was Zbaszyn not far from Katowice. My father and the rest of the community tried to help these unfortunate people. Fifty-five years later my son Danny drew my attention to a poem written by the daughter of one of these refugees:[100]

[100] Mina Friedler, *Keys* www.613.org/friedler/html accessed 5-27-1998.

"Daddy, Rabbi Friedler, strokes his cloud white beard,
eyes rivet on distant points no
present map can record
...1938...

Thursday night, the SS...
I, a student with a ticket
to Schneider's Yeshiva, England....
tricked, they said we could return,
Mother, Father and I took nothing...forced
to travel on trains...desecrate Shabbos wazzu [sic] morning...
to Polish border town, Zbanzyn [sic]...live in Stables,,,My mother
an old peasant farmer...gone when the Nazis called
our names to go to Rozhniyatov...where they would never
have let me leave...months passed...no visa, 36 zlotas [sic] we
could not stand...the conditions...rented a room...
did not have...I wrote a letter...Rabbi Chameides of
Katowice...told him I wanted to study Torah...sealed the
envelope...it came, the visa, no words, promises or cordial
invitations, what was needed...36...double chi...life...
goodbye at the train station...two weeks later, borders
closed...I worked sent 25 zlotas [sic] a month to help Mama
and Papa...never again...the Rabbi...murdered at Belzec...

Deddy's tear sounds beat against my ears
like a baby's first wails of a time just now
full circle felt
after more than 50 years,
i cry too, Deddy....no more *tzaar*...
...1996
We quiver in their steps,
ground spinning, Rabbi Chameides,
the Bluzhova Rebbe, Deddy,
Dim the lights in Hunter Shul,
twist the latch, hang the key
back on the nail with
happy kiddy days.

Tragedy also struck the family in 1938. Gertrude Thalmann (Bruno's and grandmother's sister b 1872) died in February after a short illness, and Gottfried Altmann (Bruno's brother b 1878) died of a heart attack in March. He and Artur (b 1871) left Katowice when it became part of Poland and moved about 5 km away to Beuthen (Bytom), which remained part of Germany. They established a branch of the Altmann store in the Rynek and lived in apartments above it. The German government's official anti-Jewish policies, which began in 1933, robbed them of their livelihood and, after his brother's death, Artur could no longer cope, and committed suicide in June 1938. Robert Altmann (grandmother's brother) was arrested during Kristallnacht (November 9, 1938), and sent to Buchenwald concentration camp. His body was returned to his family in a sealed coffin, which they were ordered not to open.[101] The family had to pay a ransom for his body, and the Jewish community of Germany was sent a bill by the government for the destruction that took place during Kristallnacht.

In Poland, too, life was becoming increasingly more precarious for Jews. There were boycotts of Jewish businesses, strict quotas were established for university admission, and Jewish students were segregated and forced to sit in the back benches. Jews were afraid to walk on the street at night and a bomb was thrown into our synagogue on December 5, 1935. "Anti-Jewish agitation became so pronounced in

Polish Upper Silesia during December [1935] that a delegation from the Katowice Jewish community and the Silesian Union of Rabbis requested the Polish Governor to take measures to put it down."[102] As Polish-German relations deteriorated, speaking German in public was outlawed. This affected me greatly because German was my mother tongue and the only way I could speak with my mother. I could not understand why I had to be completely silent on our shopping excursions. Everyone frantically tried to emigrate, but most countries would not admit Jews.

In the spring of 1939, a few months prior to the outbreak of the war, my father went to England, allegedly to appear before a Parliamentary Committee on behalf of Jewish German refugees who attempted to enter Britain. Aunt Lotte told me that after he finished his business in London he came to Newcastle. At that time Lotte and her husband lived with other members of her husband's family in a tiny flat. The front doorbell rang at 2:00 AM and, when Aunt Lotte opened the door, she was surprised to see my father. He was very tired, but all the beds were taken. Two girls slept in one bed in the living room, two other girls slept in a bed in the kitchen, and Aunt Lotte and her husband were in the bedroom. Father suggested that he sleep in the bathtub but finally managed to rest on a divan. Everyone urged him to stay and he was said to have been offered a position as Rav in Dublin, but he insisted on returning to his family and his community.

---

[101] Yehudah Altmann Personal communication.
[102] *American Jewish Yearbook* (Jewish Publication Society of America 5696 1936) 332-33.

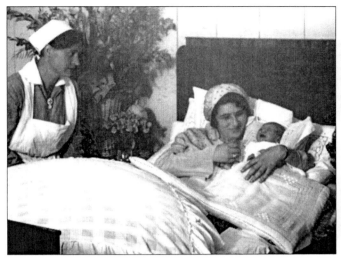

My mother a few days after either Herbert's or my birth.

My mother and Herbert welcoming me (1935).

Three generations: On right: Grand-mother and Grand-father Koenigshoefer and below my father, and Grandfather Shulim. The baby is either Herbert or me.

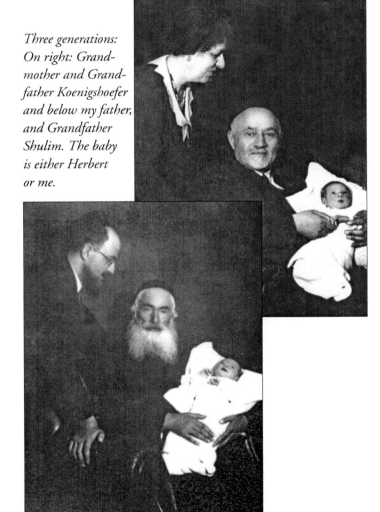

My mother with me on the potty.

Herbert (left) and I in 1937.

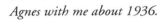

Agnes with me about 1936.

Herbert (left) and I about 1937/1938.

Herbert (right) and I about 1937/1938.

Herbert (left) and I with unidentified baby

Herbert (right) and I about 1938.

Herbert on right and I about 1937.

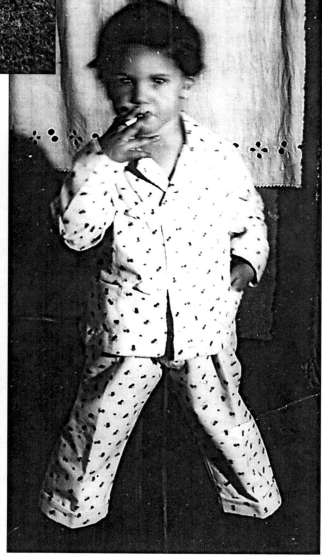

Herbert on Purim.

Uncle Beniu (father's brother) with Herbert around 1932.

Purim 1937 or 1938. Herbert is sitting in front; I am the "Mexican" is in the first row on the right. Behind me is Werner Thallman; Kurt Thallmann is next to him (in top hat).

Herbert lighting Hanukkah Menorah about 1935/1936.

My mother and I in Katowice about 1937/1938.

V

FLIGHT TO THE EAST

———— • ◆ • ————

Shortly before Germany attacked Poland on September 1, 1939 we closed the door to our apartment, took the few belongings we could carry, and left Katowice by train heading east. We left behind most of our belongings, my father's library, our family photographs, as well as other personal items, but, most importantly, we left our home. It has been my observation that no matter how transiently settled one becomes later in life, a home, once lost, is never recovered. Those who have lost it are destined to become strangers in strange lands even if they return to their former homes.

According to a then secret supplement to the non-aggression pact signed by Foreign Ministers Molotov and Ribbentrop on August 23, 1939, Poland was divided by the Soviet Union and Germany. The Soviets occupied the eastern part, which was now our destination. We first fled to Tarnów where we stayed with the family of Uncle Beniu's fiancé, a beautiful girl named Klara, whose family owned an inn (karczma). We then fled to Lwów and stayed with my father's sister, Rivka Karl (d 1942), her husband Elias (d 1942), and their two children, Binyomin (1927-1942) and Mała (d 1942) in their apart-

Herbert (left) with Cousin Mała about 1934 or 1935.

ment at 7 Żeromskiego Street. I am sure that Mała was a nickname and not her given name, since it means "small" in Polish, but that is what we called her when we played. The apartment was located in a building at the dead-end of the street. As I remember, it was very small and, especially after we came, very crowded. It was located in the Kleparów section of Lwów, an area destined to become part of the ghetto, not far from the railroad tracks. I remember hearing the train whistle, especially at night. The train station in Kleparów would become the final embarkation point for Jewish victims taken from Lwów to the extermination camp at Bełżec. Somewhere in the vicinity there must have been a tar factory because I remember its smell quite distinctly.

When Jean, David, and I visited Lviv in October 2007 we searched for Żeromskiego Street but were told that it no longer existed. We did visit the Kleparów rail station and a tablet on the wall informed us that in a two year period (1941-1943) 500,000 Jews passed through the station on their way to their deaths in Bełżec. These must have included many of our relatives.

The first three weeks of September were frightening as the outnumbered Polish forces desperately tried to defend their homeland with cavalry and ancient rifles against the superbly trained and equipped German panzer and air force divisions. Beginning on September 1, squadrons of German planes came over Lwów in waves and bombed us daily and far into the night. In addition to bombs, they used incendiaries, which caused many fires throughout the city. The high whistling scream of the approaching bombs, their explosions, the anti-aircraft artillery, and the response of fire brigades were constant and for days we were unable to leave the shelter of the cellar. Thousands of refugees fleeing the German invasion poured into the city, almost

doubling its Jewish population within a few days. By the second week of September there was no electricity or gas and food was in short supply. The Germans broke through the Polish defenses on September 19, and the following day, the Soviets entered the city and the Germans withdrew.

I have only hazy memories of these frightening three weeks but their legacy has remained with me. After the fighting subsided I do remember very clearly looking out the accordion-like metal grate (sometimes called a scissor-gate) that protected the kitchen window and seeing prisoners of war being led through the streets. These must have been Polish prisoners captured by the Russians. I remember wondering where they were being led to and tried to imagine what they must have felt like.

The legacy of the three-week bombing that has remained with me has been a life-long fear of sudden sharp noises and especially the discharge of a gun, even on stage. Over the years, my wife Jean has had to leave many a theater performance with me because a gun appeared on stage. As our children were growing up, I wanted so much to take them to watch fireworks on the fourth of July, but I could not do it. Balloons became especially frightening to me. The high pitched sound of a balloon filling with helium must remind me of the terrifying whine of a falling bomb, not knowing where it would hit. At the sound, my muscles tense, my heart begins to race, I sweat, and I panic. Over the years, Jean and I have had to discretely walk out of a number of parties and *simhat torah* celebrations because of my reaction to balloons.

After the Soviets occupied the region, we moved to Szczerzec, my father's hometown, to live with my paternal grandparents, Shulim and Miriam. We were now stateless, without resources, and without belongings. The banks were closed to us. For a few days the Polish złoty and the Russian ruble were equivalent, and then, one day, the złoty became worthless and could no longer be exchanged.

Our coming was a mixed blessing because my grandparents were very poor, and lived from hand to mouth. In addition, there was a tremendous cultural gap between us. They spoke no German and we spoke no Yiddish. That they didn't speak German was understandable to us, but that their grandchildren didn't speak a word of Yiddish was, at least in my grandmother's eyes, sacrilegious. Her attitude and actions gave a clear message that she never approved of my mother as a fit partner for her oldest son.

The entire setting must have been a great shock for my mother who grew up, and had always lived, in cosmopolitan cities. Szczerzec was a small village with dirt streets, unpaved sidewalks, and horse carts. After the spring thaw and the fall rains, thick, sticky mud made the streets almost impassable. My grandparents lived in a small one-story house with a thatched straw roof. One entered the house from the street through a small "hallway." The compacted earth floor was kept clean by sprinkling water to keep the dust down, and then sweeping it with a straw broom. The walls were whitewashed and one had to be careful not to brush against them, because the whitewash was easily transferred to whatever touched it. To the left of the "hall" was a room with a wood-burning stove. This room was used as a kitchen only on Pesach. To the right of the "hallway" was a similar room also with a wood-burning stove used for cooking and for warmth in the winter. The stove had a *pripichik* (a sort of step) where one could curl up and keep warm, and I believe that my grandmother slept there, especially during the winter. This room served as kitchen, dining room, sitting room, and, after we came, as my grandparents' bedroom. A table, some chairs, a cupboard, and a bed in the corner completed the room's decor. Near the bed was a door leading into another small room, which was originally my grandparents' bedroom, but now became ours.

A covered shed open on three sides stood at one end of a small back yard. Inside, was a clay trough that my grandfather used to slaughter chickens. Since he was the community *shochet*, the community paid him 108 złotys a year (according to 1935 community budget) for maintaining this facility. At the other end of this small yard stood another shed. This was the outhouse that served the family in all weather.

There was no running water. An old man ("Yankel der krimmer") bent under his burden, carried a wooden yoke on his shoulders with a wooden bucket suspended on each end, and brought water at irregular intervals. During the winter he wore a great coat full of holes and gloves without the "fingers." There was no electricity, telephone, or radio (we had these conveniences in Katowice; our telephone number was 3 43 26). Light was provided by kerosene lamps, and one of my "jobs" was to clean the sooty glass shades periodically and very carefully with old newspapers and trim the wick so it would not smoke when lit.

My grandfather was a tall, distinguished looking man with a long white beard and peyot (side-curls). His eyes twinkled, and I remember him as a warm and kind person. I can still see him in my mind's eye, carefully trimming his fingernails with a pocketknife. He always did this on Thursday so that they would not have a growth spurt on the holy Shabbos. The evening before he went to slaughter animals, he would take out shiny knives that to me seemed huge, and carefully sharpened them on a long stone, putting a few drops of water on the stone first, and then meticulously and rhythmically gliding the blade over the stone – there on one side and back on the other. Periodically, he would glide the sharp blade across the nail of his index finger, which he deliberately left longer than the others, to make sure that the blade was sharp and perfectly smooth. The cut on the animal's neck had to be clean and swift without ripping. I was occasionally allowed to feel

Black and white rendition of a painting of a water carrier in Kazimierz by Adolph Behrman (Abraham Berman) 1876-1942.[103]

the smoothness of the flint stone, but I was never allowed to touch the knives.

When I grew older and thought about Jewish life and culture I began to appreciate the role of the *shochet* in Jewish society. In most societies, animal slaughtering is performed by its lowest elements - people without much education, honor or respect. In contrast, in Jewish societies it required a person of high

[103] Original in the Jewish Historical Institute, Warsaw.

learning, respect, and sensitivity to be entrusted with the awesome task of taking of a life, even that of an animal.

I am afraid that my memories of my grandmother are not pleasant. I don't remember her ever smiling or saying a kind word. That is probably a harsh and unkind judgment because I knew her only during a most difficult and trying time. I was also aware that their poor relationship caused my mother a lot of aggravation. My grandmother had no patience for Herbert or me, especially for me because I was rather boisterous and unruly. Things became so strained that, one day, she forbade us to go through their room. The only exit from our small room was now through the window, which is probably why I remember it. Herbert told me that if I climbed out a window, I would not grow unless I re-entered the room exactly the same way. This made me very anxious so I kept track of exactly how many times I climbed in each direction. I must have kept proper score because I did eventually grow to become 6 foot 4 inches tall. After a short period of time, we moved out of my grandparents' home into nearby rented quarters.

We had no source of income or savings, so my father left to seek work in Lwów, where he had contacts. There was no question about the rabbinate or other Jewish communal work since the Soviet authorities regarded such work as "parasitic." My father did eventually get a job in a state store selling jams, which afforded him time, between the infrequent

customers, to learn (Talmud). He returned to Szczerzec only on weekends.

The Soviets looked askance at any outward religious manifestations, although religious life continued within the home and synagogue. While we still had them, my mother and grandmother lit candles every Friday evening to usher in the Shabbat. There was always a sense of mystery as they cast their magic spell over the candles with waving hands that transformed the hovel into a palace. But soon, candles became unobtainable. I remember scraping together wax from the burned candles, mixing it with soil and rolling it around a piece of string. I managed to make two rather odd and dirty looking "candles," about 3 inches in height and perhaps a quarter of an inch in diameter, and proudly presented these to my mother so she could light them.

Herbert was of school age, but I was still too young. My parents did try to send me to a *heder* but I rebelled against that and refused to go, undoubtedly causing them a great deal of worry about my religious future. Children were forbidden by the authorities to miss school on religious holidays, and I remember that on Rosh Hashana (1940) my mother carefully bandaged Herbert's right hand. He was instructed to tell the teacher that he had cut his hand, and therefore could not write. If he had to desecrate the *yom tov* by attending school, he would at least not desecrate it by also writing.

That Yom Kippur, I went to *shul* with my mother and recall sitting next to her playing with her glasses, which folded into a monocle known as lorgnette. I know that it was Yom Kippur because the men were passing around sweet smelling snuff to allay the pangs of hunger from the fast. I recall a great deal of crying, especially during the *untaneh tokef* prayer, when the *hazzan* intones that on this day God decides "how many shall leave this world and how many shall be born into it; who shall live and who shall die; who shall live out the limit of his days and who shall not; who shall perish by fire and who by water; who by sword and who by beast; who by hunger and who by thirst; who by fire and who by plague; who by strangling and who by stoning; who shall rest and who shall wander; who shall be at peace and who shall be tormented; who shall be poor and who shall be rich; who shall be humbled and who shall be exalted." All these previously theoretical possibilities had taken on a terrible reality.

The seemingly indiscriminate fates of families was evident daily as families considered to be bourgeoisie, namely private businessmen, the unemployed, intellectuals, and former leaders were deported to the Russian Far East. Recent studies suggest that a total of 330,000 people, 63% Poles, 21% Jews, were deported in three waves.[104] Every evening, the adults, with much whispering and sighing, would tell stories about those rounded up in the last 24 hours. These were considered the "unfortunate" ones; we did not

realize then that they would survive and most of those "fortunate" enough not to have been deported would not. One of the few weapons that the weak have is to make fun of the powerful, and Jews have been especially adept at this art form. There were many jokes about the Soviets as peasant bumpkins. It used to be told that they were so naïve and uncultured that they used night pots for cooking, and that their women wore nightgowns to restaurants thinking that they were evening gowns.

After the war, my maternal grandparents gave me a few post cards they received from my parents in those times. These were, of course, censored and had to be carefully written, but could still be sent because the Soviet Union and England were not at war. A recurring topic was the many attempts to get exit visas. Apparently, someone had promised to obtain one for us and had not kept his word. I understand that my father had befriended the British consul in Katowice, who had been a frequent guest at our home. In April 1940, my father wrote: "We have experienced difficult times. May God continue to keep us under his protection." In June (1940) my mother wrote: "We have not yet experienced hunger, thank God. The children don't lack anything. I have nevertheless lost a lot of weight. 30 kg until now. When I have an opportunity, I will send you a photo of all of us. How are you? Do Gella and Betty have enough to eat? I am very

---

[104] Philipp Ther, "War versus Peace: Interethnic Relations in Lviv during the first half of the Twentieth Century" in Czplicka (ed) 265

worried about all of you." This message has to be carefully analyzed. My mother stated that "we have not yet experienced hunger," but went on to state that she has lost more than 60 lbs. Just to make sure that the message was clear, she asked whether Aunt Gella, who was in Palestine, and Aunt Betty, in unoccupied Hungary, had enough to eat, which suggested that they should all indeed be worried about us. Ominously, father adds a postscript, "Hoffentlich sehen wihr uns mahl noch" (hopefully we will see each other once again).

I remember my mother sewing us clothes from material she salvaged by ripping apart old clothes. I especially recall a green sweater she knitted out of pieces of yarn from an old sweater she carefully unraveled. The yarn kept tearing, but she managed to place all the knots that held it together on the inside of the sweater; on the outside it looked brand new. During one of these sewing sessions, my mother must have pricked herself, and she became very ill. Her finger became infected and the infection spread up her arm. I remember the red tract on the inside of the arm that I now recognize as thrombophlebitis. She was feverish and must have been septic. There were, of course, no antibiotics. Writing a postcard to England in May 1940 my father des-

perately wrote: "Ihr durft nicht ruhig bleiben. Trude muss wieder gesund werden. Das meine ich buchstablich, nicht bildich. Helfet!" (You must not remain silent. Trude must once again regain her health. I mean this literally and do not exaggerate. Help us!). Thankfully she gradually recovered.

My maternal grandparents had apparently suggested that Herbert and I should be sent abroad. Perhaps they had heard of the Kindertransport, an emergency evacuation of children, without their parents, primarily from Germany and Austria. The United Kingdom agreed to admit 10,000 children, who were then boarded in British foster homes. The Kindertransports ceased with the beginning of hostilities and were, in any case, never available in Poland. In an almost exasperated tone father replied: "We cannot send the children abroad from here. In the place where Szulimson lives, conditions are totally different from elsewhere. It is apparent that you are not aware of this. Only God can help." My grandfather's name was Shulim (or Szulim in the Polish spelling) and "Szulimson" was, therefore, my father. What he said in code was, "You don't seem to understand and cannot even imagine the difficult conditions we are living under here."

Postcard to my grandparents in England: "4-4-1940. My Dear Ones! For a short time I have been in transit and next week I will travel to Lwow. Trude has written me about the efforts you have made concerning our journey [from here]. I hope that the matter has moved forward in the meantime. The documents will have to be sent to the consulate in Moscow and perhaps a certified copy sent to us at the same time. Hopefully we will have the luck happily and in good health to see you soon. I was happy to hear that Mr. Bornstein is concerned about us. Please coordinate your actions with his. We have experienced difficult times. May God continue to keep us under his protection. Heartfelt regards for all of you, Kalman."

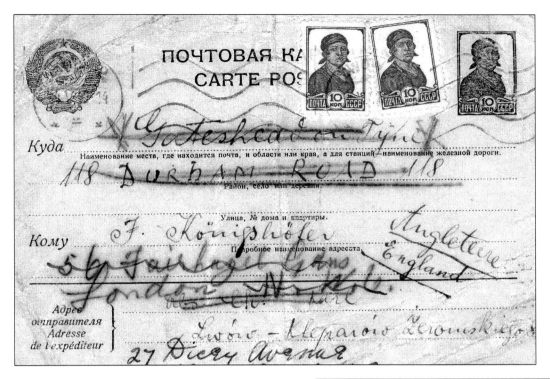

"22 April 1940. Dear Parents and Siblings! I thank all of you for your concerns [efforts]. I am very happy when I receive mail. Tomorrow, God willing, is Pesach. I will travel to Szczerzec and will remain there until our voyage [abroad]. Kalman has written to the Consul. He has not yet answered. Kalman has also made other efforts. Soon I intend to approach Kornitzer, if I am successful in getting to see him. Betty [mother's sister in Hungary] writes diligently. What do you hear from Gella [sister in Palestine]? How are Arnold Cohn and family? Did Thwaites write to the Consulate? One can only leave if one has a passport. If Thwaites wants to do it, it can be arranged. I wish you dear Johni and dear Klara a heartfelt mazal tov and much happiness on your wedding. Be truly happy. When I have more peace I will write about everything. Best Yom Tov wishes, Trudi."

"*May 12, 1940. Dear Parents! We have just received your letter of April 4. Thwaite's colleague in [?abbreviation] does not answer. From what I hear he also hasn't answered others who have turned to him [for help]. He appears not to want to bother with any of us. As a result we are very disturbed. What can we do? This is the time when we could achieve our goal [of emigrating]. We could get authorization to have our old documents recognized. But what use is it when K. is silent. In my opinion only you from where you are can undertake the necessary energetic steps. If you could only send us a permit directly from there. In the final analysis, even Betty [in Hungary] is very far away. I believe that Thwaite is not sufficiently interested in this matter. He appears to have forgotten how vigorously we — Trudi and I - have worked on behalf of others in the past. We dedicated ourselves day and night for the sake of others. Today we are not worthy enough even to receive a reply from a colleague. Please tell him that calmly in my name. You must not remain silent. Trudi must regain her health. I mean that literally and not figuratively. Help! We wish dear Johni and Klara a heartfelt mazel tov. I am sorry that I can not be there. That is what God wanted! We are once again in Szcz [Szczerzec]. Write us in Szczerzec. With heartfelt kisses, Kalman*" The crayon mark over the text is a sign that the card has been read by a censor.

"*June 10, 1940. Beloved Parents! I received mail from you and from Betty [sister in Hungary]. Many thanks. Is Ulu [sister Lotte's husband who was traveling to England from Germany] still in transit? Here many have shared the fate of Pystian [a resort town on the border of Hungary and Germany where many, including Betty and her son, Dov, were stuck in no man's land]. We are, thank God, healthy and well (not in transit) [reference to forced evacuation to Siberia]. I am now diligently searching for an apartment and my husband for a job. Hopefully we will succeed in both soon. The children have, touch wood, developed wonderfully. We have not yet experienced hunger, thank God. The children don't lack anything. I have nevertheless lost a lot of weight. 30 kg*

up until now. When I have an opportunity I will send you a photo of all of us. How are you? Do Gella [in Palestine] and Betty [in Hungary] have enough to eat? I am very worried about all of you. Lots of kisses to all and to Lotte. Trudi

Heartfelt regards. In order not to have to undertake the voyage that others have [to Siberia] we have accepted local documents. Hopefully we will see each other again. Best wishes to all of you Kalman." [For unknown reasons, the return address notes the sender's name as Trude Bernet and not Trude Chameides. Bernet is the last name of my mother's sister. Lotte, who was at that time fleeing Germany for England.]

Postmarked June 1940. "Dearest Parents and Siblings! Your letters give me great pleasure. Kalman of course writes you daily. I am here with the in laws. I want to have the children near me. Thank God they have developed well. Johni, I think of you often. I am not sure when your wedding is. In any case I wish you lots of mazal. Why does Lotte not write? I have written her a number of times. Betty writes often. The old Warshauer, mother of Aunt Frieda [wife of Gottfried Altmann] has died and I received mail from Bruno [Altmann]. I wonder whether we will ever have all of our wishes granted. Twaith's friend has not yet answered. Heartfelt kisses to all, Trude

In the meantime we received news from

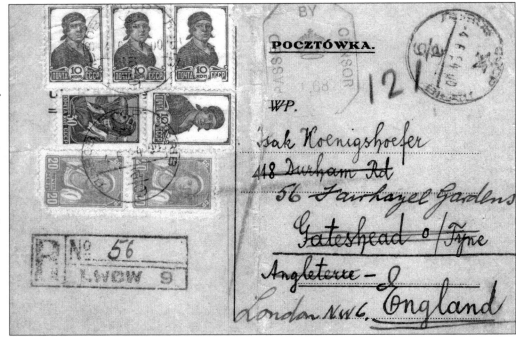

you that the consul has answered. Please God a permit may soon be granted. It would be important for us to have proof here that our documents are in order, even if we cannot travel at this time. We cannot send the children abroad from here. In the place where Szulimson lives [the son of Szulim, namely where we live] conditions are completely different than anywhere else. It is apparent that you are not aware of this. Only God can help. Heartfelt regards, Kalman."

Herbert and I made friends with the neighborhood children and had plenty of fun. Every so often, we would watch as a car came into this small village. When the car stalled, which seemed to happen with some regularity, the driver would have to get out and start cranking the crank on the front to try to get it started, all the time sweating and cursing. We liked to watch the village smithy shoe horses, and every now and then, horses would get "spooked" and rear at the sight of a car or oncoming train near the railroad tracks. We heard stories about horses kicking farmers in the head, and this provided fodder for a lot of imaginative conversation. We once stopped to watch a group of muscular young peasants compete with each other in lifting heavy weights. They were planning a long bicycle ride, and the strongest would take a little girl, who was also watching the proceedings, on his bicycle. We watched as they competed good-naturedly. I remember the little girl's delight, when her father lifted the heaviest weight, and got to take her. One of our favorite games was most annoying to the adults. We found that if you took a key, which in those days was hollow, and filled it with match heads, you could attach a nail with a string, and cause a small explosion by hitting it against a rock or, better still, against the house where it caused a small hole.

Uncles Ajzyk and Beniu were the only members of our family, besides our grandparents, whom we now saw occasionally. I am not sure where they lived, but I remember visiting uncle Ajzyk and his new wife, Aunt Zipporah. I remember that they had a bear rug and I enjoyed playing with the bear's head and occasionally lost sticky candy in its hair.

In October 2007 Jean, David, and I visited Szczerzec, now known as Shchirets, a small town with about 10,000 inhabitants. There are still a few elderly Polish residents, but the majority are Ukrainians. Zwi (Herbert's current name) was kind enough to draw a map for us from memory, and we were astounded at how accurate it was, down to the curvature of the streets. Without it, it would have been impossible for us to orient ourselves. We found the street where my grandparents lived, but unfortunately their house is no longer standing, having been replaced by an alley. The synagogue and mikveh have been replaced by a school. In short, except for the cemetery (see next chapter), there is, today, no evidence that Jews had lived in Szczerzec for close to 700 years, and had constituted a majority of its occupants during much of that time.

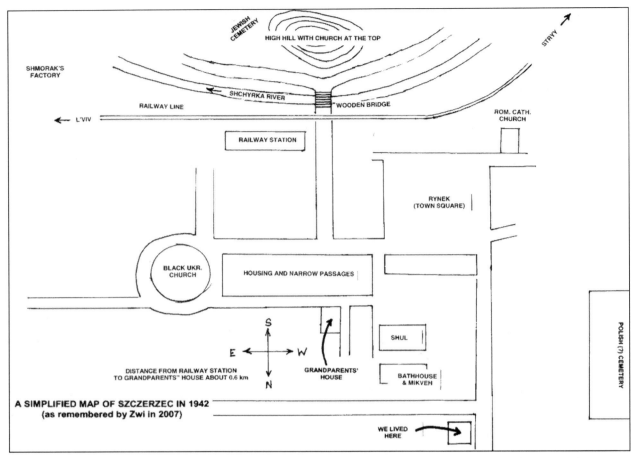

Map of Szczerzec drawn by Zwi Barnea (Herbert) from memory in 2007. We found the map to be extremely accurate and could orient ourselves very well with its help.

VI

GERMAN INVASION

— • ◆ • —

The grown ups in Szczerzec became very agitated on June 21, 1941. Everyone who had a radio, and there were not many, sat huddled around it anxiously listening to the news. That was the day operation Barbarossa, as the Germans named their attack on the Soviet Union, began. I remember bragging to my friends that I wasn't afraid because I spoke German and, should they invade, I would undoubtedly be able to make friends with them. Sometime before the invasion, there was a dog fight between a German and a Russian airplane over the village of Szczerzec. No one in the village had ever seen an airplane before, and so a crowd gathered in the square to watch. One of the airplanes (I forget which) was hit and began a nose dive into an empty field, black smoke trailing behind him. The pilot ejected and as the parachute opened "Roite Malke" was heard to exclaim: *"kik ahin, afilu a sonnenshirm hot er!" (look at that, he even has a sun umbrella!)* She was known as "di roite Malke" because she had red hair, to differentiate her from "die schwartze Malke" who had black hair.

The Soviet army started to retreat on June 27, and by June 30, the retreat was complete. The first German troops en-tered the Lwów district on July 1. Prior to their retreat, the NKVD (Narodnyi Kommisariat Vnutrennykh Del – The People's Commissariat for Internal Affairs or Soviet secret police) massacred thousands of Ukrainian political prisoners. When the victims were discovered, the Ukrainians vented their rage on the local Jewish population. They organized anti-Jewish riots, including beatings, looting of property, and murder, in all the surrounding towns and villages. In Szczerzec, Jews were herded into the town square and, under the watchful eye of local brutes, were forced to wash the cobblestones with toothbrushes.

My mother, Herbert, and I managed to hide in a nearby cellar in the home of an acquaintance. I remember the terrifying dark as I huddled as close to my mother as possible saying the *shema* and hearing the screams, and occasional shots from above. Suddenly there was banging on the cellar door, loud barking shouts, and a crash as the door was smashed open. A shaft of light that made us squint pierced our darkness, and I heard the noise of many boots running down the steps. As we were hauled out, I looked at my mother and almost didn't recognize her. Her *perukkeh (shaitel)* must have fallen off in the commotion. I had never seen her without it. How strange she looked! We had a pre-arranged plan that if we were discovered, Herbert and I were to run as fast as we could to a pharmacy on the town square. The pharmacist was a friend of ours. I believe he was a Jew, but he and his family were left alone by the mob as a sign of respect for the important role that a pharmacist plays in a small town. As soon as we were out, Herbert ran to the pharmacy, but I refused and felt very proud that I stood my ground. That stubborn streak served me well in subsequent years. When we were finally allowed to return home, we discovered that my grandmother had been beaten. She was disfigured, bloody, and most of her teeth had been knocked out, but she was as feisty as ever and proud of the fact that the Ukrainian thugs were unable to dislodge her from her home.

The Germans did not stop the Ukrainian anti-Jewish riots until July 10, by which time approximately 10,000 Jews had been murdered in the Lwów region. My father was still in Lwów and we heard little from him. The Germans now posted a continuous stream of daily orders: Jews had to hand over all radios, furs, jewelry, etc. We were not personally affected by these because we had so little but the level of fear noticeably increased. Words like "transport" and "resettlement" took on a new and ominous meaning. One day, a terrified, bleeding girl, who turned out to be a distant relative, ran into the house. She told an un-

believable story of deportation, transport, and death. I remember her sitting in my grandmother's Passover kitchen surrounded by the family. She had huge frightened eyes and blood was oozing from the many scrapes she had sustained in jumping from a train as it passed near Szczerzec. The guards shot at her and left her for dead, and so she managed to escape temporarily. I say "temporarily" because the Germans had us trapped like animals and, if they didn't get us one day, they were sure to get us the next. Unfortunately, I don't even remember her name or how she was related to us and so, to my knowledge, except for this fragment, all evidence of her existence on earth has been erased.

We now saw even less of my father than before, since he continued to work in Lwów. I remember one visit when I barely recognized him. He had lost so much weight that his clothes hung on him; he had trimmed his beard and looked very gaunt. I think that he was very aware what was going on, and had a clear idea what Germany's ultimate plan was for us. On that visit, he insisted that we needed a hiding place. Our rented home consisted of a long room and a kitchen. A door from the kitchen opened into a shed used as a pantry to keep food cold. He suggested that we brick over the outside shed window, and build removable shelves in front of the door. We could then hide there in case of an emergency. I remember being outside on a moonlit night while my father, Uncle Ajzyk, and my grandfather blocked off

Family portrait of my parents, Herbert (left front) and me (right front) taken so it could be cut into individual passport photos.

the window with bricks. None of them, of course, had done such work before, and I remember looking at the window when the job was finished and thinking that this would not fool anyone, because the outline of the previous window opening was still clearly visible. I was, however, very impressed with their job in camouflaging the door to the pantry. Standing in the kitchen one saw shelves with pots and pans but could not tell that there was a door behind them. At that time, I often engaged in some creative daydreaming, and would imagine a window in the wall that I could magically open and on the other side was – England! England, in my imagination, had taken the place usually reserved for the Garden of Eden.

On another occasion, my grandfather decided that they should hide their "valuables" and so I again remember standing at night, this time in back of my grandparents' house, as they dug a hole in the ground to bury a Kiddush cup, some bales of cloth, and the Shabbat candlesticks. I have often wondered what family treasures and mementos, and how many Shabbat candlesticks must lie buried deep under Ukrainian and Polish soil.

My father continued to make efforts to obtain papers for us leave. Travel to the west was now impossible, and so the efforts were directed at trying to get to a neutral country, like Switzerland, or to join Aunt Betty in Budapest, which was not yet occupied. On one of his visits to Szczerzec, we went to a photographer for a family portrait. The family was carefully positioned in such a manner that each could be cut out and made into a passport photo, but since they were afraid to share the true purpose with the photographer, there is some overlap. The opportunity to use photos for a passport never presented itself.

It was around this time that, lying in bed, I discovered something crawling over me. With great alarm I woke Herbert and asked him what it was. He examined it carefully and pronounced it a louse. He then showed me how to kill it by squeezing it between two fingernails until there was a distinctive cracking sound. If the louse had recently had a meal there would be some blood, which, Herbert told me, was very valuable because it was used for making lipstick. I was always impressed with Herbert's vast knowledge, and for a long time wondered how people were able to collect enough lice to make all the lipstick in the world.

On July 8, 1941 proclamations were

Verordnung

Die jüdische Bevölkerung über 14 Jahren, welche sich in der Stadt oder im Bezirk Lemberg aufhält, hat ab 15. Juli 1941 als Kennzeichen eine weiße Armbinde mit blauem sechseckigem Stern ✡ (Davidstern) auf dem rechten Oberarm zu tragen.

Jude ist, wer von mindestens drei der Rasse nach volljüdischen Grosseltern abstammt.

Als Jude gilt auch der von zwei volljüdischen Grosselten abstammende jüdische Mischling,

a) der der jüdischen Religionsgemeinschaft angehört oder noch in sie aufgenommen wird,

b) der mit einem Juden verheiratet ist oder sich noch mit einem solchen verheiratet.

Juden, die das Kennzeichen nicht tragen, werden bestraft.

Ausländer fallen nicht unter diese Verordnung

DER KOMMANDANT
der Stadt Lemberg.

РОЗПОРЯДОК

Жидівське населення в літах вище 14, що перебуває в місті Львові або у львівській окрузі, має, починаючи від 15. липня 1941 р., носити як відзнаку на правому рамені білу перев'язку з синьою, шестикутньою зіркою ✡ (зірка Давида)

Жидом є кожний, хто походить від щонайменше трьох за расою чистожидівських предків.

За жида треба вважати теж жидівського мішанця, що походить від двох чистожидівських предків,

а) того, хто належить до жидівської релігійної громади, або буде принятий до неї,

б) того, хто з жидом одружений або одружиться з жидом.

Жиди, що не носять такої відзнаки, підлягають карі.

До чужоземців цей розпорядок не відноситься.

Командант м. Львова.

Rozporządzenie

Ludność żydowska powyżej lat 14, przebywająca w mieście Lwowie albo w powiecie lwowskim, obowiązana jest nosić, począwszy od 15 lipca 1941, jako odznakę na prawym ramieniu białą opaskę z niebieską sześciokątną gwiazdą ✡ (gwiazda Dawida)

Żydem jest każdy, kto pochodzi od conajmniej trzech rasowo czystożydowskich przodków.

Za żyda należy również uważać żydowskiego mieszańca, pochodzącego od dwóch czystożydowskich przodków,

a) tego, kto należy do żydowskiej gminy wyznaniowej albo do niej przyjęty zostanie,

tego, kto pozostaje w związku małżeńskim z żydem albo związek małżeński z żydem zawrze.

Żydzi, nie noszący takiej odznaki, podlegają karze.

Cudzoziemców rozporządzenie to nie dotyczy.

KOMENDANT
miasta Lwowa.

Proclamation of July 8, 1941 in German, Ukrainian, and Polish.

"Decree

Jews above the age of 14 residing in Lwów or its environs are required, beginning July 15, 1941, to wear a white armband with a blue six-pointed star (David's Star) as a badge on their right arm.

A Jew is defined as anyone who has a minimum of three pure bred Jewish grandparents.

A person is also considered a Jew if he is a mixed breed with two Jewish grandparents,

a) and is a member of the Jewish religious community or will be accepted as such

b) one who is or will be married to a Jew

Jews not wearing such a badge will be punished.

This decree does not apply to foreigners.

Commander of the City of Lwów

posted that required all Jews to wear an identifying mark. Today, this is usually considered to have been a yellow patch or star, but the design was determined locally and, in our region, it was a blue *Magen David* on a white armband. The armband had a required width and the *Magen David* a required size and I remember mother sitting with white cloth and blue thread carefully measuring, drawing, and stitching the *Magen David* and then sewing it onto her right upper sleeve.

In August 1941, the German authorities established a Judenrat in Lwów (officially known as Judische Gemeinde der Stadt Lemberg) with Dr. Yoseph Parnas as its first Chairman. Dr. Parnas was arrested by the Germans in November 1941 and shot to death for refusing to give the Germans a list of Jews. Father was appointed to the Religious Affairs Department of the Judenrat, which was responsible for religious matters within the community. The other members of this department were Rabbi Moshe El-hanan Alter, Rabbi Israel Leib Wolfsberg, Rabbi Nathan Nute Leiter, Rabbi Shmulke Rappaport, Rabbi Moshe Ehrenpreiss, Rabbi Hersh Rosenfeld, Rabbi Anschel Schreiber, and Rabbi Dawid Kahane.[105] Rabbi Kahane was the only one to survive the war. Establishment of the Judenrat satisfied the Germans' need for order. When they wanted to round up Jews, they would place their order with the Judenrat, which had to agonize whom to turn over, knowing full well what their fate would be. The actual round-up was carried out with the help of the Jewish Police and Ukrainian Auxiliaries. One can only imagine the intrigue and bribery that this system encouraged.

In March 1942, as part of their practice of deception, the Germans announced plans for "resettlement" and asked the Judenrat to prepare lists of Jews, and participate in the roundup. After two days of discussions, the members of the Religious Affairs Department decided to send a delegation to Dr. Landesberg, then Head of the Judenrat, to warn him that such participation was not in accord with Jewish Law. The delegation consisted of Rabbis Yisrael Leib Wolfsberg, Moshe Elchanan Alter, Kalman Chameides, and Dawid Kahane.[106] "We explained that in times

of trial such as these we were duty bound to draw attention of the leader of such a large Jewish community to the enormous responsibility associated with complying with the German orders. According to Jewish law and morality, he was to seek other ways. When our enemies come to us saying: 'Bring one of you so that we may kill him. If not we will kill you all' — it is better that all die and not one Jew be delivered to the enemy. This is what the Halakah rules."[107] Dr. Landesberg was sympathetic to the Rabbis' views but was not in a position to disregard the German order. The March *Aktion* started with a roundup and murder of those on the list, but continued and included many others.

Postcards could no longer be sent to England since we were now part of the "Generalgouvernement"[108] and therefore at war with that country. Postcards and letters could, however, still be sent to neutral Switzerland, and I have three pieces of correspondence written by my parents to Mr. Alfred Schwarzbaum in Lausanne. Alfred Schwatzbaum, a native of Będzin, whom my father probably knew, was a functionary of a Jewish organization in Switzerland and apparently, through his numerous connections, was able to get some exit visas. In the first, a postcard, written by my father in June 1942, he asks for "acts of charity," namely food parcels. Four parcels were apparently re-

[105] Dawid Kahane, *Lvov Ghetto Diary* (The University of Massachusetts Press, Amherst 1990) 23-24.
[106] Philip Friedman, *Roads To Extinction: The Destruction of the Jews of Lwów* (The Jewish Publication Society 1980) 269.
[107] Kahane 43-44; 156-157.
[108] The Generalgouvernement or General Government was created by the Germans on October 26, 1939 as a semi-autonomous unit under German leadership, which was initially divided into four districts: Warsaw, Kraków, Radom, and Lublin. After the Germans attacked the Soviet Union, Eastern Galicia was made into a fifth district.

Postcard written by my father to neutral Switzerland. Note the German General-gouvernement stamp and the Judenrat return address.

ABSENDER

Judenrat Lemberg für

K. Chameides

POSTKARTE

Alfred Schwarzbaum

Av. Villamont 23

Lausanne

Schweiz

23. VI. 942.

Lieber Freund!

Von Onkel Bruno hörte ich wiederholt, daß Sie sich nach unserem Befinden erkundigt haben. Ihre Anhänglichkeit hat uns sehr gerührt. Wir sind gtt. gesund. Für Liebesgaben oder sonstige materielle Unterstützung werden wir Ihnen sehr sehr dankbar sein. Die Adresse unserer Verwandten dürfte Frau Lotte Felsenstein (Tochter von Bruno Altman) Ihnen angeben koennen.

Wir werden uns aufrichtig freuen, von Ihnen direkt eine Nachricht zu erhalten.

Sie koennen an den Judenrat Lemberg für mich adressieren. Ebenso koennen Sie an meinen Schwager E. Karl Lemberg Zeromskig. 7 schreiben.

Ihrer frndl. Antwort entgegensehend verbleibe ich mit herzlichsten Grüssen

Ihr K. Chameides.

June 23, 1942

Dear Friend,

I have repeatedly heard from Uncle Bruno [Altmann] that you have inquired about our circumstances. Your devotion has moved us very much. We are, thank God, healthy. We would be very grateful to you for acts of charity or other material support. As to the addresses of our relatives, Lotte Felsenstein [Bruno Altmann's daughter living in London] can give you these. We would be genuinely happy to hear from you directly. You can write me at the Judenrat in Lemberg. You can also write to me at my brother-in-law, E. Karl Lemberg Żeromskig 7

I look forward to your reply and remain with heartfelt regards,

Yours,
K. Chameides

4. VIII. 942.

Lieber Freund!

Herzlichsten Dank für Ihre w. Karte. Die nach Lemberg geschickten Sardinen und Mandeln kommen sämtlich an und sind für uns von größter Wichtigkeit. Bitte uns öfter zu schicken. Diese Woche bekamen wir 4 Sendungen. Isak koennte ja dafür bezahlen und uns auf diese Weise behilflich sein. Unsere Bilder haben wir vorläufig keine Gelegenheit Euch zu schicken.

Wir sind gesund und wohlauf. Guttman's sehe ich hier nicht.

Herzlichsten Dank für Ihre Bemühungen.
Bleiben Sie herzlichst gegrüßt
von Ihrem
K. Chameides
Lemberg-Kleparów
Żeromskig. 7

Dear Friend,

Heartfelt thanks for your card. The sardines and almonds sent to Lemberg arrived in their entirety and are of utmost importance to us. Please send us [parcels] often. This week we received 4 packages. Isak [grandfather in England] could pay for these and thereby be helpful to us. So far we have not had an opportunity to send you our photographs.

We are healthy and well. I do not see Guttman here.

Heartfelt thanks for your efforts.

With heartfelt regards,
    Yours,
    K. Chameides
    Lemberg-Kleparów
        Żeromskig 7

It is clear from this veiled message that there was a tremendous shortage of food and that my father is pleading for them to send more. The statement, "I do not see Guttman here" is strange. This could refer to a person, but may also be a hint of difficult conditions (i.e., there are no good people here).

Sehr geehrter Herr Schwarzbaum!

Gestern konnte ich durch Bruno Altmann Ih..
u. Adresse erfahren & zugleich den Namen des Spende..
der Ölsardinen hören. Innigsten Dank dafür. Wa..
~~Sie uns damit halfen~~ ist nicht zu erzählen. So hab..
ich doch für einige Male Abendbrot für die Ki..
der. Ich erhielt 2x je 2 Schachteln. Ein Abse..
der war nicht aufgeschrieben, so daß ich den
Empfang nur bei der Firma bestätigen kon..
Wie geht es Ihnen? Ich war vor einigen Wochen
bei meinem Mann. Er sieht so schrecklich
aus, nicht zum Wiedererkennen. Na, es ist wei..
fit kein Wunder. Bitte sind Sie nicht böse, wen..
er nicht schreibt oder nicht schrieb. Ersten..
wußten wir Ihre Adresse nicht & dann hat er das..
zu viel Sorgen. Falls Sie Lotte Felsenstein meine Schwester
schreiben, veranlassen Sie sie bitte, mein..
Eltern aufzusuchen & ihnen nützlich..

..wir gottlob alle gesund sind. Auch
meine Schwester Betty ist gesund. Vielleich..
..einer neue Eltern Ihnen schreiben & bitte..
..den sie mir dann den Brief ein.. man..
..soll mir nur familiäres schreiben. Besten
~~Dank für die Besorgung. Entschuldigen Sie~~
bitte den halben Bogen. Ich habe keinen
anderen zur Hand & will schon an Sie
schreiben. Unsere Kinder entwickeln
sich gottlob sehr gut. ... noch Bekann..
te in der Lausanne? Mein Mann arbeit..
dort im Judenrat. Ich spreche ihn 2x wöch..
lich telephonisch. Sobald ich einen Passier..
schein bekomme werde ich wieder be..
ihm sein. Es tut mir unendlich leid so..
getrennt zu sein, was kann man mache..
Die Verantwortung ist augenblicklich sehr
groß. Bleiben Sie recht gesund. Nochmals
innigsten Dank
            Ihre
            T. Sch.

Very Dear Mr. Schwarzbaum,

Yesterday I found out your address and the sender of the
oil sardines from Bruno Altmann. Sincere thanks for this.
You cannot imagine how much you have helped us with this.
This has provided me with several suppers for the children. I have received 2 parcels twice. Since there was no
sender's name, I could only acknowledge its receipt at
the [parcel] company. How are you? A few weeks ago I visited my husband. He looked so terrible; almost unrecog-
nizable. But then it is no wonder. Please don't be angry
that he does not write. First of all, he didn't have your
address and besides he has so many worries. If you happen
to write to Lotte Felsenstein [Bruno Altmann's daughter
in London] ask her to please look up my parents and tell
them that we are, thank God, all well. My sister Betty
[Gluck in Hungary] is also well. Perhaps my parents could
write to you and you could be kind enough to send the
letter to me. They should write only about family matters.
Thank you very much for your troubles. Please excuse
that I write on half a sheet of paper but I have no other
at the moment and want to send this out. Our children
are thank God developing very nicely. Are there any
other acquaintances in Lausanne? My husband works in the
Judenrat. I speak with him twice a week by telephone. I
will join him as soon as I receive a pass. It causes me
unending sorrow to be separated but what can I do! At the
moment his responsibility is very great. Be well. Once
again, most heartfelt thanks,
                    Yours,
                    Trude Ch.

ceived, which included some sardines and almonds, and my father expresses his gratitude for these in a postcard written in August. My mother also sent a letter of thanks ("you cannot imagine how much you have helped us"), and informs Mr. Schwarzbaum that she was able to stretch the sardines into "two meals for the children." I remember those sardines; they have remained one of my favorite "comfort" foods to this day.

During the summer of 1942, the administration of Jewish affairs in the Lwów district (including Szczerzec) was transferred to the SS. A massive, systematic, and well planned Aktion started on August 10th, lasted until August 29, and resulted in the deaths of 50,000 - 60,000 Jews. Victims included hospitalized patients, infants in delivery suites, and children in orphanages. Prior to August, killing of Jews had been sporadic and random and the mood remained optimistic that the free labor the Jews provided would somehow allow most to survive.[109] The cruelty, brutality, and organized killing during the August Aktion destroyed any illusion and convinced most Jews that none of us would survive. That this almost became a reality is borne out by the statistics. In October 1941 there were 119,000 Jews in Lwów (some figures are as high as 150,000); by November 1942, only 29,000 remained.[110, 111]

The ghetto was liquidated in April 1943 and the remaining 8,000 Jews were forced into labor and extermination camp on Janowska Street. When Lwów was liberated by the Soviet army on July 27, 1944 only 823 Jews, those who managed to hide with Aryan papers or in the sewers, remained alive.[112, 113]

In October 2007 Jean, David, and I visited Szczerzec, now known as Shchirets. As I stood in front of the alley where our grandparent's house once stood, I wondered whether the workmen building that alley ever found the treasures that my grandparents buried there. An elderly Polish lady told us that the Germans rounded up the remaining Jews in 1942 and forced men, women, crying children, the elderly and the young into the synagogue where they remained without food for 10 days. They were then taken to the railroad station and "taken away." The synagogue was destroyed, and a man in the village told us that he remembers his father dismantling the foundation stones and using them to build the houses that now stand across the street from what used to be the synagogue. The Rynek, which Jews were forced to scrub during the first pogrom, is still there, although without cobblestones, and so is the pharmacy to which we were supposed to run. I could not definitely identify the house where we hid.

---

[109] Filip Friedman, *Zagłada żydów Lwowskich* (Wydawnictwa Centralnej żydowskiej Komisji Historycznej przy Centralnym Komitecie żydow Polskich # 4 Lódz, 1945) 15.
[110] Philip Friedman, *Roads to Extinction* 288.
[111] Filip Friedman, *Zagłada żydów Lwowskich* 23.
[112] Filip Friedman, *Zagłada żydów Lwowskich* 25.
[113] Robert Marshall, *In the Sewers of Lvov* (Charles Scribner and Sons, NY 1990).

We made our way up the hill and over a bridge to the cemetery. An old lady in her eighties, Mrs. Stefania Kokurudza, was standing over a well bringing up two pails of water. David immediately offered to help carry them to her home, but she refused his help. When she arrived at her small house, she spilled a handful of water from each pail in a deliberate and superstitious act. She told us that she lives alone since her husband died, and all night, she fights with demons that come in through the window from the cemetery. She pointed an arthritic finger in the direction of a wooden platform and said, "Do you see them over there? You probably don't see them, but I do. These are small demons, but when they come into the house they are much bigger." She told us that her parents had been paid by the Jewish community to care for the cemetery, and when they died she took over the job even though she no longer gets paid. She thought that the cemetery is about 700 years old and that it contains about 1500 graves. She pointed to a clearing and told us that the Germans rounded up a group of 42 Jews in 1942 and shot them there. We went into the woods and saw mazevoth (tombstones) everywhere. The cemetery is overgrown.. Many of the mazevoth are falling down, and most are covered with a thick layer of moss making the inscriptions almost impossible to read. Those that are not, show amazingly detailed and beautiful art work.

The pharmacy to which Herbert and I were supposed to run if our hiding place was discovered (photo 2007).

The Shchirets Jewish cemetery in 2007.

VII

HIDING

—•◆•—

The Uniate, or Greek Catholic Church, as it became known in the 18th century, was established by the Treaty of Brest in 1596 as a union between the Orthodox and the Roman Catholic Churches. The new church was allowed to maintain its Orthodox traditions (language and manner of prayer, priests allowed to marry) but recognized the supremacy of the Pope. Andrei Sheptytskyi (1865-1944), had attained the highest ecclesiastical position within the church and held the title of Metropolitan-Archbishop of Lviv and Halych with jurisdiction over the province of Galicia in western Ukraine, for more than four decades (1901-1944).[114] Before WW II, Metropolitan Sheptytskyi had maintained warm relations with the Jewish community, contributed to the welfare of the Jewish poor, and showed evidence that he knew both spoken and written Hebrew.[115, 116]

Rabbi Jecheskel Lewin, religious leader of the Lwów Jewish community, my father's predecessor in Katowice, and a long-time friend of the Archbishop, approached him during the Ukrainian anti-Jewish pogroms in the wake of the Soviet retreat in June 1941. He asked the Archbishop's help in stemming the campaign of terror and murder unleashed by Ukrainian nationalists against the Jewish community. The Metropolitan made no commitment, but urged Rabbi Lewin to remain in the safety of his residence. Rabbi Lewin replied that he did not come to seek personal shelter, that his mission was accomplished, and that he would rejoin his community. On the way home, he was attacked and beaten by the Ukrainians, and taken to the Brygidki prison where he was murdered.[117]

In the somber atmosphere of the summer 1942, the Religious Affairs Department of the Lemberg Judenrat appointed a delegation, consisting of Rabbi Dawid Kahane and my father, to approach Metropolitan Andrei Sheptytskyi to ask his help in hiding several hundred Torah scrolls that the Jewish community had

[114] Paul Robert Magocsi, *Morality and Reality. The Life and Times of Andrei Sheptyts'kyi* (University of Alberta, 1989).

[115] Shimon Redlich, "Sheptyc'kyi and the Jews During World War II" in Magocsi, *Morality and Reality* 145-162.

[116] Phillip Friedman, "Hurban Yehudei Lvov" *Enziklopedia shel Galuyot* Jerusalem, 1955 670.

[117] Kurt I. Lewin, *Journeys Through Illusions* (Fithian Press, Santa Barbara, CA 1994) 36.

accumulated at 12 Bernstein St.

Rabbi Kahane and my father had been colleagues at the Vienna Rabbinical Seminary, which required each candidate for *semicha* (ordination) to write an original research paper. Rabbi Kahane's advisor suggested that he learn Church Slavonic, an ancient Slavonic language used by the Uniate Church, in order to study one of the earliest translations of Josephus and determine whether references to Christianity in his writings were part of the original or were later additions.[118] After Rabbi Kahane's appointment to his first pulpit in Lwów, his knowledge of Church Slavonic helped him develop close relationships with Uniate priests.

A Ukrainian Uniate Priest, Dr. Gabriel Kostelnik,[119] helped arrange the meeting with Metropolitan Andrei Sheptytskyi, which took place on August 14, 1942. The Archbishop agreed to hide the Torah scrolls if the community could arrange for their transport.[120] In the course of the meeting, the Metropolitan inquired about the rabbis' personal welfare and offered his help. He offered to shelter the rabbis, their wives, and their daughters, but was afraid to hide boys since their cir-

cumcision would easily identify them as Jews. However, after consulting with his younger brother, the Archimandrite or Superior, Ihumen Klement (1869-1951), head of the monasteries, he also agreed to hide their sons.

Under the Metropolitan's leadership and with the cooperation of the church hierarchy, especially his brother Ihumen Klement (now St. Klement), about 100-200 Jews,[121, 122] including Rabbi Kahane, his wife and two daughters were saved. It is impossible from this distance of time to be sure what the Archbishop's motives were in saving so many Jews. We do, however, know what he told Kurt Lewin, the oldest son of Rabbi Jecheskiel Lewin: "I am not undertaking this for money or for any other anticipated reward. I am doing this solely for the love of God and my fellow man. My obligation, if I have the ability, is to save my fellow human beings whose lives are threatened....I have never even thought about conversion; that would only constitute another form of payment and would be imposed. If I am successful in saving you and you live through the war and you are convinced about the correctness of my faith,

---

[118] Rabbi Dawid Kahane, Personal communication.

[119] Dawid Kahane, *Lvov Ghetto Diary* 57-58.

[120] The community could not arrange the transport and the Torah scrolls were apparently buried for safekeeping. Moshe Maltz, *Years of Horror; Glimpse of Hope* (Shengold Publishers 1993) 143 writes of his visit to the only remaining synagogue in Lwów after liberation: "A side room of the synagogue is filled with Torah scrolls that were buried in the ground to hide them from the Germans and have just been dug out. There are altogether 500 of these scrolls, still damp and smelling of the wet soil."

[121] Phillip Friedman, "Ukrainian-Jewish Relations," *YIVO Annual of Jewish Social Science* (YIVO Institute for Jewish Research, New York 1959) 259-296.

[122] The individuals that I know of who were saved include: Oded Amarant, Zwi Barnea (Herbert Chameides), Leon Chameides, Rabbi and Mrs. Dawid Kahane and two daughters, Kurt Lewin, Nathan Lewin, Anna and Joseph Podoshin, Lily (Stern) Pohlman, Adam Daniel Rotfeld, Cecylia Stern.

[123] Kurt I. Lewin, *Przeżyłem* (Fundacja Zeszytów Literackich Warsaw, 2006) 120. This is the original Polish version of an autobiography written in 1946 and published in a Hebrew translation: *Aliti miSpecia* in 1946.

Icon of St. Klementii Sheptytskyi, beatified by Pope Paul II in June, 2001.

then we can discuss it."[123]

Metropolitan Andrei died in 1944 after the Soviet liberation. His brother, Klement, was arrested by the NKVD (Soviet secret police) in 1947, sentenced to eight years of hard labor, and died in 1951 in the Vladimir prison, the same prison where Raoul Wallenberg was incarcerated. Archimandrite Klymentii (as he is known in Ukrainian) Sheptytskyi was beatified by Pope John Paul II during his visit to Lviv on June 27, 2001.

Klement Sheptytskyi has been recognized by Yad Vashem in Jerusalem with the title of "Righteous Gentile," but his brother Archbishop Andrei, who was the head of the Church and without whose permission and encouragement no Jews would have been saved, has not been so honored, despite repeated attempts by the survivors to reverse the decision. The main reason given by Yad Vashem for their refusal was a letter that the Metropolitan wrote in 1941 asking the Ukrainian population to co-operate with the new regime and hailing the Germans as victors and liberators.[124] The suffering and murder of Ukrainians at the hands of the Soviets is now conveniently forgotten as is the end of the same letter in which the Metropolitan asks the new government to treat the population equally, without regard to differences in nationality or religion. Dr. Mordechai Paldiel, then head of Yad Vashem, once wrote me that had he been a private individual, the Metropolitan would surely have been honored since there is no dispute about the fact that he saved Jews, but that more was expected of him as head of his church, and as an example he cited the actions of a Bishop in France. I answered him that his statement is not in keeping with our tradition. I pointed out that the Bible calls Noah righteous in "his generation," and the great medieval commentator Rashi explains that had Noah lived in Abraham's generation he would not have been considered righteous. What could be done in France would never have been allowed in Ukraine. In reaction to an article[125] in which Dr. Shevah Weiss, Chairman of Yad Vashem

124 Mordechai Paldiel, "Andrei Sheptizky – Collaboration with the Enemy?" in *Saving the Jews* (Schreiber Publishing Rockville, MD 2000) 245-256.
125 Shevah Weiss, "Ukrainian Schindler" *WPROST* #1192 October 9, 2005.

Board, called Metropolitan Andrei a "collaborator" on the basis of that 1941 letter, I replied that it is less important what he wrote in 1941, when no one, including Jews could have imagined the Germans' murderous plans, than what he did in 1942,[126] when the German aim became clear. The ingratitude of our people, as expressed by the refusal of Yad Vashem to honor such a deserving man, is a shameful blot on the Jewish nation.[127]

I was much too young to fully appreciate the process by which my parents reached the agonizing decision to hide my brother and me under the protection of the Church, but they must have reached the conclusion that we would not otherwise survive. What courage, driven by fear and realism that must have taken! I imagine that my mother argued against it, and that my father, both a pragmatist and realist, must have convinced her that it was the only course. Kurt Lewin[128] describes his mother's agony when faced with a similar situation. Even though she was convinced that they would not survive, she could not get herself to agree to hide her two youngest children in a monastery for fear that this would be a Jewish spiritual death sentence. Eventually, Kurt managed to get his 9 year old brother, Nathan, into hiding without telling his mother, but she would not allow her youngest child to go. That child was shot by the Germans.

In September 1942, my father made two dangerous journeys to Szczerzec, and took Herbert and me separately to Metropolitan Sheptytskyi's residence at Sw. Jur (St. George) in Lwów in a truck transporting laborers. The human mind has a way of protecting us from severe emotional pain; I remember many of the events of those days as if they happened yesterday, but my mind is totally blank on that last good-bye with my mother. I cannot imagine her emotional state as she sent two children, aged 7 and 9, into a Christian environment. I have no doubt that she gave me instructions not to forget that I was a Jew and to say the *shema*, but I remember nothing. I cannot count the number of nights during which I have tried to dredge up something about that moment from the depth of my memory. But there is a complete blank. In contrast, I remember my goodbye from my father quite clearly.

I made the journey from Szczerzec to Lwów standing in a truck carrying Jews to forced labor. The adults pressed all

---

[126] In August 1942 the Archbishop wrote a letter to the Pope in which he reported: "Liberated by the German army from the Bolshevik yoke we felt a certain relief which did not last even a month or two. Little by little the Government instituted a regime of terror and corruption that is beyond belief and which becomes, day by day, more oppressive and more unbearable. Today the whole country agrees that the German regime is to a larger degree than the Bolshevik, bad, almost diabolic. For the past year not a day passes without the most horrible crimes of murder, robberies, rapes, confiscation of property and concussions being committed. The Jews are the first victims."

[127] The non-recognition by Yad Vashem, including a translation of the 1941 letter is thoroughly reviewed by Julian Bussgang, "Metropolitan Sheptytsky. A Reassessment" in *Polin* vol 21 (The Littman Library of Jewish Civilization, Oxford 2009) 401-425.

[128] Kurt I. Lewin, *Przeżyłem* 133-134.

Metropolitan Andrei Sheptytskyi (1865-1944) as he appeared about 1943 (right) and in an official portrait (above).

around me so that I was completely hidden from view; had we been stopped by a German or Ukrainian patrol I would surely have been shot along with those hiding me. It was hot. I could barely move as my face pressed against various parts of the anatomy of those sheltering me. The smell was almost unbearable. After what seemed like an interminable time, the truck slowed to a crawl, but did not stop completely. My father cautiously looked out; the street was deserted. He took my hand and we jumped out of back of the barely moving vehicle. We approached the huge wooden doorway of the church compound and my father pulled a chain ringing a bell inside. After a few moments we heard rustling and a small window opened. My father identified himself, the door was opened by a priest wearing a long black cassock and a large cross, and we crossed the threshold into a new world.

This world, in contrast to ours, was serene and quiet. The halls were carpeted and people whispered so as not to disturb the peace. There was a smell of incense and age in the air. The walls were lined with portraits of icons. We were ushered into the Metropolitan's book-lined study. An old, grey-haired man was sitting in a wheelchair covered with a blanket. He motioned me to come to him and patted my head. My father kissed me and said good bye. It suddenly dawned on me that I would be left here and I started to cry. My father took a handkerchief from his pocket, wiped my tears, and gave me the handkerchief, which I still have.

I was just a little over seven years old and I was now alone in a new and strange world. My childhood and all the people I loved and implicitly trusted were left behind in that other world. I can see now that throughout my life I have been searching for that other world and have tried, unsuccessfully, to recreate it. As each of my children and especially my grandchildren reached the age of seven, I would stare at them and marvel anew that I was able to adapt, but my life depended on a successful adaptation. I had to learn to speak Ukrainian and to read my prayers in Church Slavonic (written in a variation of the Greek alphabet). Instead of the shema, I had to learn "Ojcze nasz" (Our Father) and "Bohoroditse Divo" (Ave Maria). I had to remember never to go the bathroom while other children were about, never to bathe with other children; to make sure, at the penalty of my life, that one part of my body was never seen. I had to remember never to speak about my past, my parents, and my customs. Even my name was changed, and I repeated it over and over so it would roll off my tongue naturally. I immediately had to learn how to answer common questions asked of children: What is your name? Levko Chaminskyi; How old are you? Seven years old. Why don't you speak a better Ukrainian? We spoke Polish at home. Where are your parents? My father died when I was a baby and my mother was killed in an air raid.

I was first taken to an orphanage in Brzuchowice, where I was briefly reunited with Herbert. This orphanage was under the auspices of the Ukrainian Women's League who were not happy with sheltering Jews and I stayed there until shortly after Christmas (1942). Conditions here were difficult. The boys were rough and food was scarce. I remember sitting on my bed with a piece of bread, on guard lest it be stolen by another child, while trying to make it last as long as possible. First, I slowly bit off small pieces of crust working my way

around in a circular fashion, and then the soft center until it was all gone. I can still taste that piece of bread and feel the ache of hunger in my gut that the lone piece of bread did not pacify. One of my prized possessions, a watch given to me by Uncle Ajzyk was soon stolen. My mother must have known where we were because one day I was called into the Mother Superior's office and she handed me a piece of candy from a bag that my mother had sent; I never received the rest. I became ill and lice crawled all over my body. I don't in fact know whether these were real or a product of my feverish state. The sisters were in a terrible dilemma because they were afraid to call a doctor who might discover my circumcision, which would jeopardize everyone there since the penalty for hiding a Jew was death.

In December 1942 or the beginning of 1943 it was decided to move me to a monastery in Univ, a small village southeast of Lwów. Herbert was moved to various locations including a village of Paniwei Zeleni (in Podole) in the Carpathian Mountains. Brat (Brother) Marko Stek accompanied me to Univ. We first went by tram to the railroad station in Lwów, then by train to Przemyślany. Finally, we walked the remaining 7 km to Univ. In Lwów, an SS officer sat down next to me on the tram. He spoke small pleasantries and pinched my cheek in a way that adults, but not children, consider cute; perhaps I reminded him of a son left behind in Germany. Brat Marko must have frozen in his seat. I, of course, understood the officer's German and was glad to hear a familiar language but, if I had answered, he would have suspected that I was Jewish because Ukrainian children did not speak German. I played dumb and Brat Marko relaxed and gave me a smile of approval.[129] We got off the train at Przemyślany and began walking. After a while, I became tired and did not want to walk further. In my stubborn way, I sat down in the snow and refused to move. Exasperated, Brat Marko broke a branch off a tree and gave me a good thrashing. I was shocked never having experience anything like this before. I got up quietly and walked the rest of the way.

Brat Marko Stek was a remarkable man. He had a good sense of humor and a smile that immediately won your confidence. He used to befriend the local militia, both German and Ukrainian, drank with them and found out in advance when the Germans would raid the monastery looking for Jews. I would be immediately hidden either in the monastery itself or outside it. On one such occasion, I was awakened in the middle of the night and told to get dressed in a hurry. I was then taken to a house, which I found out later belonged to one of Brat Marko's relatives. That must have been on a Saturday because the next morning the family went to church, and locked me in the house. While they were gone, I had to relieve myself, but I could not get to the outhouse since all the doors were locked. In those days I wore clogs with canvas tops and wooden soles since leather and rub-

ber were in short supply. Since I did not have socks, I wrapped my feet in two rectangular pieces of cloth. After an uncomfortable and anxious time, I relieved myself in one of these pieces of cloth and then threw the entire contents into the fireplace. There were two unpleasant consequences of this action: the odor, and the realization that I now had no covering for one foot to protect it from the fierce Ukrainian winter. I subsequently alternated wrapping my feet, and developed frostbite in both feet. During the cold months my feet would swell and blister, and it became painful to walk.

After the war, Brat Marko immigrated to a Ukrainian monastery in Canada. He visited New York in the early 1950s, and I visited with him. In the course of the conversation, he suggested that after I married and had children, I should send them for summer vacations to his monastery in Canada. After a moment's hesitation he added, "Don't worry I won't try to convert them; I'll even build a *heder* for them." He followed that up with a story about a recent visit to Israel. A Jew approached him through an acquaintance and asked for help in obtaining a visa to Canada because of the difficult economic circumstances then prevailing in Israel. With his great and hearty laugh he continued, "I told him that I risked my life to protect Jews from the Germans, but to protect Jews from Jews, they will have to do it all by themselves."

There were perhaps 20-25 children (either orphaned or from families unable

---

[129] This recollection was confirmed by Kurt Lewin who heard it from Brat Marko.

to care for them) in the Monastery of the Assumption of the Virgin Mary in Univ. Brat Danil,[130] a tall priest with a balding head and a full black beard, was in charge of the children. He was a kind man but a strict disciplinarian who enforced obedience with a cane that hung in his study. I remember having a confrontation with him once. I believe that I had bragged about something to one of the other boys, which might have revealed my identity and endangered all of us. I left his ofice-cell enraged and determined never to speak a word about my past again. On December 31, 2008, Brat Danil was recognized as a Righteous Gentile by Yad Vashem, as a result of testimony of the survivors.

Shortly after arriving in Univ my head was shaved, probably as a hygienic measure, and remained that way for the duration of my stay. Watching my locks fall to the ground was very traumatic for me; another piece of my identity was being stripped away. At a later time, some of the older children were allowed a narrow growth of hair in the middle of their heads, much like the Apaches, and I remember being very envious of them. I didn't quite realize the extent of the trauma that losing my hair caused me

Children in front of the "cerkva" (church) in Univ in a photo taken in the autumn of 1943 or the spring of 1944. At left is Brat Danil (Temchyna). First row standing, 3rd child from left is Danyło Czerwiński (Daniel Adam Rotfeld) and 4th from left is Dorko Brorowicki (Oded Amarant). I am standing in the second row between them.

[130] On our visit to Lviv in October 2007, we found out that his last name was Temchyna. He was arrested by the Soviets in 1947 and sentenced to 10 years of hard labor in Siberia. He died in 1972.

Ihumen Venedict (left) and I in front of the same cerkva wall in 2007.

until many years later when our daughter, Debbie, decided to shave our grandson's head for the summer. The first time I saw him I became extremely upset. I tried not to show it, but my emotion was clearly out of proportion, and recurred every time I saw him. I spoke with Debbie about it and she replied, "Dad, it's only hair – it will grow back." She was, of course, absolutely right.

There were two other Jewish children in the Univ monastery, Dorko Brorowicki (Oded Amarant) and Danyło Czerwiński (Daniel Adam Rotfeld). I don't know that we ever spoke about it but there is no question that I knew they were Jews. The three of us became separated after the war but I always thought about them, won-

dered where they were, and hoped that someday I would meet them again. That would not happen until the early 1990s.

For some reason I remembered Dorko's real last name, and whenever I traveled I would look in the phone book for him. In the early 1990s I was visiting my cousin Dov in Gedera, Israel and realized that I had never looked in the Tel Aviv telephone directory. When I did so, I found an Adolph Amarant and telephoned him. An old man answered, and after hearing my story, told me that he was 89 years old and the person I was searching for was his nephew who lived in Tel Aviv. He had an unlisted telephone number but he was kind enough to give it to me. The following evening, I met Oded and his family and we had a memorable and emotional reunion. He told me that he was born in Palestine and that in the summer of 1939 his mother took him to Poland to visit his grandparents. His mother returned home and left him for a longer visit. The outbreak of the war trapped him. He showed me a "wanted" poster the Germans had produced looking for a "Palestinian." Following liberation, he was reunited with his parents in Israel, studied there, and received a degree in engineering. In the course of the evening his wife mentioned that she was concerned that Uncle Adolph was not answering his phone. I suggested that we go over immediately, and when we entered his apartment, found him dead on a couch. I would estimate that he had been dead for about 12 hours since rigor mortis had set in. As we waited for the *hevra kadisha,* we speculated that he must have been kept alive just long enough to give me Oded's telephone number.

Daniel was more difficult to find because neither Oded nor I could remember his last name. We went to see Rabbi Kahane, by then quite elderly, but he too could not remember his name. Several months after my visit, Oded was invited to appear on a television panel to discuss Louis Malle's prize-winning movie about hidden children in France, "Au Revoir, les Enfants." In the course of the discussion, Oded mentioned our meeting and the fact that we were looking for the third child. A businessman, watching in Haifa, was preparing to go to Poland the next morning and, impressed by the story, made inquiries, which identified the third child as Adam Daniel Rotfeld. Initial contact with Daniel was through his relative in Italy because, as a member of the Polish Foreign Service, Daniel was afraid to receive mail from the United States. After the dissolution of the Soviet Union in 1989, we corresponded directly and eventually met.

Before the war, Daniel's father, a prominent attorney, had represented the legal interests of the Studite Order of the Uniate Church, and after the German invasion of eastern Poland, he entrusted Daniel's older brother to the protection of the church.[131] His parents considered 3-year old Daniel too young to be sent away from home. Unfortunately, his older brother was so homesick that he had to be returned to his parents. As the priest was about to leave, he noticed Daniel, and suggested that he take him. The en-

Daniel and I finally met in 1994 (top). When he met with Pope Paul II in 1999 (below), he expressed our gratitude to the Greek Catholic Church.

[131] *POLITYKA* #7 (2491) 19 February 2005 70-73.

tire family, except for Daniel and a sister, perished. Since no one knew of Daniel, he was left in the monastery in Univ after liberation. As a former Polish citizen, Daniel was repatriated to an orphanage in Poland. He was so unhappy there, that in January 1947 he and two friends ran away, and walked back to the monastery in Univ. When Ihumen Klement, Metropolitan Sheptytskyi's brother, was arrested in 1947, Daniel used to bring him food packages prepared by the sisters. He remained in the monastery until its dissolution by the Soviets, after which he lived with his surviving 17-year old sister.

Daniel was one of 3,000 children repatriated to Poland in 1950. When the transport arrived in Krakow, only four children were not claimed by family. Daniel was one of the four, and so he was sent to an orphanage. Conditions in this orphanage were better, and he was encouraged to pursue higher education. He graduated from the University of Warsaw and received a PhD with a thesis on the right of self-determination of people in modern international law, from the Jagellonian University in Kraków in 1969. The 1960's were a difficult time for Jews in Poland and Daniel was unable to get a position. He was finally accepted into the Foreign Service and gradually rose in rank. His natural talent, intelligence, and hard work resulted in many diplomatic positions and honors. He was appointed Professor at the University of Warsaw in 2001 and became an authority on world peace and peaceful cooperation among

nations. He has published widely and was appointed to two unprecedented five-year terms (1991- 2000) as Director of SIPRI (Stockholm Institute of Peace Research), a Swedish organization that studies and promotes world peace. He then served as Poland's Undersecretary of State and finally as Foreign Minister from January to October 2005, when his party was defeated at the polls. He has since been a member of many diplomatic missions and Poland's chief negotiator with Russia. Daniel's life was again saved when he missed the airplane that carried the Polish president and much of the government to the forest at Katyn where it crashed on April 10, 2010. He had accompanied the Polish Prime Minister and President Putin of Russia to a preliminary commemoration earlier in the week, and President Putin suggested that Daniel accompany him to Moscow to continue their discussions. As a result, Daniel arrived back in Warsaw too late to catch the ill-fated flight.

In honor of Daniel's 65th birthday, his diplomatic friends published a book, which was supposed to be a humorous "collection of documents and memos found in his KGB file." The editors asked me to contribute a piece for the volume and I wrote the "memorandum" reprinted below.[132]

In 2005 I discovered that another little boy, the Nobel laureate in chemistry and poet, Roald Hoffman, was also hidden with his mother in the same village of Univ. They were hidden by our village

---

[132] *Podwójne Życie – Double Life- ADR's File* (Wydawnice Magnum, 2008 Warsaw, Poland).

From: Levko Chaminskyi aka Dr. Leon Chameides
Re: Danyło Czerwiński, aka Adam Daniel Rotfeld
Date: November 12, 1944

BEFORE IT IS TOO LATE

I would like to draw your attention to a highly suspicious and potentially dangerous individual known as Danyło Czerwiński. I have known him for about two years during which time we resided in the Studite Monastery of the Ukrainian Catholic Church in Univ. He blends perfectly into his environment, speaks colloquial Ukrainian, and prays flawlessly. Under this camouflage, he has successfully evaded the Gestapo and SS for over two years. No one here has the slightest suspicion that he is undercover; that he really is someone else. I believe that he has the potential for becoming highly dangerous to organized hierarchical authority and a potential threat to the Party's noble socialist goals for Europe in the near future and could undermine the Party's plans for the eventual perfection of all humanity.

I know that when you investigate him thoroughly you will think that I exaggerate. You will conclude that he could not possibly be as dangerous as I believe he is, since he is only six years old. Such a conclusion would be a great mistake. I would like to remind you that successful and driven people with a mission are not born that way. Given an innate high intelligence and sterling character, of which he has already shown evidence even at his tender age, successful and driven adults are a product of their experiences. Daniel is an extremely sweet boy who manages to get along with everyone despite being quite stubborn and opinionated. As you know, one-and-a-half million Jewish children have been slaughtered in the last three years and only a handful, such as Daniel, have remained alive. Studies have shown that, having remained alive, such children tend to become highly focused and driven. They try to justify their survival with a life-mission and develop an especially keen sensitivity to justice, freedom, equality, truth, and conflict resolution by peaceful means. I predict that he will defend these principles with an almost religious (if you pardon the expression) zeal. Theoretically, these are of course also important concepts for the Party but compromises must sometimes be made in the short-term in order to achieve long-term gains. It would not surprise me if an intelligent boy like Daniel, despite all odds, goes on to attain a higher education and eventually becomes a leader for these causes. Someday he might lobby for world arms control and human rights; become a diplomatic leader, perhaps even a foreign minster, and I can assure you, from what I see in him now, that if the Party's representatives ever face him across a table and he perceives injustice, inequality, discrimination, falsehood, or armed conflict they will not prevail.

I urge you to take action now before it is too late!"

Fields of Vision

From the attic the boy
watched children playing, but
they were always running
out of the window frame.
And the weathered shutters
divided up space, so
that he couldn't often tell
where the ball Igor kicked
(he heard the children call
Igor's name) would end up.
The boy was always moving,
one slat to another,
trying to make the world
come out. He saw Teacher
Dyuk's wife with a basket,
then he saw her come back
with eggs; he could smell them.
Once he saw a fat goose,
escaped from her pen, saved
from slaughter, he thought.
Once he saw a girl, in her
embroidered Carpathian
vest. He couldn't see the sky,
the slats pointed down; he
saw the field by the school,
always the same field, only
snow turned into mud into
grass into snow. Later
the boy grew up, came
to America, where he
was a good student, praised
for his attention to facts;
he taught people to look
at every distortion
of a molecule, why
ethylene on iron
turned this way, not another.
In this world, he thought, there
must be reasons. His poems
were not dreamy, but full
of exasperating
facts. Still later, he watched
his mother, whose eyes were
failing, move her head,
the way he did, to catch
oh a glimpse, the smallest
reflecting shard of light
of our world, confined.

schoolmaster, Mikola Dyuk, in the attic of the school, and he used to peek out between the slats and look enviously at the schoolchildren, perhaps including us, running around "free." He describes this in his poem *Fields of Vision*[133] in which he compares his attempts to see the world between the attic slats, to his later attempts to explain chemical structures so others could see, and to his elderly mother trying to get a glimpse of her immediate world with failing eyes.

I have often thought about the achievements and contributions that we, four Jewish children, hidden in this small village have made and I cannot help but wonder and imagine the potential achievements and contributions of the one and a half million children whose lives were snuffed out.

The monastery at Univ was run by the Basilian Brothers of the Studite Order. The Studite Order was named for Theodore the Studite (d 856), who established monastic life for the Eastern Church. His monastic rules were introduced into Ukraine in the 11th century but disappeared from the Greek Catholic church until they were resurrected at the end of the 19th century by Metropolitan Andrei Sheptytskyi. The central activities of the Studites consisted of agriculture, caring for orphaned children, and prayer. The Univ Monastery, a walled compound first built in the 13th century, located in a beautiful valley in the foothills of the Carpathian Mountains surrounded by

---

[133] Fields of Vision, *Michigan Quarterly Review*, 39(2), 244 (2000); in M.A. Safir, Ed., *Connecting Creations: Science-Technology-Literature-Arts*, (Santiago de Compostela: Centro Gallego de Arte Contemporáneo 2000). With permission of Prof. Roald Hoffman.

fields and forests became the mother monastery, and the center of monastic revival. The compound consists of a number of buildings, including living quarters and a cerkva (church). There were also barns for cows and chickens, and in the kitchen courtyard there was a hand water pump. We took turns pumping water, and its ingenious arrangement always fascinated me. There was a spigot that, when turned, directed the water into a holding tank high in the building. The holding tank supplied water by gravity to the bathrooms and kitchen. Pumping was part of our job and we had to pump until the tank was full, indicated by an overflow of water through a pipe onto the roof. How thrilling it always was, especially in the freezing winter, to see that trickle of water.

Because farming made the monastery almost self-sufficient in food, we did not suffer food shortages until the latter part of 1943 and early in 1944, when the Germans confiscated our livestock and the church bell. We went to school down the dirt road, and we also had daily farm chores. We worked in the fields, picked fruit, cared for the animals, mainly horses, cows, and sheep, and took turns peeling potatoes. During the winter, the potatoes were stored in the cellar and had to be carried up to the kitchen. As the winter wore on, many of the potatoes rotted, and some sprouted new growth. In the first year, when food was plentiful, we would discard these, but during the latter part of the war, when food became scarce, we were grateful even for the rotten potatoes.

My introduction to farming came shortly after I arrived in Univ. I was sent to the barn to throw down bales of hay from a loft to feed the cows. As a city-reared child, I had never as much as seen a cow, let alone get close to one. My first problem was to squeeze by one of the cows to reach the ladder. I managed to do that and slowly, with my heart pounding, I climbed the ladder. One rung at a time, the floor receding from me, I finally made it and heaved a sigh of relief. I grabbed a rope holding the bale of hay and, by pulling and shoving, got it to the edge and, with one final effort, throwing my entire seven-year old weight against it, threw it over the edge. I was thrilled at this accomplishment until I looked down and saw that the cow, smelling food, had taken up a position next to the ladder. I had no idea how to get down, and I started to cry, but soon realized that this would do me no good since no one could hear me. I dried my tears and began throwing handfuls of hay to coax the cow away from the ladder. After what seemed like an eternity, the cow moved slightly. I could now descend from the safety of my perch, but I didn't know how. I had never seen anyone come down a ladder so I didn't know that I was supposed to come down backwards. After almost falling several times, and holding on for dear life, I slowly descended and squeezed by the cow who didn't as much as give me a look of thanks for my efforts. I suspect I would never have remembered this affair if it had not been so terrifying for me.

I gradually got used to and even started to enjoy some of the chores, especially during the long days of summer and early fall when, while watching the animals at pasture, I could lie on the soft grass, smell the freshly mowed hay or the sweet smell of hemp, look up at the sky, and dream. There was a fast flowing stream at the foot of the monastery, and we would amuse ourselves by throwing stones into the swiftly moving water. Sometimes we were sent down the dirt road past the schoolhouse to the mill to get the wheat ground into flour. We would then watch a bored and tired horse go round and round dragging a large millstone, placed on top of another, grinding the wheat between them. We gradually learned which wild berries we could pick and eat; I remember picking sweet wild strawberries (poziomki), raspberries, boysenberries, gooseberries, and many others whose English names I never learned. In contrast to the summers, the winters were brutal with subzero temperatures, and frequent snow storms, made worse by our inadequate clothing. I had only one thin blanket at night. During the day, I had no gloves, socks, boots, sweater, or overcoat. The winter of 1943-1944 was unusually cold and snowy, and our misery was compounded by hunger. My hands and feet became swollen and developed open and oozing sores. It took quite a few years after liberation for my hands and feet not to swell in winter.

Religion was a large part of our lives. I was baptized early during my stay and gradually became a religious little boy. Every morning, we were awakened by a monk with a wooden clapper (two pieces of wood held together with a piece of

leather) chanting "molytvy chas" (it is time for prayers). We would hurriedly get up in the dark, splash some cold water on our faces, and go to chapel. We attended the stone church (cerkva) only on Sundays and religious holidays. Until early 1944, we had a church bell and, as a special privilege, we might be allowed to ring it by swinging from its rope. Outside the church was a babbling brook. Inside, I liked to watch the shadows cast by the many candles, listen to the tinkle of tiny bells, and smell the sweet incense from the censer swung by the priest. The service was in Church Slavonic, which I learned to follow from the small prayer book I was given. At appropriate times during the Mass, we would answer "hospody pomyluj" (Lord have mercy on us) and, if I went to confession first, I was allowed to have Holy Communion. The priest would place the wafer on my tongue, and I would allow it to dissolve slowly in my mouth. I was especially careful not to bite it, since it was the "body of the Lord." I always went to confession because I wanted that wafer, but I always agonized, because I didn't know what sins to confess to. Generally I stuck with the reliable ones of lying and thinking bad thoughts. Fortunately, the Priest never asked me to elaborate.

We slept, dormitory style, in a long room with the beds close to each other. The "mattresses" and "pillows" were sacks filled with straw, which poked us each time we turned. One day, the other boys told me that I sometimes talked in my sleep. This concerned me very much and therefore, before going to sleep, I would kneel by my bed, cross myself according to the Ukrainian *minhag* (custom) by apposing the thumb, index, and middle fingers to represent the Trinity, close my eyes, and pray "with all my heart and with all my soul" to Jesus and Mary to protect me during the night from talking in my sleep and revealing that I was a Jew. I did not appreciate the irony at the time.

Mother Mary was a most important figure for us. Once, during a thunderstorm I explained to my friends that I had heard that thunder was due to Mother Mary wheeling baby Jesus' carriage up in heaven. One of the reasons Mary became such a significant figure was, I believe, that we lived in a totally male society, and suffered from a lack of love, warmth, maternal concern, or a tender touch. One day, I was called to the main hall to meet a visitor. As I came into the room I noticed a tall woman in a nun's habit, a large cross dangling from her braided belt. I glanced at her face which, even after more than sixty years, is vivid in my memory. The white of her wimple pressed against, and framed her face. The few hairs that I could see from under her wimple were definitely black as were her eyebrows. Her eyes were brown and I saw in them a look of concern, compassion, and tenderness I had not seen in a long time. Trying not to stare, I glanced at her features and thought they resembled my mother's but, to my horror, I discovered that the memory of my mother's features was be-

coming hazy. Nevertheless, I convinced myself that this was indeed my mother in disguise, despite the fact that the nun spoke to me in unaccented Ukrainian, and that my mother had never been able to learn any language except her native German. I quickly looked away so that I would do nothing to jeopardize her disguise and give away her new "identity." I never saw the nun again and I remember nothing of our conversation, but my conviction as to her "true" identity helped me many times over the next two years.

My only other "contact" with my family took place a few days after my arrival in Univ. I was rummaging around a top shelf of the closet and suddenly saw something familiar. I tugged at it and pulled out a pair of short trousers. As soon as I saw them, there was no question in my mind that they belonged to my brother, since no Ukrainian peasant child would have shorts embroidered with velvet. My major concern was where to hide them so no one else would find them, and I finally stuffed them into a corner of the attic. Many years later, my brother told me that before my arrival, he was taken to Univ but only stayed there for two days.

I was not consciously aware of the tragic events that were taking place on the "outside." One day, as I was on my way to the mill, I passed a family, a man with a short beard, a woman with her head wrapped in a babushka, a small boy, and an older girl. They were huddled in a wagon and something about them seemed vaguely familiar. I obviously identified with them since I remember them so vividly, but I don't know whether I recognized that they were Jews. I tried to look for them whenever I passed that way, and then they disappeared. We found them on an outing into the woods, sprawled on the forest floor, dead. The father's abdomen had been torn open, and his intestines were spread before him on the forest ground.

We could sense changes in the spring of 1944. Food became scarce and we foraged for any plant that could be eaten. Mealtime became noisy as children scrambled to beg for more food, and banged wooden spoons on tin plates. I always stood in the back; no matter how hungry, I could not get myself to beg. We began seeing Ukrainian peasants don German uniforms and heard German soldiers sing sarcastic songs, one of which began: "Es ist alles vorüber, es ist alles vorbei; den Schnapps von Dezember bekommen wir in Mai…" – "It is all over, all washed up; the whiskey rations from December, we don't get until May…" We often heard rifle fire, the rat-tat-tat of submachine guns, and, less frequently the explosion of a bomb.

As the front drew closer, an increasing number of wounded were brought to the monastery. Most of these were Ukrainian peasants from nearby villages who either fought with the partisans sabotaging the Germans or, just as frequently, with the Germans against the advancing Russian army. One man,[134] I am not sure whether he was a physician or a physician's assistant, known in Russian as a *feldsher*, was put in charge of the wounded. He had little equipment, and almost no medications. For some reason, he appointed me to help him. My job was to wash the bandages. As soon as someone died, I would take the bandages off, wash them, hang them to dry, and then roll them so they would be ready for the next victim. Sometimes, I would be allowed to bandage a wound, and I soon learned that if a wound had a greenish tint and a sweet smell, the victim would soon be dead. I did not learn until I was in medical school that that was almost certainly due to a pseudomonas infection, for which there was then no treatment. Sometimes, after a battle, when the shooting had died down, I would be sent to the forest to look for dead German soldiers and try to find bandages.

This job gave me much satisfaction and self-importance, but much more importantly, it gave me food because when the families came to visit their sons and husbands, usually on Sunday, they would bring me farm produce. I would receive gifts of eggs, cheese, and bread from them. I soon learned how to make a hole in an egg with a pin or needle and suck out its delicious contents. I also learned that one person's misfortune can be another's salvation.

The Soviet army liberated our region in July 1944 and brought with it a new

[134] On our October 2007 visit I was told that his name was Vitaly Matkowski and that he was not a physician but an experienced medic. He was arrested by the Russians, spent years in the Gulag and returned in 1991. He died a few years ago.

fear. The Russians were determined to stamp out religion in general, but especially the intensely nationalistic Ukrainian Greek Catholic Church. They arrested priests and eventually outlawed the Uniate Church, and confiscated its properties. The Church was not allowed to function again until the Soviet Union imploded in the early 1990s. The Soviets first converted the monastery in Univ into a concentration camp for priests, and later into an asylum for insane women. Many years later, Daniel Rotfeld told me that when he visited the monastery as a Polish diplomat, he could barely keep from laughing as he realized that a gold statue of Lenin occupied a place of honor on what had been the farm manure pile in the middle of the courtyard of an insane asylum. How appropriate!

In the Fall of 1944 (I think it was in September), I was told to walk to a nearby village from which transportation would be available to St. Jur in Lwów. I took Dorko (Oded) with me and, with our few belongings, we began walking. We were soon stopped by two Russian soldiers. When we told them where we were headed, they conferred with each other and made a decision. One went off, perhaps to ask his superiors what to do, while the other, a young teen-aged lad, stood watch over us. We were forced to crouch by the side of the road with our arms in the air while he stood over us with his submachine gun. To offset boredom, we struck up a conversation and I suggested that we all go to a nearby farmhouse. I pointed out that we would all be

more comfortable, and he could watch the door and even lock it. The young guard liked the idea, and marched us off to the farmhouse. The farmer welcomed us and offered us something to eat. While we waited, Dorko and I had a disagreement as to whose prayers, mine to Jesus or his to Mary, were responsible for this stroke of good luck. At last, the other soldier returned and informed us that we could go no further; we were to return to Univ. I asked him for a written pass in case we were stopped by another patrol. The poor fellow had no paper, and was probably illiterate so we never got that pass. Our return journey must have been uneventful since I don't remember it.

Shortly afterwards, I was put on a horse drawn wagon and made the trip to Archbishop Sheptytskyi's residence at Sw. Jur (St. George) in Lwów. It was there, while attending morning Mass in the chapel that I looked up and saw two boys come in. I immediately recognized one as Herbert, my brother. The other was Nathan Lewin. They motioned to me and we went to the kitchen, where I ate breakfast. They then told me to get my things together. That was rather easy. I was wearing all the clothes I owned - no underwear, a peasant shirt, a pair of pants made of sackcloth held up by a rope, and wooden-soled cloth shoes without socks. I wrapped up all my possessions - a book of Ukrainian fables (borrowed from the Monastery library), my small prayer book, my black rosary with a cross on the end, a photograph of all the children with Brat Danil taken in front of the church in

Univ, and the handkerchief that my father gave me when he left me at St. Jur - into the blanket with which I had covered myself in Univ. I still have the book, photo, handkerchief, and blanket, and I was very pleased when we used the blanket during my grandson Ilan's *brith mila*.

Herbert, Nathan, and I went directly to see Rabbi David Kahane, who told us that no one from our family survived, and gave us a note written by our mother. I remember this meeting quite vividly, but, strangely, I don't remember having any emotion when told that my parents, grandparents, aunts, uncles, and cousins were dead. It almost seemed natural; as if I expected as much and would have been surprised had it had been otherwise.

In October 2007, Jean, David, our younger son, and I visited Sw. Jur and spent an afternoon in Univ. The visit brought back many memories and emotions. We were accompanied to Sw. Jur by Myroslav Marynovych, Vice Rector of the Catholic Ukrainian University in Lviv. Myroslaw was a sensitive and informed guide. He had been active in advocating for human rights included in the Helsinki accords, as a result of which he was arrested by the Soviets in 1978, and found guilty of anti-State activities. He was sentenced to 10 years in the Gulag followed by two years of exile in Kazakhstan. When asked whether he would demonstrate for human rights again if he had known what awaited him, he replied "Without hesitation, I would do it again." He said that he found prison a "deeply spiritual experience."

As we waited for Myroslaw in the yard of Sw. Jur, I searched for the entrance that

my father and I had used, but could not locate it. A large cross stood in the courtyard and people going into the church genuflected and crossed themselves before it. We entered the church and the surroundings of dim light, flickering candles, beautiful singing in the minor key, and above all the smell of incense transported me back in time. We followed Myroslaw down the stairs into the crypt where the church fathers including Sheptytskyi are buried. I stood before his tomb, and was surprised at the deep emotion I felt. This was, after all, the final resting place of the man to whom I owed my life. Myroslaw then took us to the private quarters. Many of the rooms had been changed and renovated for the visit by Pope Paul II in 2001. Unfortunately, the library has been moved to Kiev along with the seat of the Church, and so I could no longer identify the room where the Archbishop received me. I did, however, immediately recognize the beautiful chapel and where I sat when Herbert and Nathan Lewin came to pick me up.

We met Ihumen (head of a monastery) Venedict, the current head of the Univ monastery, outside a hospital in Lviv. He had been hospitalized as a result of an automobile accident suffered some months before, but he insisted on signing himself out so he could personally accompany us to Univ. He is a man probably in his early forties with a black beard and high hat of his rank. Quiet in his demeanor, he asked intelligent and penetrating questions throughout the afternoon.

I learned that the Studites are trying to resurrect their church after being suppressed by the Soviets for so long, and they are anx-

ious to hear about their history. They are especially thirsty for evidence that would vindicate them of charges made against the behavior of Ukrainians during the war. In general, I found that, in regard to the murdered Jewish population, the Ukrainians are about where Poland was 10 years ago. They realize there is an empty spot in their history—in speaking about Poland I once described it as the pain of a phantom limb, it is there but you can't scratch it—but they have not yet been open enough to try to identify and understand the missing parts.

Univ is a very small village, really one road, with about 250 households. We passed the schoolhouse where we went to school and where Roald Hoffman had been hidden in the attic, and then we saw a clearing and, nestled into the mountains, was the white wall of the monastery compound. It is as beautiful as I remember it, but much cleaner and smaller than I had imagined. For example, I was impressed at

how close the bell tower was to the church. When I was small, I thought it was much further away. Some things have changed. The barn has been moved across the street, and its former space has been turned into a conference center. The kitchen, dining area, and the pump are gone. The buildings we lived in have been turned into a garage, and the monastery no longer has an orphanage. A stream with a statue of Mary flows outside the compound wall. Visitors come to the stream and fill bottles with water. We were told that the source of the stream is under the cerkva (church) and that there is a story of a miraculous healing by some who have drunk the water from it. I recognized the stream and am quite sure that this was the location of my baptism. The church was exactly as I remembered it, with flickering candles and a smell of incense. The sun was

Sw. Jur (St. George) Cathedral as seen in 2007.

*Crypt of
Archbishop
Andrei
Sheptytskyi at
the Cathedral
of Sw. Jur.*

priests were either killed or sent to the gulag from which few returned. The Church itself was outlawed and its property, including its churches, was confiscated. When Ukraine regained its independence after the fall of the Soviet Union, the Church was once again made legal and its property returned. They are trying to reconstitute it, but it will take much time as they try to reestablish a tradition and re-educate their leaders.

Myroslav invited me to address the faculty and students of the Ukrainian Catholic University, and I was happy to do so. I spoke for about an hour to a most attentive and interested group who asked excellent and intelligent questions. I tried to convey the cultural richness and size of the prewar Jewish community of Lviv, and its decimation during the war. I gave them an outline of my own story and emphasized the role that their church played in my survival. I stressed that the behavior of the Studites was in contrast to that of most of our former neighbors, who either turned their backs on us or even participated in tormenting us. I have been told that my talk had a profound effect on them.

On the way back from Lviv we stopped in Warsaw and spent three days with Daniel Rotfeld. This gave me an opportunity to get to know him a little better, reminisce about our common experiences, and learn his views about the world from the vantage point of someone who has known and worked with most of its leaders. It is quite remarkable what he has been able to achieve considering that he spent his entire childhood and youth in orphanages.

setting and a stream of light entered the church and allowed particles of dust to dance within it. A most beautiful sight! Ihumen Venedict had a lunch prepared for us and assured us that it was all vegetarian, and all grown locally. It was most delicious.

During lunch, Ihumen Venedict told us that the Soviets first turned the monastery into a concentration camp for priests and later into an insane asylum for women. The

Black and white copy of Getto IV 1956 by Marek Oberlander (1922-1978) depicts his memorial to the martyred Jews of his hometown of Szczerzec. The horizon is overwhelmed by the sad eternal eyes of the Jew as witness. The crowded ghetto is hemmed in by crosses, which become barbed wire in the foreground. (Reproduced with permission of Muzeum Narodowe, Wrocław).

VIII

MY FAMILY'S FATE

———•◆•———

Except for that piece of candy I received shortly after arriving in Brzuchowice, I had not heard from my parents or from other family members since I left home in September 1942. Rabbi Kahane told us in the fall of 1944 that no one survived, but I only learned snippets of their ultimate fates later.

Uncle Ajzyk was sent to the notorious Janowska Camp in Lwów[135] where he became ill with typhus, which left him almost completely deaf. Somehow, my father managed to get him out, and brought him to Szczerzec. Herbert told me: "Our grandparents and Uncle Ajzyk apparently hid in their proposed hiding place in a double wall of the *sukkah* which was always set up in a house with a metal roof which could be opened, and in case of rain, closed from the inside. The *sukkah* was behind the chicken slaughtering place and served during most of the year for wood storage. The false wall, which grandfather built and showed me before I left, was, like the rest of the place, built of wood, and some boards could be grasped by protruding nails and removed. The space behind this false wall was quite narrow. Wood was stored in front of the wall to make it look quite natural. When I was first shown the wall, I could not recognize any change." Apparently the Germans never found the false wall and my grandparents and Uncle Ajzyk remained there some weeks after Szczerzec was declared Judenrein. They were apparently shot by the local Ukrainian militia when they came out in search of food. Uncle Ajzyk was then barely 31 years old. According to a note left to us by our mother (see below), my grandparents died on the fourth day of Chanukah (December 7) 1942.[136]

Most of the remainder of the family, including the Karls (my father's sister and her family) and the Bittersfelds (Uncle Ajzyk's wife and her family), were taken to the notorious extermination camp in Bełżec during the great Aktion in August/September 1942 and were not heard from again. I never found out Uncle Beniu's fate, but he was not yet 30 years old and never married his beautiful fiancé.

---

[135] The Janowska Camp was named after the street on which it was located and had the reputation of being one of the cruelest of German extermination camps where inmates were literally tortured to death. Approximately 25,000 Jews went through the camp and the most optimistic numbers are that no more than 350 survived.

[136] According to another source (Forum Żydów Polskie http//tzp.net.pl/spot24.htm accessed on 5-19-2009), Uncle Aizyk and Aunt Zipporah were killed in 1943 when he was 32 and she was 30 years old.

```
                    V e r z e i c h n i s
           -------------------------------------------

der bei den Judenrate Lemberg beschäftigten unentgeltlichen Arbeitnehmer
               \        für Oktober 1942.


F R I L D H O F S A B T E I L U N G     Gruppe "U"
----------------------------------------------------------------

  1. Barach Feiwel
  2. Jachnis Baruch
  3. Horowitz Saul
  4. Seidenfrau Isak
  5. Reiss Ignacy


F R I E D H O F S A B T E I L U N G     Gruppe "R"
----------------------------------------------------------------

  1. Seidmann Isak
  2. Ropschitz Rosa
  3. Fleischmann Antonina
  4. Chameides Kalman
  5. Bergner Abraham
  6. Kamm Berisch
  7. Leder Regina
  8. Schein Mendel
```

Document from the files of the Holocaust Museum in Washington, DC dated October 1942 showing that Kalman Chameides was assigned to work in the cemetery in Group "R".

The Lwów ghetto was closed on September 7, 1942 and shortly thereafter the Judenrat was disbanded. Only Jews with a specific work assignment were allowed to live for the time being. In October 1942, my father's name appears on a list[137] of "unentgeltlichen Arbeitnehmer" (uncompensated workers) in "Friedhofsabteilung Gruppe R" (cemetery workers group R)— Jews assigned as grave diggers. I am overwhelmed every time I think of that gentle scholar who loved books and people, of that great orator who moved grown men to tears, digging graves.

On October 26, 1942 my father wrote a remarkable letter to Metropolitan Sheptytskyi. It must have been smuggled out of the ghetto, and was found among the Metropolitan's papers by Bishop Michael Hrychyshyn, who kindly sent me a copy. The following is a copy of the letter and my translation of it.[138]

[137] United States Holocaust Museum Washington, DC.

[138] Leon Chameides, "Kalman Chameides – One of the Last Spiritual Leaders of Katowice. A Tribute," in Marcin Wodziński and Janusz Spyra (ed) *Jews in Silesia* (University of Wrocław, Research Centre for the Culture and Languages of Polish Jews, Kraków 2001) 401-416. I made some errors in the translation that appears in that article. I believe this translation to be truer to the original.

Lemberg, den 26 Oktober 1942.

„ Und der Gerechte lebt in seinem Glauben "
Hab.

Exzellenz!

Infolge der Tücke der Verhältnisse war es mir bis heute nicht vergönnt, Ihnen, Exzellenz, meinen innigsten Dank für die warme brüderliche Aufnahme abzustatten, die ich bei Ihnen in der Stunde der Not gefunden habe. Aus der Tiefe meiner betrübten Seele habe ich damals Gottes Segen auf Sie, Exzellenz und Ihr Haus herabgefleht, als wir älterer Freund und ich in Ihrer Nähe von den Mühsalen der grausamsten aller Verfolgungen wenige Tage hindurch ausruhen durften.

Unser Exodus erfolgte leider zu früh! Mein Leidensgenosse ist nicht mehr da. Aber auch ich habe Monate schweren Ringens und bitterer Erlebnisse hinter mir. Nur der Glaube an Gott war meine Stütze! Nur die Hoffnung auf die baldige Offenbarung Seiner Huld war mein Leitstern in diesen vom Tode überschatteten Wochen!

Wenn mein lieber Kollege, dr. Kohane und ich uns nun — im Einklang mit der mündlichen Erklärung des H. dr. Kohane Seiner Eminenz Pater ... gegenüber — unter die Fittige der Kirche zu begeben entschlossen haben und um Ihre Zuneigung und Ihren Beistand bitten, so geschieht dies nicht allein aus dem uns allen angeborenen Selbsterhaltungstrieb heraus, sondern gleichzeitig in der festen Zuversicht und Hoffnung, daß es uns in der Zukunft gegeben sein wird, für das Wohl der Menschheit und einer im Glauben geeinten Welt im Geiste der unsterblichen Lehre der alle Wesen versöhnenden und erlösenden Nächstenliebe zu wirken. Wir wollen an der Errichtung des großen erhabenen Domes der Liebe teilhaben, in dem alle, die guten Willens sind, Platz finden werden.

Wer wie wir vermag so tief die Leidensgeschichte des großen göttlichen Dulders nachzuempfinden? Wer wie wir vermag das Licht zu erfassen, das aus Seinem vom Schmerz gezeichneten Gesicht uns entgegenstrahlt? Gleich Ihm rufen wir täglich und stündlich: „ eli, eli, lama schebaktani!" Unter den Bildern der unzähligen Märtyrer unseres schwergeprüften Volkes, die uns vor Augen schweben, wenn wir die Dornenkrone auf unserem gebeugten Haupte den Spott einer haßerfüllten Welt zu ertragen haben, ragt Sein vom Glorienschein des göttlichen Martyriums umgebenes Bild tröstend hervor!

Exzellenz! Eile tut not! Noch koennten Sie uns dem Abgrund entreissen, der seinen Rachen nach uns auftut!

Mögen Sie uns bald dazu verhelfen, diese Zeit des Weltbrandes zu überdauern, auf daß wir als treue Diener Gottes und Seiner Willensvollstrecker auf Erden den heranbrechenden Morgen einer geläuterten Menschheit im Verein mit allen Gläubigen begrüßen dürfen ! —

K. Chameides

Lemberg, October 26, 1942
"And the righteous lives by his faith"

Hab.

Excellency!

In view of the treacherous circumstances, I have not had an opportunity until today to express to you, Excellency, my deepest gratitude for the warm, brotherly reception that I received from you at a time of affliction. From the depths of my sad soul I prayed for God's blessings for you, Excellency, and for your household, while my elder friend and I were allowed to rest in your presence over a few days from the vicissitudes of the cruelest of all persecutions.

Unfortunately, we left too soon! My fellow-sufferer is no longer here. But I too have suffered through months of difficult struggles and bitter experiences. Only my faith in God has sustained me! Only hope in the speedy revelation of His grace has been my guiding star during these weeks, overshadowed by death!

If my dear colleague, Dr. Kohane and I - as stated in a personal oral explanation by Dr. Kohane to his eminence Father...- have now decided to place ourselves under the protection of the Church and to ask for your sympathy and aid, it is not only because of an inborn instinct for self-preservation common to all of us, but also from a firm faith and hope that in the future we might have an opportunity to work for the welfare of humanity and for a world united in faith in the spirit of that immortal doctrine which reconciles and liberates all people - love of one's fellow man. We want to participate in the establishment of a large sublime dome of love under which all people of goodwill will find a place.

Who can sympathize as deeply as we with the tale of woe of the great divine sufferer? Who, better than we, can capture the light shining from his face engraved by pain? Like he, we cry daily and hourly: "eli, eli, lama schebaktani!" His comforting image, encircled with a halo of divine martyrdom stands out among the images of countless martyrs of our sorely tried nation hovering before our eyes, when we have had to bear the crown of thorns on our bowed heads - the derision of a world seething with hatred!

Excellency! Haste is essential! You can still snatch us away from the abyss whose jaws are about to swallow us!

May you soon help us to outlast this time of world conflagration, so that we, as God's faithful servants and executors of his will on earth, may be allowed to greet the approaching dawn of a refined humanity in community with all the faithful!-

K. Chameides

Translation of letter that my father sent to Metropolitan Sheptytskyi in October 1942.

The letter is beautifully handwritten in an elegant German. Each word was obviously very carefully chosen for maximum meaning and emotion for its recipient as well as to emphasize the common bond of faith, humanity, and brotherhood of the writer and recipient despite their different theological world views. The letter must therefore be read very carefully with great attention to detail.

The letter opens with a quote from Habakkuk 2:4 "and the righteous lives by his faith." This could be viewed as a challenge to the faith of the recipient. In other words, a truly righteous person is challenged to put his expressions of faith into action. However, considering the care with which my father selected every word, it is important to examine the context (in the book of Habbakuk) in which the sentence appears. It will then be understood that this is both an expression of the writer's despair as well as his faith in the eventual victory of good over evil. Habakkuk prophesied about Nebuchadnezzar's invasion of Judea, the resulting suffering of the Jews, and the eventual downfall of the aggressor at the hands of Persia and Medea. The prophet complains to God about the apparent lack of justice; that the wicked seem to prosper while the righteous suffer. He is advised to wait with patience for the eventual victory of good over evil. Habakkuk's description of the despair of his day, so similar to that of the German occupation, must have given my father a measure of comfort and

allowed him to use this phrase as an expression of spiritual defiance. The Jews must have patience, for in the end they will survive as a people even though many individuals will not.

That this quote from Habbakuk was a summary of my father's faith can also be surmised from a discussion in the Talmud and an essay he had written: "Habakuk came and grounded them [the Torah and the commandments] upon one [principle], 'and the *tzaddik* (righteous person) lives by his faith.'"[139] Approximately 10 years earlier, in 1932, my father wrote an article in which he enumerated attempts by the Rabbis to summarize the entire Jewish religion in as succinct a manner as possible: "Finally, Habbakuk condensed them into one rule 'the righteous shall live by his faith (in God)'. Thus it is established that faith in God and trust in Him is the last link in the chain of regulations and maxims with which our sages strove to express the essence of our religion. One word: 'Emunah', which in Hebrew means faith, trust, loyalty, and constancy, reveals itself in the final analysis, as the most appropriate and exact description of the Jewish entity."[140] My father's expression of faith in God is undoubtedly an expression of his feeling, but it is also a means of establishing a common link with a prince of the church.

Apparently out of fear that the letter might get into the wrong hands, only the author's name is mentioned. Metro-

---

[139] Babylonian Talmud 24A.
[140] Kalman Chameides, "Jewish Ethics" in *UGGIK* #5 March 1932 5.

politan Sheptytskyi's name does not appear in the letter and the author deliberately misspells Rabbi Kahane's name as Kohane, and leaves a blank for the intermediary priest's name.

The first paragraph is an expression of gratitude to the Metropolitan, undoubtedly for hiding Herbert and me, for his warmth and understanding, and apparently also for sheltering him and his friend for a few days. I don't know when these few days took place. My father did not stay when he took me so it must have been afterwards. The "älterer Freund" (older friend) must refer to Rabbi Dawid Kahane since the two went to see the Metropolitan together, although Rabbi Kahane was a year younger (b 1903) than my father. Perhaps their relative ages were a topic of discussion with the Metropolitan or it may simply mean a longstanding friend. The temporary feeling of peace that he describes finding in the Metropolitan's presence is reminiscent of Rabbi Kahane's description of one of his visits. "The walls of the Jura Mountain palace left an odd impression on me. It seemed as if I had been suddenly lifted from a raging sea whose mighty gales threatened to overwhelm everything in their range, onto a quiet and peaceful island where every tree, every blade of grass, every flower seemed to ask in astonishment: 'Is it really true that a terrible storm rages out on the sea?' The stillness prevailing among these walls was so soft we could hear

clearly the beating of our hearts. After a wild, nervous tumult of the ghetto, I really thought we were walking on a different planet."[141]

In the second paragraph my father laments that he and his friend left the protection of the Metropolitan too soon because the persecution of Jews continued and his "fellow sufferer" was no longer with him. I don't know who this "fellow sufferer" is since my mother was still alive at the time. The time frame must have been the terrible *aktionen* of August and September. It is possible that he lost contact with Rabbi Kahane and thought that he had become a victim.

The third paragraph suggests that Rabbi Kahane and my father had decided to seek refuge with the Metropolitan. This is confirmed by Rabbi Kahane[142] and I don't know why my father never took advantage of that. He seems to feel a need to justify his decision, which, he states, is based not only on an instinct for self-preservation, but also on the contributions that they could eventually make towards creating a world of peace and harmony.

The fourth paragraph is indented and therefore stands out from the rest. My brother, Zwi (Herbert), and I think that the indentation serves the same function as the Hebrew word להבדיל which is used to contrast anything Jewish with something not Jewish, a stylistic defiance. This paragraph is clearly written with the Metropolitan's faith in mind. My father tries to make the Archbishop understand

141 David Kahane, *Lvov Ghetto Diary* 58.
142 David Kahane, *Lvov Ghetto Diary* 57.

the full force of Jewish suffering and therefore uses a symbol with which a Prince of the Church can have empathy – the suffering and death of Jesus. But my father, like Mark Chagall and Arthur Szyk in art, reclaims Jesus as a Jew and depicts him as only one in a long line of persecuted Jews throughout the ages. By painting an image of a despised and persecuted Jesus as just one in a long line of suffering Jews, he reminds the Archbishop that were Jesus alive today and under German occupation, he would be suffering together with his fellow coreligionists. He reminds him that true Christianity is a religion of compassion and love as preached by Jesus, which must be extended to his suffering people.[143] This serves as an introduction to the next paragraph.

The final two paragraphs are a plea for help and an expression of hope in a hopeless world; a conviction that those who have suffered so much, have derived a unique insight and perspective from that suffering, for perfecting the world.

In November 1942, Metropolitan Sheptytskyi published a pastoral letter, "Thou Shalt Not Kill" in the *Lwiwski Arkhieparkhialni Widomosti,* the organ of the Galician Uniate Church, in which he stressed the importance of this commandment and threatened all those who disregarded it with excommunica-tion.[144] The pastoral letter was written "in order to fulfill our duty to the Almighty as shepherds of souls and preachers of the Gospel, to warn our faithful, with heaven and earth as our witnesses, against the evil deeds which have recently spread among us so frightfully, and call for penitence on the part of persons who committed the sin of murder."[145] It is not known whether the timing or publication of this pastoral letter was influenced in any way by my father's letter, nor is it clear whether he is referring to the murder of Jews, of Ukrainian political rivals, or both.

Throughout his letter, my father chose his words carefully to evoke a clear emotional response in a prince of the Church. For example, in the fourth paragraph the word "Leidensgeschichte" (tale of woe) is used in Christian theological terminology for Christ's Passion. In the third paragraph the word "Dome" (dome) can also refer to a Cathedral. In the fourth paragraph the phrase "Dornenkrone auf unserem gebeugten Haupte" (a crown of thorns on our bent heads) would evoke a sympathetic understanding in a Christian theologian. In the fourth paragraph he quotes the Aramaic "eli, eli, lama schebaktani" (My God, Lord why have you forsaken me), which, according to the Gospels of Mark[146] and Matthew[147]

---

[143] Equating the suffering of Jesus with the suffering of the Jews is within the context of Christianity. Jesus is quoted as saying: "whatever you have done to the least of these… you have done to me" (Matthew 25:40).

[144] Phillip Friedman, *Ukrainian-Jewish Relations* 291.

[145] David Kahane, *Lvov Ghetto Diary* 159.

[146] The Gospel According to St. Mark 15:34.

[147] The Gospel According to St. Matthew 47:46.

Copy of page from death list in Lviv archive. Note #5981. My father is listed as Dr. Kalman Chamajdes –Luft (using his mother's maiden name for identification). The dates of death and burial are 25/XII (December 25).

were Jesus' last words, rather than the Hebrew version from Psalms 22:2 ("Eli, eli lama azavtani").

On November 18, a new registration of Jews took place in the ghetto and those working in military factories received the letter W (Wermacht) and those working in defense industry received the letter R (Ruestungsindustrie).[148] My father apparently acquired a work certificate from the Rohstoff Company.[149] My father died of typhus on December 25 (18 of Teveth). My mother, I was told, carried his body on her back to the cemetery to assure a proper burial. She placed bottles containing his name at his head and feet,

so his body could be identified.

I don't know exactly when or where my mother died. She was still alive in April 1943, when she gave Rabbi Kahane her last note to us. The Germans liquidated the Lwów ghetto in April by rounding up all Jews still alive. Those deemed fit for work were taken to the Janowska Camp and marched each day to work until they either starved to death or were killed. Those not deemed fit for work, including all children and most women, were shot immediately. The Germans then went through the ghetto and used flame throwers to flush out anyone still hiding within. I don't know

[148] Filip Friedman, *Zagłada żydów Lwowskich* 21.
[149] David Kahane, *Lvov Ghetto Diary* 84.

how my mother died. I don't know if it was by gas in an extermination camp or by a bullet at the edge of a pit or in the streets of the ghetto. I am sure, however, that her last words were the *shema* prayer and her last thoughts were about her two children in a Christian monastery.

At the time of their deaths, my father was 40 and my mother was 38 years old. I don't know whether there is an afterlife or a heavenly tribunal but if there is, God had some explaining to do.

When we met with him on October 30, 1944, Rabbi Kahane handed us two notes written by my mother in pencil on a scrap of paper. The following is a translation from German: "My husband died on the 18th of Teveth or December 25, at 11 in the evening of typhus. My in-laws died on the 4th day of Chanukah. Kalman was buried near Rabbi Laib Braude and Dajan Ehrenpreiss. At his head and feet is buried a bottle containing the name Kalman Ch." Rabbi Kahane added in Polish: "Mrs. Trude Chameides wrote this testament in her own hand in my presence. She gave this to me in April 1943. Signed by Kahane, David in Lwów on October 30, 1944."

On a separate piece of paper my mother wrote: "My parents are named Isaac Königshöfer and live in London. The address can be obtained from Rabbi Dr. Hertz. Also that of my brother, Jonas Königshöfer in London. My sister, Betty Glück lives at 41/III Nagymero street in Budapest. I have left the following assets: With Siegfried Freudenthal in Jerusalem at 8 or 20 Keren Kayemeth Street – 220 pounds

With Isaac Königshöfer, London – 200 pounds

With L. Bornstein, London 34 or 42 Exeter Road NW 2 – 186 pounds, a diamond ring of ¾ carats and sapphire stones, as well as a gold man's watch[150]

With Adolph Felsenstein in London, the address can be obtained from the Königshöfers or Rabbi Dr. Hertz – 354 pounds."

In October 2007 Jean, David, and I visited as many of the sites as possible in Lviv. As I mentioned previously, the street on which my father and the Karls lived, Żeromskiego, no longer exists. We did walk along the streets of the former ghetto although there are no signs indicating its borders. The old cemetery of Lviv, with matzevot (tombstones) dating back to the 14th century, no longer exists. The Russians dismantled it, used the mazevot as building materials, and covered it with cement to serve as an outdoor market. We saw it surrounded by its ancient wall but did not choose to enter it. We were told that a huge statue of Lenin was erected in the center of town near the Opera House and when it was dismantled, it was discovered that its foundation consisted of mazevot from the old cemetery.

We went to the Lviv Archives and verified that my father was buried in the

---

[150] When they were approached about these items after the war, the Bornsteins claimed that they lost them (I suspect they didn't think anyone would survive), but that they would replace them. The replacements were given to Herbert.

Last testament written by my mother, Gertrude Chameides, in pencil on a scrap of paper and handed to Rabbi David Kahane in April 1943 (see text for translation).

Janowska cemetery. Unfortunately, because of lack of space, people were subsequently buried on top of the old graves; all the mazevot there date from after the war. It was therefore impossible to identify the exact spot where my mother buried my father.

We visited the site of the notorious Janowska concentration camp. The Germans had demolished it and all that remains is an empty field. A small plaque at the entrance notifies the visitor about its previous function. Garbage lay strewn here and there. In the distance we could see a group of loud men sitting and drinking and, to our left, we saw a woman who had appropriated a small plot of land on which to grow vegetables. I am sure that the earth was very fertile.

Jerusalem 20. September 1945
Liebe Lotte,
Ich hatte in der hiesigen Zeitung gelesen,dass für Isaac Koenigshoefer bei der hiesigen Aguda eine Nachricht liegt. Ich bin darauf heute dort gewesen und fand folgende
Nachricht vor: "In Jerusalem wohnt eine Familie Isaac K. aus Fuerth 1/B. Wollen Sie
ihr bitte folgende Mitteilung zukommen lassen. Ihr Schwiegersohn Rabbiner Chameides
aus Katowice ist im Jahre 1943 im Lemberger Ghetto an Typhus gestorben. Seine Frau
(die Tochter von Fam. K.) und die beiden Jungens blieben zurück . Beide Jungens wur
den dann später in einem ukrainischen Kloster in Brzuchowice bei Lemberg untergebracht
Unser Gewährsmann berichtet uns,dass er Frau Rabbiner Chameides später noch öfter gesprochen hat,bis dann jeder Kontakt abgerissen wurde. Er ist aber sicher,dass sie zu-
letzt nicht mehr in Lemberg war. (Sie hatte die Absicht nach Budapest zu gehen) er
fürchtet aber ,dass sie nicht mehr lebt. Es ist Pflicht,die Familie K. hiervon zu ver
ständigen ,damit sie sich um die Enkelkinder kümmert. Wollen Sie auch bitte die per-
sönlichen Grüsse des Unterzeichneten bestellen.
Die Mitteilung kam von der"Hyefs " (Schweizer Hilfsverein für jüdische Flüchtlinge
im Auslande) unterzeichnet war der Brief von einem Dr. Landau, Montreux.
Wegen der Jungens habe ich mit l. Leo eingehend gesprochen. Leider ist augenblicklich keine Möglichkeit,die Jungens aus Polen herauszubringen,da keine Certifikate da
sind. Aber er behält die Sache sehr im Auge und wird bemüht bleiben,sobald sich eine
Möglichkeit bietet. Es ist schrecklich,was die Juden durchgemacht haben und noch durch
machen müssen nachdem der Krieg schon zu Ende ist. Und nachdem sie das Volk sind,das
die grössten Opfer an Gut und Blut gebracht. Man macht einigen Dutzend Vrbrechern
heute unter grosser Aufmachung den Prozess weil,sie Juden in unmenschlicher Weise
zu Tode gepeinigt haben und hinschlachteten und an dem Reste dieser Unglücklichen,
die bis jetzt dem Tode getrotzt,aber hinsiechen,versündigt sich die Menschheit und
damit auch diejenigen,die sich jetzt zum Richter aufwerfen wollen. Es ist ein be-
schämender Beweis für den niederen Kulturstand der Menschheit. Ich habe Deine beiden
Airletters nicht zur Hand,ich habe sie Leo gegeben und der ist über Jomtow nach einem
Kibuz verreist und so kann es sein,dass ich etwas zu beantworten vergesse.
Ich hoffe,es geht Euch gesundheitlich ordentlich,auch bei uns ist G.s.D. soweit alles
in Ordnung. Jomkippur haben wir gut verbracht. Diese Tage waren besonders schwer,mei-
ne Schwägerin Else Kahn in Haifa wollte dass wir über diese Zeit nach Haifa kommen
sollten,wir wollten aber nicht. Wir brauchen Ruhe, das tut uns am besten.
Hoffentlich bringt das jetzt begonnene Jahr für das gesamte Judentum die einzige
Lösung,die es zu beanspruchen das Recht hat,und die so schwer von den Völkern zu
erringen ist,den materielle Interessen höher stehen. Hoffentlich wird diese Frage
mit G'ttes Hilfe recht bald in unserem Sinne ihre Lösung finden. Von Jony hatten wir

*Part of a letter sent by Meir Koenigshoefer from Jerusalem to Lotte Bernet in England with the first information
about our survival:*

"*September 20, 1945. Dear Lotte, I read an announcement in the local paper that there was a message in the Jerusalem
Agudah office for Isaac Koenigshoefer. I therefore went there today and found the following message: "In Jerusalem
there lives a family by the name of Isaac K. originally from Fuerth, Bavaria. Please inform them of the following: Your
son-in-law, Rabbi Kalman Chameides from Katowice, died of typhus in the Lwów ghetto in 1943. He was survived
by his wife (the daughter of family K.) and two children. Both children were subsequently sheltered in a Ukrainian
monastery in Brzuchowice near Lwów. Our informant tells us that he spoke with Mrs. Chameides often afterwards
until all contact with her was broken. He is however sure that she is no longer in Lwow. (She intended to go to Budapest)
but he is afraid that she is no longer alive. It is important to notify the family K. of this so that they can concern themselves with the grandchildren. Please also transmit personal greetings from the undersigned." The information came
from "Hyefs", the Swiss Aid Organization for Jewish Refugees and was signed by a Dr. Landau from Montreux.*

*I spoke extensively with Leo [his son-in-law] in regard to the children. Unfortunately, at the present time, it is
impossible to bring the children out of Poland since it is impossible to get certificates here. But I will keep the matter in
mind and will be ready to act when an opportunity presents itself. It is terrible what the Jews have suffered and continue
to suffer even after the end of the war. After being the nation that made the greatest sacrifice in life and property. Nowadays
they have huge show trials for a few dozen criminals who tortured Jews to death in an inhuman fashion while humanity,
and all those who believe in the rule of law, sin against the remnant of those unfortunates who have defied death but are
downtrodden. It is shameful evidence of the low cultural level to which humanity has sunk…*"

The Bełżec extermination camp in 2007. A central area of volcanic ash is surrounded by plaques with names of communities from which Jews were brought for final disposal. Some plaques include the date of the transport.

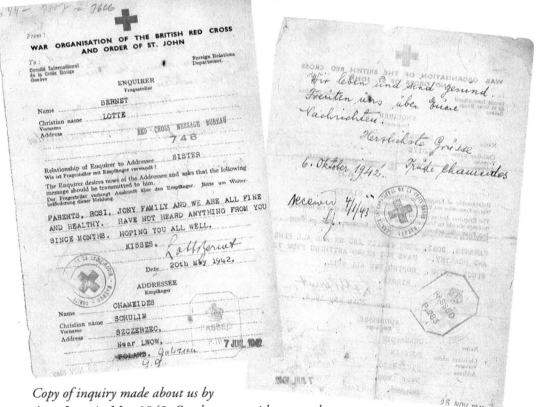

Copy of inquiry made about us by
Aunt Lotte in May 1942. On the reverse side my mother wrote:
"We are alive and healthy. We are very happy to hear news from you.
Heartfelt regards, Trude Chameides."

IX

A NEW HOME

———— • ◆ • ————

While Rabbi Kahane tried to find a home for me, I stayed temporarily with the Frost family on Małeckiego 5. Józef and Wilma Frost had survived the war together with their son, Adam (Adek), and had provided a home for Herbert. Mr. Frost was a lawyer, but also learned how to bake from his father. That skill was responsible for saving the family's lives. They had a small dog, a cocker spaniel, with whom I enjoyed playing. Herbert and I considered Adek to be a spoiled brat, perhaps because he spent the war years with his parents, and never had to fend for himself. To us he seemed childish, interested in playing pranks, but, in retrospect, perhaps it was we who were abnormal, having been robbed of a childhood and children's interests. Herbert did not like living with the Frosts; in fact, he resented them.

Our war experiences, the loss of our parents, and the separation from our family had a profoundly different effect on Herbert and me. This was undoubtedly partly due to the two-and-a-half year age difference between us, but I think that it was also due to our very different personalities. I have always tended to be upbeat, to accept situations and move on, and to be optimistic in life. Herbert has always been brooding, analytical, and somewhat more pessimistic. One of his tragedies is an excellent memory; he can recall detailed conversations from his early childhood. I, on the other hand, tend to forget unpleasant experiences.

A few days after I arrived at the Frosts', Mrs. Frost told me that a friend of hers, a Mrs. Tola Wasserman, would be coming to meet me, and, if everything

Tola Ashkenazy and Albert Wasserman at their wedding in 1937.

Tola Ashkenazy (left front) with her mother and one of her brothers about 1919.

Shimon Ashkenazy, Tola's father.

worked out, I might go home with her.

Tola Ashkenazy Wasserman was born in Lwòw on April 29, 1909 but always celebrated her birthday on May 3, Polish Independence Day. She was a "change of life baby" so her siblings were considerably older, as were her parents, especially her father, Shimon, for whom this was a second marriage. Her family's poverty and her father's death when she was only six years old, forced her to end her formal schooling at the age of 13. She married Albert Ignacy Wasserman on August 8, 1937. He was a boxer who came from a completely assimilated Jewish family. Before agreeing to marry him, Tola made him promise that he would confine himself to being a referee. As an officer in the Polish Army reserves, he was called up in 1939 when Germany attacked Poland,

and was never heard from again.

Tola's mother died when she was over 90 years of age on *erev* (eve of) Yom Kippur (September 22) 1939, the day the Russians entered eastern Poland. Mother Tola always told me how grateful she was that her mother had died peacefully before the German invasion. In the fall of 1941, Tola was forced to leave her beautiful apartment at Asnyka 7 to her maid, Kazia, and move to the ghetto, into an apartment with 6-8 others without water, heat, or indoor toilet. Every day, as part of a work brigade, she would leave the ghetto and go to work in a factory sewing German uniforms. The man in charge of the factory was a middle aged German who took a liking to her and, one day, warned her not to go back to the ghetto. She hid in the factory overnight, and was

Tola Wasserman in 1939 (left) and in 1945.

spared a major *aktion*. In April 1943, the Germans liquidated the ghetto by rounding up the remaining Jews and setting the ghetto on fire. Fortunately, having been warned of that possibility by her German supervisor, she hid in the factory basement. Having nowhere to go and unable to return to the destroyed ghetto, she went to her former home and pleaded with her maid, Kazia, to hide her, her sister-in law, and her infant niece. Kazia agreed, and for the next 15 months they stayed in a backroom, which was somewhat separated from the rest of the apartment. Every day, Kazia brought them food and took out their waste discreetly, so that her neighbors would not become suspicious. During the German retreat, a bomb destroyed their hiding place, but, miraculously, they were spared, and all three survived. Tola's entire family including her four brothers, a sister, and nephews were killed. The only survivor was a half sister, Rose Pasternak, who had emigrated to Brooklyn many years before the war. Tola later wrote, "I was undernourished and weighed only 84 lbs. I was sick, had boils and a rash all over my body

and was not able to walk straight since my right leg was sore and swollen for about a year. But I thanked God that I was alive. The worst time in my life, I think was the day I came out on the street. For the first time in almost 15 months I was again able to breathe the fresh air, to see the sky and the sun, some green leaves and children in the streets, a sight I missed so much. I also, however, felt very sad and could not believe I had nobody — no family, no friends, and I wondered of what use so much suffering was. I had nothing left to wear except one skirt, one blouse, and two changes of underwear, which I shared with some of the survivors who didn't even have that much."

I shall never forget November 6, 1944, the first time I met her. She was about 5'4" tall, with a lovely figure, jet black hair, and a pretty face with a mole on her right cheek. She was soft spoken and had kind eyes. At the end of the visit, she put her arm around me and asked if I would like to come home with her and I answered, yes. We came to her apartment at Asnyka 7, she drew a hot bath for me and scrubbed my neck and ears - my first bath in over two years - gave me a pair of pajamas, and fed me supper. I will always remember that supper — I can taste it even now. It was served on a real china plate with a shiny metal knife and fork. The mashed potatoes were pure white, the eggs were fried, and the wild mushrooms were the most delicious I had ever tasted. After dinner, she handed me a toothbrush and tooth paste and asked me to brush my teeth, something I had not done since

I left home over two years before, and then led me to a bed with a white sheet. I lay down on a soft mattress, put my head on a feather pillow, and covered myself with a yellow eiderdown. She leaned over, called me her "shaifele" (little lamb), hugged me and kissed me. It had been over two years – a long time in the life of a 9-year old – since someone had hugged or kissed me, or said a kind word to me. I had almost forgotten how warm and soft a woman's face was. I went to sleep thinking that this was either a dream or I had died and gone to heaven.

When we first met we discussed what I should call her and we decided on "ciocia," aunt. Some time later, I asked her if "ciocia" minded (in Polish the third person is used when a child addresses an adult) if I called her "mamusia" (mommy). Her eyes filled with tears that overflowed onto her cheeks. I was concerned that I had said something inappropriate and hurt her, but she reassured me with hugs and kisses.

Here is how she remembered our first meeting:[151]

"I heard about many children whose parents had been killed but who had survived and were now in orphanages, and some with good people. And then I started to think about taking under my care one of these unhappy children and give them what they most needed – loving care. My friends thought I should not do that, being alone and not having anything except my salary

as a saleslady, not even a room of my own. But despite their attempts at persuading me, I felt very much a need to have someone to live and care for.

"I was introduced to the rabbi, Rabbi Dr. Dawid Kahane, who was one of the survivors and who was trying to place many of the orphaned children in homes. He did not manage to place too many of them, because most of the survivors were single men and women who also lost everybody. The Rabbi knew my family and he tried to explain to me all the great responsibilities I would be taking over, but I was determined to take a child. I wanted a child of such an age that I would be able to continue working and provide for the two of us.

"October 6,[152] 1944, a few weeks after I was again free, was my luckiest day. On that day I got a son. I was called by the Rabbi, Dr. Kahane to come to my friend's, Dr.Frost, house and see there the child whom he brought for me from an orphanage. I went there straight from work. Coming into my friend's house, I had to pass a kitchen and a small room. In that room was my son, standing near my friend's son. I just passed by with my heart beating and tears coming to my eyes and hoping that I will make him a good mother. My dear son was at that time nine years old, a tall but very thin, quiet and frightened child. I went into another room where the

[151] Tola Stark, Unpublished letter June 16, 1954 written at the suggestion of a lawyer whom she consulted when authorities at Yeshiva University questioned whether I should remain with her (see below).
[152] I remember it as November 6.

Rabbi was already waiting for me. I was left alone with the Rabbi. He asked me maybe I would prefer a little girl. My answer was that even if I would, I want the child who is waiting in the next room. I felt that it is not an object to be put up for sale and that I would never let the child think that he is not wanted. He was already very unhappy. After that I was told by the Rabbi all about him. The Rabbi told me that his name was Leon and that he was the son of a famous Rabbi in Poland, and that he survived with his brother, three years older than he, who will stay with my friends, so that they will see a lot of each other. Then the Rabbi suggested that I may take the child from my friends' home after work in the evening, and I answered that I will be happy to do so. I came back that evening, and took my son home, after having spent a few hours with him in my friends' home so that we got to know each other a little bit. As I wrote above I was still living with my former maid. The room in which we were living now was a very large one. We had one bed and one sofa. My good former maid agreed to sleep with me on the sofa so that my son could have a bed of his own. That first night my dear son and I will remember all our lives. First of all, I washed and scrubbed him, washed his hair, applied ointment to the chilblains on his hands and his sore feet, and took care of his skin rash. Then I made supper for him, some fried mushrooms and

bread and butter and milk. At that time it was a real luxury. Every day we got closer and closer to each other, he still called me Auntie."

I started attending a Russian school and, despite a new language, I made excellent progress. In addition to reading, writing, and arithmetic, we spent a good portion of the school day learning Communist propaganda especially about Lenin and "Batko" (Father) Stalin. Lenin and Stalin were depicted almost as gods and the stories about them were similar to some Hasidic tales: Lenin, dressing up as a peasant and going to the woods to chop wood for some unfortunate poverty-stricken widow. These stories, intended to inspire us with a love for the Soviet system, were reinforced in the communist youth group, meetings of the Young Pioneers, that I had to attend several evenings a week. I was very proud of the red kerchief and insignia with a hammer and sickle that I wore to these meetings.

I was also very pleased that, with Mother Tola's careful attention, my hair started to grow back. I tended it like one would a beloved garden. I raked it with a comb several times a day, watered it carefully in the morning and then tried to train it to fall back by tying a cloth around my head. Mother Tola was a strict disciplinarian and began teaching me good manners. Her ideal in men's fashions and behavior was the Duke of Windsor, the darling of women in the 1930s because he gave up the throne of England for "the woman I love." This

Front (right) and back (above) of report card issued on June 19, 1945 from the #16 Stalin District Middle School in Lviv. The back shows my name as Leon Kalmanovitch [patronymic] Chameides. The front shows four marking periods (I started in the second) and the final mark. Grades are 1 to 5 with 5 being the highest. Subjects in which I received a mark are (from the top): Ukrainian Language (oral, written, and overall); Russian Language (oral, written, and overall); Polish Language (I started out weak and rapidly improved); Arithmetic; Civics; Geography; Art; Music and Voice; Physical Education; Behavior; Absences (note that I missed 28 days during which I was riding the trams). At the bottom is a note that I passed to the fourth grade.

was, of course, before it was generally known that his character was somewhat flawed, and that he was a Nazi sympathizer. Mother Tola never tired of telling me to emulate royalty, to walk and speak like a prince. Through rigorous practice, I learned how to greet a lady: bowing, clicking my heels, and kissing her hand when it was offered to me. I learned how put on a tie properly - a full Windsor knot for formal occasions, and a half Windsor knot for less formal ones. I learned how to set a table, which utensils to use, and how to use each one. These were reinforced when we ate out several times a week. Mother Tola felt that we needed good food to rebuild our bodies. There were no restaurants yet, but people did make "restaurants" in their homes for extra income. During these meals, I would be carefully observed and if I made some error of etiquette, one look from Mother Tola would set me straight. This sounds harsh, but it was done with love and her often repeated conviction that if I knew how to do things properly I would never feel out of place in any society. Time has proven her to have been correct. By the time we finished dinner, it would already be dark, especially during the short days of the fall and winter. Mother Tola was very nearsighted and could not afford glasses so I would hold her arm and say, "nadół" – down and "do góry" – up as we stepped down and up the pavement. When we got back to our apartment I helped her take her boots

At the end of WWII, the Polish borders were moved westward by drawing a line through Brześć (Brest Litovsk) in the east and incorporating part of Germany up to the Neisse river into Poland in the west. As a result, Lwów now became part of the USSR. This border change resulted in a massive westward population shift including about 12 million Germans.

off; in the fall and winter these were Russian high boots that were very stiff and required one person to pull and the wearer to push. Before going to sleep I would polish our shoes until I could almost see my reflection.

I remember those days as extremely happy ones, but I must also have had some inner conflicts because I did act out. Surreptitiously, I would skip school and ride the trams of Lwów. I made friends with the conductors and they would let me ride free and let me watch as they turned the power conducting cable in the opposite direction with a long string at the end of the line. It was not long before someone saw me and snitched on me. Mother Tola confronted me and was furious. My conflicting emotions got the better of me and, for the only time in my life, I considered suicide. In retrospect, I was feeling sorry for myself and the consideration was not a serious one; I certainly did nothing about it and it soon passed. Considering what I had already gone through in the short nine years of my life, it is not surprising that I had some emotional turmoil but, with Mother Tola's help and her unconditional love, I managed to resolve them.

At the 1943 Tehran Conference, the Western Allies agreed to grant the Soviet Union sovereignty over most of the areas of eastern Poland that it had annexed in 1939, including the Lwów district. Churchill and the other western leaders were, however, determined not to repeat the errors of the post World War I agreements, which plagued interwar Poland,

namely national borders with mixed nationalities. As a result, the Polish Committee of National Liberation (Polski
Komitet Wyzwolenia Narodowego), the
precursor of the new (communist) Polish
government, signed Evacuation Treaties
with the Soviet Republics bordering
Poland in Lublin in 1944. One provision
of these treaties was that ethnic Poles and
Jews would be repatriated to Poland from
those parts of former Poland annexed by
the Soviet Union or its republics.

The repatriation started early in 1945
and the Frosts, taking Herbert with
them, were among the first to take advantage of it. Mother Tola's maid, Kazia,
was not very happy with my arrival.
Their relationship became strained since
Kazia was both her maid, and her savior.
When the Frosts left for Poland and their
apartment became available, Mother Tola
gave Kazia her apartment, and we moved
to Małeckiego 5. This apartment, although considerably larger, was not as
nice as the one we had left. We only had
one bed and mother insisted that I sleep
in it, while she slept on the floor. The
government decided that the apartment
was too large for two people, so they bil-
leted several Russian soldiers with us. I
don't remember exactly how many there
were, but I believe there were four including a father and son. My favorite was
Tolek who used to tease and tickle me.
At that time, there was always a sense of
sadness around Russian soldiers, despite
their outward coarseness. They had gone
through so much and had lost so many
friends and family members. Many of the

soldiers sent back from the front had
been wounded, some with amputated
limbs, and ours were no exception. We
had great sympathy for them as fellow
sufferers and we were, of course, grateful
to them as our liberators. We got along
quite well and they had great respect for
Mother Tola.

One day, in autumn, the older soldier
asked me to guard the door of the
kitchen and warn him if any of the
younger soldiers, especially his son, approached. He went into the kitchen, leaving the door slightly ajar. I stood on the
other side as a lookout. After a while I became curious. I peeked into the kitchen
and was astonished at what I saw. His
head and shoulders were completely enveloped in a large white shawl-like cloth
with black stripes and strings on the cor-
ners. He swayed rhythmically and read
from a book in a sing song fashion. That
gently swaying shrouded figure seemed
vaguely and uncomfortably familiar to
me, but I couldn't remember where I had
seen it before. I sensed danger in this
clandestine act, so I quietly closed the
door and continued my guard duty until
he came out.

On May 7, 1945 one of the soldiers
came home with a bottle of vodka and
announced that the Germans had surrendered, and that the war was over; "Batko"
(father) Stalin would be speaking over the
public address system to announce it.
Mother Tola was skeptical and didn't
want to deal with a drunken soldier, so
she took the bottle away from him,
locked it in the closet, and told him that

they would go together to hear the address, and if what he said was true, she would not only return the bottle, but would buy him an additional one. At the appointed time, we joined crowds of people congregating in the park-like setting in front of the opera house. A hush fell over the crowd as "batko" Stalin's voice came over the loudspeakers, and announced VE Day. One cannot imagine the joy in that park. Soldiers started to

Two Soviet officers and I posing in front of the Lviv Opera House (1945).

play accordions, and the crowds broke into song and dance. There was spontaneous laughter over the joy of victory, and tears at its huge cost. And yes, Mother Tola did indeed give the soldiers two bottles of vodka. I was impressed that the soldiers held her in such high regard that, when she confiscated their favorite drink, they did not object.

Mother Tola worked in a store just up the street from the Rynek selling cosmetics and eau de Cologne. After school I would go past the old Town Hall with its tall spire and clock and join her in the store. There were no cash registers and all addition was done on an abacus. I was fascinated how rapidly fingers would fly over the abacus and arrive at a correct sum. Every so often, a soldier would come in, buy a bottle of cheap perfume, break off the glass nozzle and drink it down; anything containing alcohol was fair game. At other times, a civilian or soldier would come back from Germany wanting to sell goods on the black market, and Mother Tola would resell them "under the counter." Big sellers included any alcoholic beverage, costume jewelry, nylon stockings, and above all, for some inexplicable reason, mother of pearl buttons. One day, I was standing behind the counter when an inspector walked in. One of the salespeople in a panic handed me several hundred mother-of-pearl buttons sewed on cardboard. She must have thought that the inspector would not search me, but a telltale bulge under my shirt was too obvious to ignore. Mother Tola and I were invited to the NKVD

(Narodny Kommisariat Vnutrennich Del or People's Commissariat for Internal Affairs[153]) office in the Town Hall. Greatly worried about a charge of black marketeering and smuggling, we walked to the office of one of the inspectors with great trepidation. He had the evidence before him and asked us to sit down. He asked whether we knew that what we had done was illegal, and we acknowledged that indeed we did. He then rose, closed the door, came back, put out his hand and said, "vi chochyte zit, a ya tozhe" (you want to live, so do I). Mother Tola greased his palm, he kept the buttons, and we were led out of his office.

On another occasion, two Russian officers came into the store. They seemed more refined and well educated that most, and Mother Tola later told me that she thought they might have been Jewish. They spoke with great nostalgia about their children whom they had not seen for a long time, and asked Mother Tola's permission to take me out for something to drink. They took me to what had once been one of Lwów's most elegant hotels, Hotel George. We listened to the orchestra play mournful Russian songs and tangos, and each of us had a beer (I believe it was my first). On the way back, we cut through the park (then known as Wały Hetmańskie and now Prospect Svobody) in front of the Opera House, and noticed a street photographer. One of the officers suggested that we have a photo taken, and each of us got to keep a copy. I have always wondered what happened to them

and I suspect they have wondered the same about me.

Our social life revolved around the other few survivors. There were no concentration camps in the Lwów region, only extermination camps such as Belżec and Janowska, from which almost no one returned. And, with the liquidation of the ghetto in 1943, all Jews, with the exception of the few who were hidden by gentiles or survived in the sewers, perished. We would meet someone on the street and the exclamation of surprise was always the same, "You survived! How about so-and-so? Did you see him? When did you see her last?" Everyone was constantly searching for a brother, a sister, a parent, an aunt, an uncle, anyone. Lists of names hung on the walls of the one remaining synagogue, and there were always people anxiously searching, always searching. At gatherings, the topic was always the same. Each survivor in turn told his story of near death experiences and miraculous, seemingly insignificant events that saved him. There were stories of cruelty and, occasionally, of kindness. There was always the story of the mother who awoke from a nightmare of seeing her trapped child, ran to the place in her dreams and indeed found her child. I would listen quietly but never took part; it was not polite for a child to speak in the presence of adults unless spoken to first. Except for brief factual outlines, children were not given the opportunity to tell their stories for, after all, we were just children. I didn't mind; I

---

[153] Secret police, the forerunner of the KGB.

was, after all, used to being in hiding.

One of the people we met at such a gathering was Cesia. Cesia Stern, a kind and pleasant survivor who was saved with her daughter, Lily, by the wife of a Gestapo officer, Frau Irmgard Wieth. Cesia was an excellent seamstress and sewed clothes for the wives of the German officers stationed in the region. When events turned against the Germans, mother and daughter had to leave their hiding place and found shelter at Sw. Jur. After liberation, Cesia made a beautiful dress for Mother Tola from the lining of the blanket I brought from the monastery, and made me a beautiful suit from a German uniform. Interestingly, we had no problem with this, but when we came to England, this so outraged my family that they forced Mother Tola to throw out my suit. Cesia and her daughter eventually emigrated to London, and when Mother Tola became ill in 1963, Cesia came to New York for several weeks to take care of her.

When the first cinema reopened, I very much wanted to go since I had never seen a movie. I approached Mother Tola about this, but she explained that she did not yet feel right about going to something enjoyable. She, like everyone else, was struggling with the issue of how to reenter life after such a catastrophe. We have rules of mourning for one individual, but how does one mourn for an entire family, an entire community, an entire world? She agreed to let me go with Maya, a Russian teenaged relative of one of the soldiers who now also lived

with us. The film was an American movie, "The Great Waltz," which depicted the life and music of Johann Strauss. I was enchanted with the music, the costumes, and the ability to show motion on a screen seemed magical.

Sometime in the spring or early summer of 1945, I developed a fever and respiratory symptoms. Mother Tola became alarmed because, before antibiotics and the availability of modern medical diagnostic and therapeutic techniques, every illness had the potential of being fatal. Memories of widespread, and often fatal, epidemics of typhoid, cholera, and other diseases were still all too recent and vivid. A number of preventive health practices, a mixture of the rational and superstitious whose aim was to ward off illness, were still rigorously enforced. For example, it was said to be bad to drink too much water, especially shortly after eating certain foods, such as cucumbers or fruit. I remember sometimes being so thirsty that, when it rained, I would stick out my tongue to catch a few raindrops. So when I developed the above-mentioned symptoms, Mother Tola asked a doctor to make a house call. He came, examined my tongue carefully, and announced that I had pneumonia and needed cupping, called "bańki" in both Polish and Yiddish. This was an ancient, and probably useless, but harmless remedy. He took out a large number of glass cups, swabbed each in turn with alcohol, lit the alcohol with a flame from a small alcohol lamp, waited until the flame was extinguished, and then applied it quickly to my back. The flame, having used up the oxygen in the cup, created suction, which gently pulled on my skin. He did this until my back was completely covered with these suction cups that were supposed to draw out whatever was causing me to be ill. This was not painful but did cause a peculiar pulling sensation and left a red ring when the cup fell off. When he finished with the back, he proceeded to repeat the procedure on my chest and then announced that I would recover in a few days. He was correct; the cupping clearly worked.

In August 1945, we were notified that our turn had come for repatriation to Poland. Mother Tola decided that before leaving her native city, she should get certain documents from the Soviet authorities. These included a birth certificate and adoption papers for me, and a death certificate for her husband. She explained that the adoption papers were important so that we would not be separated and, whereas, these papers would also change my name legally to Wasserman, she did not expect me to use it, and urged that I continue to use my family name to honor the memory of my parents. In order to fill out the papers, I needed my date of birth. Herbert was quite certain that I was born in 1935, but he couldn't remember the month, so I picked April because I liked the color of the blooming of daffodils after a long winter.

The legalization of my status was also necessary because a few months before, certain rabbinic authorities attempted to remove me from Mother Tola on the

grounds that, as a son of a rabbi, I should be brought up in a religious home. That, of course, was after I had regained my strength, my looks, and my hair; before that, they didn't seem all that interested. This issue would come up again in 1954 when I was a student at Yeshiva College. I was called in to see Mr. Max Baer, the dormitory supervisor, and told that it had come to his attention that my adopted mother was not Jewish and that he would make alternate living arrangements for me. I simply laughed at him and told him that he should have been there to convince the Germans, since they had obviously killed her entire family in error. Mother Tola, however, took this very seriously and contacted a lawyer. I should perhaps express gratitude to Mr. Baer, for otherwise, I would not have Mother's recollections of our first meeting, the writing of which was suggested by her lawyer.

We heard horror stories about the train trip to Poland, especially from a letter sent by the Frosts after their arrival in Kraków. People were generally transported in open cattle cars even in winter, and the train would stop, sometimes for days, in the open fields while the engineers got drunk. We were, fortunately, going during good weather and we had another stroke of good luck. A physician acquaintance was appointed as physician for this transport. He was entitled to travel in a covered cattle car with a large Red Cross, and he invited us to join him. He also bought a large supply of vodka, and the first time the train stopped in the

Russian certificate of birth issued in Lviv on July 21, 1945 giving my birthday as April 15, 1935 and my name as Leon Albertovich Wassermman.

Russian certificate of adoption issued in Lviv on July 21, 1945 changing my name from Leon Kalmanovich Chameides to Leon Albertovich Wasserman.

middle of nowhere, this gentleman stood on top of the car and threw a bottle against a rock, smashing it and spilling its precious contents. He then informed the engineer how many bottles were left, and that he would destroy two bottles each day they stopped; the engineer would receive all the remaining bottles when we arrived at our destination. We completed the trip, which before the war took a few hours, in a few days rather than the few weeks that was now common. My last memory of Lwów is riding in a horse drawn carriage (droszka) to the railway station. Maya was standing on the balcony of our apartment whistling a beautiful sad Russian song that blended perfectly with the clip-clop of the horse's hooves on the cobblestone roadway.

In October 2007 Jean, David, and I visited as many of the places as possible that I remembered from Lviv. Fortunately for us, but not for its current residents, very little has changed in the old part of town. The streets were still paved with the 17th and 18th century cobblestones, the buildings from the 16th century and those built by the Austrians in the 18th and 19th centuries continue to be beautiful but like an old dowager showed their age. I had not been sure whether we had lived at 5 or 15 Małeckiego but the issue was easily settled when I recognized # 5 and there was no #15. I found the courtyard to be considerably smaller than I remember it but the building on the outside is the same. We did not try to see the inside of the apartment. I anxiously looked out the car window for Asnyka 7. I remembered it being set back from the street and suddenly there it was, set back almost in a cul-de-sac. Again, we did not try to see the apartment.

I did not find the location of the store but the old Town Hall, which had served the Poles, Austrians, Poles again, Germans, and Russians when we were there, was now serving the same function for the Ukrainians. The buildings have remained, only the masters have changed. The park-like setting in front of the Opera House continues to serve as a meeting place for all ages. We saw people walking, men arguing politics, people challenging each other at chess, checkers, and dominoes, children chasing each other and driving miniature electric cars. Photographers still stood ready to take your photo, I am sure now with a digital camera. The Opera House is surely one of the most beautiful in the world. We were able to get tickets for a concert and so I saw the inside for the first time. The elegance of the foyer, the painted ceilings, and the gentle curve of the banisters complement the external appearance.

X

REPATRIATION TO POLAND:
ANOTHER CAMOUFLAGE

$$\cdot \blacklozenge \cdot$$

Our Polish destination was Bytom, about 5 km from Katowice, since the Frosts had settled there. Like most of Upper Silesia, Bytom was a coal mining center. It remained part of Germany (then called Beuthen) after WW I, but with the shift of the German-Polish border westward after WW II, it became part of Poland.

I was excited to be reunited with Herbert, although we had spent so little time together that we barely knew each other. The Frosts managed a consignment store, and I used to enjoy going there to play with the telephone and to see all the treasures that people were trying to sell. There was little work and most of the surviving Jews tried to earn a living as small time merchants. Mother Tola and I used to go to the outdoor market and search for items we could buy cheaply and then resell them. We once found a pair of men's shoes for an excellent price, and we were eagerly making a mental note of the profit we could make by reselling them when, on closer examination, we discovered that we had bought two left shoes. The seller of course disappeared immediately. Dejected, we told the story to the Frosts. Herbert was listening and piped in, "give them to me

and I will sell them." And so he did to another unsuspecting buyer.

We found a furnished two room apartment at 4 ul Koszarowa, which we shared with Mother Tola's girlfriend, Wanda, who used to call me "czarny łebek" ("little black head") because of my jet-black hair. The apartment was heated by a coal burning stove and there was only one toilet in the hallway down a flight of stairs, which served the entire building. In winter, I tried to wake up before Mother Tola so I could start a fire in the stove to warm up the freezing apartment. Mother Tola worked in a delicatessen, a side benefit of which was that we enjoyed leftover sausages and hams. The owner rode a motorcycle and loved to give me rides and, much to Mother Tola's horror, I enjoyed many exciting excursions through the narrow winding cobblestone streets of Bytom.

We didn't own a radio but every once in a while Mother Tola would splurge and buy a newspaper, and that is how we learned about the Nuremberg trials. I remember sitting with Mother Tola and Wanda in the kitchen reading the paper and discussing the charges against the accused, and the legal manipulations used to

Registration with the Jewish community in Bytom dated October 17, 1945. We waited for quite a while before registering out of fear of having our name on a Jewish "list" but finally did so in case anyone remained alive and was looking for us.

prove them. I was especially fascinated that all-powerful men like Göring were being charged with crimes. We were, of course, familiar with some of the atrocities first hand, but not their magnitude or extent. We were astounded that a powerful country like the United States would want to go to the expense and time for a trial. The prevailing opinion in our circles was that there was not an iota of doubt that they were guilty, and that they should all be summarily hanged. In retrospect, this would have been exactly the wrong thing to do; it would have brought the civilized world to their level. At the time, we did not recognize that the trial was not about the German leadership, but about the civilized world and its need to restore respect for law, which had been so perverted.

As survivors returned, Polish anti-Semitism showed its ugly face once again, and so when Mother Tola signed me up for school she thought it best that I pose as a Roman Catholic. I was used to posing, so this did not represent a problem for me, and, to make the disguise complete, I was given a new name, Lesław Kuszarecki. I even went to a Roman Catholic Sunday Mass with a friend. As I recall, the priest spoke about how monotheism and the Trinity were not contradictory, and used the example of a shattered mirror in which one may see thousands of reflections of one entity. The issue of my date of birth came up once again when I was ready to register for school. I didn't know my birthday, and I had picked April 15 because of the pretty flowers and this date is reflected on my Lwów documents. Now, Herbert recalled that I was, in fact, born in June so I was registered with June 15 as my birthday. When we went to England, my grandparents, and a copy of my birth certificate, confirmed that my date of birth was in fact June 24.

In the fall of 1945, we were notified by Rabbi David Kahane, who was then the Chief Jewish Chaplain of the Polish army and lived in Warsaw, that an emissary was coming from England with news from my family. We arranged to meet him at the Frosts' since our apartment was small and inadequate. I was very suspicious and fearful that this represented an effort to separate me from Mother Tola, and I was determined that this would not happen. At the appointed time, the door opened, Rabbi Solomon Schoenfeld walked in, and his presence filled the room. Tall and distinguished, he cut an imposing figure and, in the opinion of the women present, was very handsome. He had a short reddish Van Dyke beard, piercing blue eyes, and, most interesting to me, he wore a uniform of a British officer. In fact, I later learned that the uniform was not that of a British officer, but was audaciously his own design. It consisted of an officer's cap with a visor and two silver medallions, a Magen David and the Ten Commandments, a leather sash across his chest, and an UNRRA (United Nations Refugee and Relief Administration) insignia on his arm. It was the Magen David that mesmerized me. To me this

was a mark of shame to be worn by edict on an armband for easy identification by the Germans. I couldn't understand how he could wear it so openly and with apparent pride. My Jewish identity was still in hiding and caused me pain and shame.

Rabbi Solomon Schoenfeld as he appeared in 1945 in a uniform of his own design.

Rabbi Schoenfeld introduced himself, and then told us that my maternal grandparents Königshöfer, Uncle Johni and Aunt Klara, Aunt Lotte, and Aunt Rosie all lived in England, and wanted to bring Herbert and me to live with them. He had already arranged for the necessary papers, and presented us with a letter stating that the "Secretary of State has decided to authorize the grant of visa facilities to enable them to journey to this country." We couldn't read English, of course, and, as Mother Tola was fond of saying in such situations, looking at the letter was like sitting through "tureckiem kazaniem" (a lecture given in Turkish). However, even we understood the names "Herbert and Leon Chameides" and the absence of the name "Tola Wasserman."

"How about Mother?" I asked through an interpreter.

"I don't have a visa for her," he replied.

"Then I am not going," I said.

There was an uncomfortable and stunned silence in the room and Rabbi Schoenfeld left.

Letter from the British Government to Rabbi Schoenfeld dated September 24, 1945 giving him permission to bring Herbert and me (but not Mother Tola) to England.

Telegrams: ALWEP, LONDON.
Telephone: CENtral 5272.

All communications should be addressed to:—
THE UNDER SECRETARY OF STATE.

Home Office,
(Aliens Department),
10, Old Bailey,
London, E.C.4.

24th September, 194[5]

Please quote the reference:—

C 20330

Your reference:—

REC/HP/FD

Sir,

     With reference to your letter of 4th September in respect of Herbert and Leon Chameides, I am directed by the Secretary of State to say that he has decided to authorise the grant of visa facilities to enable them to journey to this country.

     Instructions are being sent to the nearest British Consular representative abroad to whom they should apply.

     I am, Sir,
     Your obedient Servant,

Schonfeld,
Religious Emergency
Council,

er ich weiss dass dieser Weg laenger dauert,
s der,den ich Ihnen zuerst geraten habe,da die
suchen an alle moeglichen Departments gehen.
.Kahane wird Ihnen meines Erachtens gewiss in
eser Richtung helfen koennen. Fuer Herbert und
on haben wir die Erlaubnis rasch erhalten,da
e Kinder inbegriffen sind in einer Kollektiv-
willigung herzukommen,und Sie werden gewiss
rstehen,dass es ein Verbrechen von uns waere
ese Moeglichkeit die Kinder in eine "gesuender
ft" zu bringen verfallen zu lassen. Sollte es
her vielleicht jetzt nicht moeglich sein,dass
e den Transport von Herbert und Leon schon
gleiten koennen,so moechte ich Sie sehr bitten
n Leon Rabbi Schoenfeld mitzugeben und ich geb
nen mein heiliges Versprechen,dass ich von hie
s alles tuen werde bis ich Sie sofort nachkom-
n lassen kann,will Ihnen aber nochmals raten,
ss der beste Weg ist,als Begleiter eines Trans
rtes mitzukommen.
s Sie hier anfangen werden,darueber machen Sie
ch bitte keinerlei Sorgen.Zuerst wollen wir Si
le einmal hierhaben und dazu beisteuern dass
e und die Kinder wie Familie Frost alle die
rchtbaren Zeiten so weit wie menschenmoeglich
rgessen werden. Dass Leon Sie immer als seine
eite Mutter betrachten wird,dafuer koennen Sie
cher sein. Bitte verzeihen Sie das schlechte
utsch,aber ich habe seit Jahren kein Deutsch
hr geschrieben und die Sprache ist uns naturge
less mehr wie verhasst.
h hoffe recht bald von Ihnen zu hoeren und
zwischen bin ich mit besten Gruessen Ihr

Part of letter from Uncle Johni to Mother Tola dated October 10, 1945 advising her to let me go with Rabbi Schoenfeld and giving her his "holy word" that he would do everything possible to enable her to get to England as soon as possible.

Shortly afterwards, we received a letter in German from Uncle Johni. In it he expressed gratitude to Mother Tola for all she had done for me, and said that he stood ready to help her in every possible way. He suggested that she apply to accompany a transport of children to England but that, in the meantime, Herbert and I should come on a children's transport with Rabbi Schoenfeld. "As you know, the British government has been kind enough to allow children to enter but it is more difficult to get adults into the country." He concluded by giving Mother Tola his "holy word" that he would help her in every possible way to be reunited with me. I was furious and confused.

On his second visit, Rabbi Schoenfeld asked to speak to me alone. We went into the bedroom, and through his interpreter he explained that it was very nice of my family to invite me; that this was a unique opportunity to be reunited with my family; that this would have been my parents' wish; and that I should not be so stubborn. I looked him straight in the eye, and told him that they had already taken one mother from me and that I would not allow them to take another one. I would not go without Mother Tola and they would have to carry me out kicking and screaming. When he heard my reply, his face grew pale and, visibly shaken, he turned on his heel and left the room. I found out later that he cabled uncle Johni with my reply, and shortly thereafter we were informed that a visa to travel to England was arranged also for Mother Tola.

At the beginning of December 1945, we packed our meager belongings, and boarded a train for Warsaw. Rabbi Kahane's military driver met us at the station and took us to the rabbi's apartment/office on 16 Aleja Szucha. I looked out the window of the car and could not believe my eyes. Every building had been destroyed. Streets were torn up. People were aimlessly walking in the quiet streets, and the odor of destruction permeated the air. Television images have accustomed us to scenes of bombing and destruction, but what they cannot convey is the distinctive odor. We had seen bombed out buildings before, but never on such a scale. After the Warsaw ghetto uprising, the Germans had completely demolished the ghetto; they destroyed the remainder of the capital after the Polish uprising. The only part of the city left intact was the suburb of Praha, across the Vistula River. Russian troops had occupied Praha and watched as the Polish resistance fought against the far superior German forces without offering assistance. We now know that this was part of Stalin's deliberate plan to "soften" Poland by destroying its fighting core and making it easier to subdue.

We spent the next three weeks at the Kahane apartment waiting for a plane to take us to England. The apartment was a beehive of activity, and many refugees stayed there temporarily. People were desperately searching for family members, for a mother, father, husband, wife, or children or for any scrap of information about them. Sometimes there were joyful

Rabbi Dawid Kahane in Polish officer's uniform as he appeared in 1945.

reunions, but more often tears, as the bitter truth dashed all hope. For the first time, we met concentration camp survivors, and the evenings were filled with harrowing stories of suffering, death, and an occasional escape. I had a very pleasant voice and inevitably at the height of the tension someone would say, "Leszek, sing us a song." Reluctantly, and after much encouragement, I would stand and sing one of the popular Polish songs like "Warszawo ty mojaś warszawo" (Warsaw, you are my Warsaw) or one of the many war songs.

I also saw many weddings at the Kahane's. Some were genuine – two lonely people having already experienced hell hoped for a taste of heaven. Others were

marriages of convenience. I remember for example the sham marriage of Lonka Gruss, one of Mother Tola's acquaintances from Lwów. Her husband, Philip, had been conscripted into the Polish army (Anders' Army)[154] and fought in the battle of Monte Casino after which he was demobilized. Lonka, who was blond and didn't look Jewish, survived on Aryan papers. She wanted to rejoin her husband, but could not get a visa to Italy so she found someone with a visa and, for payment, "married" him so as to be able to be reunited with her husband. Desperate times called for desperate measures. We later met the Grusses in London, and Philip took me to Selfridge's Department Store on Oxford Street and bought me my first fountain pen (a grey Parker). It is difficult to convey to a 21st century reader what a fountain pen represented in those days. This was before the era of ball points and, of course, long before computers. Good penmanship was a much valued skill and in school we had to write with a pen and nib that had to be dipped in ink. A fountain pen, which was not allowed in school, was a symbol of education, erudition, and adulthood.

We were finally notified to come to the airport for our trip to England, but it turned out to be too foggy (this was before radar) for planes to take off. So we came back the following day, and the following, until our departures became a

---

[154] This was a Polish Army in exile under the command of General Władysław Anders and under the control of the British Eighth Army. It fought with distinction, especially in Italy. It was made up of Polish exiles many of whom escaped from Siberia and made their way to England via Asia and the Middle East.

TRANSPORT COMMAND, ROYAL AIR FORCE

AIR PASSAGE AUTHORITY № 176078

BOOKING REFERENCE.....WAR/328....

AUTHORITY has been granted by the Air Priority Authority at the place of issue for the following air passage:—

Rank, Initials, Name.	Service or Department.	Passport or Identity No.	Baggage Allowed.	Flight Nos.
MASTER. L. CHAMAJDES.		1615.	65 lbs.	CBW 52

From	Via	To.
WARSAW.	BERLIN	BLACKBUSHE

When any part of above flight is performed on a Civil Air Line, the cost will be:—

* (A)—chargeable to British Government Funds, viz., to........................Dept. (unless B.O.A.C. waiver applies to that Dept.)

* (B)—not chargeable to British Government Funds, but recoverable from........................

Chief Rabbi's Religious Emergency Committee, Bloomsbury

*Delete which is not applicable.

Signature of Issuing Officer.

F/Lt.
Assistant
Air Attaché

Date Stamp.

(S.8390A) 19,600 Bks. H.w. 8/44

P.T.O.

Royal Air Force authority to travel from Warsaw to Blackbushe Air Force base via Berlin noting that payment for passage is recoverable from the Chief Rabbi's Religious Emergency Council.

standing joke as we repeatedly said good-bye and then hello. But finally we took off on December 28, 1945 in a Royal Air Force troop carrier with canvas seats. The plane stopped overnight at an air force base in Berlin and I had at least two new experiences here, my first taste of corn-flakes (I didn't like them) and double sheets on the bed (I couldn't figure out how to climb into bed). When we arrived at the Blackbushe Air Force base in England the consular official looked at our passport and saw that it was only valid for one exit from Poland, and that our visa was for a one month visit to England. "Wouldn't you like to stay longer?" he asked. When we nodded, he entered

six months. We had already learned that decisions with major consequences, including life and death, were made with a flick of a finger at the whim of an official with a uniform and a stamp.

Jean and I have visited Poland four times, the last time in October 2007. On our first trip, to help dedicate the memorial in Katowice, we took Debbie and her new husband David with us. Danny accompanied us the second time, David, our youngest son, came the third time, and also accompanied us for one day on our way back from Ukraine. Since I had no personal memories of Katowice, nothing evoked a great deal of emotion. We did go to our former apart-

ment on Derykcyjna 10 but did not go inside. We visited the cemetery, which has remained intact and found the graves of
Leopold and Charlotte Altmann as well as
that of Jette Altmann, Bruno's first wife. We
went to the Municipal Library and I asked
the young lady if she had any historical documents about the pre-war Katowice synagogue. "A synagogue? In Katowice?" she
asked incredulously. "I don't think there
was one here." On our third visit we went
for an afternoon visit to Bytom (the former
Beuthen). The town was most depressing.
Buildings were abandoned

and everywhere one could see caved-in
streets where the coal had been removed. It
will take several generations to make this
beautiful town livable again. Warsaw has
changed most of all. The first time we were
there it was drab but on our last visit we
were impressed with the changes that have
physically transformed it into a lovely western city. More impressive has been that
Poland appears to be coming to grips with
its history and especially its important
Jewish past.

Visa page of Polish passport showing arrival
in Blackbushe and the change from a one- to
a six-month stay.

My Polish
passport photo,
December 1945.

XI

ENGLAND

— ◆ —

NEWCASTLE-ON-TYNE

We arrived in London on the evening of December 29, 1945, the end of a bitterly cold and damp day. We were used to cold weather, but not combined with the dampness of England that made it "bone- chilling." Aunt Lotte met us at the train station, took us to a hotel, and left us with one shilling. The hotel room had no central heating, and when we examined the fireplace, we discovered that there was a gas heating unit with a meter that required one shilling for one hour of heat. We inserted our only shilling and at the end of the hour went to bed. We didn't have enough money for food, and had no idea where to get it or how to ask for it. It was not an auspicious beginning.

The following day, Aunt Lotte took us to the railway station and we started a six-hour journey to Newcastle-on-Tyne, in northern England, on a train pulled by a steam engine. The remnant of the Königshöfer family, who escaped to England prior to WW II, lived in the Newcastle suburb of Jesmond. This remnant included Uncle Johni Kaye (anglicized from Königshöfer for business purposes), his wife Klara, and their children, Ruth and Naomi (David would be born in 1946), at 8 Haldane Terrace; Aunt Lotte Bernet with her two children, Manfred (Michael) and Erna, at 93 Holly Avenue; and my grandparents, Martha and Izaac Königshöfer and Aunt Rosie at 73 Osborne Terrace. It had already been decided that Mother Tola and I would live with the Kayes, and Herbert, with Aunt Lotte. Towards the end of 1946, Aunt Rosie and my grandparents were joined by Aunt Betty (Gluck) and her youngest son, Bernd (Dov), who survived the war in Budapest.

We arrived in Newcastle in time for dinner and all gathered at the Kayes to meet us. Our only common language was German, and I was pleasantly surprised that I understood it despite not having spoken it since the age of seven. Initially, I had trouble speaking, but my fluency gradually returned. The family was surprised at our healthy appearance and civilized behavior. Physically, we had recovered well from the war and were well dressed and well nourished. Throughout dinner, they stared at me and made repeated complimentary remarks at my good table manners. Mother Tola beamed.

The plan that Herbert would live with

October 1968 in Israel. Left-to-right: Lotte, Betty, Gella, and Rosie.

Left-to-right; David, Danny, Aunt Lotte and I in a photo taken in Israel in 1985.

Aunt Lotte with second husband, Max Holtzmann, during their engagement in Paris in 1950.

Aunt Lotte was unfortunate for him. Shortly after coming to England, Aunt Lotte's husband, Julius, Uncle Ulu (1898-1944) suddenly died of a heart attack and Aunt Lotte was left with two children, Manfred (Michael) and Erna. To support her family, she took charge of their factory. The factory, known as Julius Bernet, Ltd., originally manufactured wooden needlework and children's saving's boxes, and was established by Uncle Ulu in Germany in 1920/21. The company exported to many European countries and, as a result, received permission from the British Home Office to establish a branch in England, which allowed the family to come in October 1938. Many years later,

Aunt Lotte expanded the business by adding the manufacture of small souvenir dolls in native costume of many countries. Being stubborn, resourceful, and extremely hard working, she became quite successful materially, but the time and effort it took, in addition to her difficult personality, had a profoundly negative effect on her children, especially Michael. She never came to terms with the loss of her husband. I was sometimes invited to her house for a Shabbat meal. The entire house was dark, gloomy, and still in mourning more than two years after Uncle Ulu's death. There would be a table setting and chair for Uncle Ulu, and a photograph of his tombstone was placed

Uncle Julius "Ulu" Bernet.

on his plate. His clothes were kept in good order and hung neatly in the bedroom closet, and his side of the bed was made up as if he were still alive. Aunt Lotte was extremely religious, but her interpretation of Judaism was literal, fundamentalist, and somewhat naïve. This is best exemplified by a question she posed to me when she was already in her 90s and living in an assisted living facility in Jerusalem: "Tell me, Leon. How do you think I will be reunited with Ulu after I die? Will I fly up to heaven or will he meet me halfway?" Aunt Lotte had a reputation for great thrift, even stinginess, which even extended to food. Herbert was very unhappy in this environment and he was therefore not unhappy when he was sent to a Jewish boarding school, the Hasmonean Grammar School in London, which Michael also attended.

Uncle Johni and Aunt Klara about 1946.

Uncle Johni with his conducting baton.

Mother Tola and I lived with the Kaye family for the next two years. These were not happy years for me but, in retrospect, were very important for my social, religious, and educational development. As I describe our predicament, I want to emphasize my gratitude to Uncle Johni and Aunt Klara. They opened and shared their home with us at a most difficult time for all of us. But, I would be less than honest if I didn't describe the situation as I remember it.

My unhappiness stemmed primarily from the way Mother Tola was treated. She essentially became the Kaye's unpaid maid who did most of the cooking and some of the cleaning. I especially remember my Bar Mitzvah in 1948 with a great deal of bitterness. The Kayes had invited some of their friends for a small celebration in their living room. Mother Tola had no money and felt terrible that she couldn't buy me a gift. Throughout the evening she served the guests when she should have been the center of attention. Even though I tried to make her happy during those years by tokens of affection and small gifts, I was too young to fully appreciate her situation. Mother Tola was then in her thirties, widowed, alone, trapped in a foreign land without money or friends and without prospects for the future. Only Frances and my grandmother showed any measure of understanding for her predicament. Frances was the Kaye's live-in nanny who shared the attic of the house with us. She had been an army nurse before being demobilized, and eventually married a wounded Canadian soldier whom she had nursed. She used to commiserate with Mother Tola, acted as her sounding board, and occasionally would invite her to go to the movies. My grandmother was a very warm, affectionate and charitable woman. She always had a kind word, and grew to love Mother Tola. Many years later, when we were in the United States and she was facing death in Israel, my grandmother wrote a beautiful letter to Mother Tola thanking her for what she had done in caring for me, and stated that she considered her as her daughter.

Socially, this was an important time for me because it was the only time since my early childhood, that I was part of a family unit. Years later, when Jean and I were building our family, these two years were the only family experience I could draw on, and Uncle Johni was my only male role model. He introduced me to photography and bought me my first camera, a used Voigländer. He introduced me to classical music, and whenever a classical piece played on the gramophone or radio, he would take his baton (he had at one time considered being a conductor) and "conduct" it. Uncle Johni's gramophone (known in the US as a phonograph) played 78 rpm records. Each side of a record lasted only 3 minutes, and the fidelity by today's standard was quite poor. Nevertheless, we would listen to classical music, chazzanut, opera, etc. Sometime after we arrived, Aunt Klara's parents sent a portable wireless radio, which was quite a hit and fascinated me. I was technically adept and made a crystal radio. By string-

ing a long antenna in the attic, I would try find the most distant radio station I could hear.

The Kaye family lived in a large 3-storey house. Despite outward appearances, there was a great deal of tension in the household. Uncle Johni had established a factory, Eldon, which manufactured nail files, but business was not going well, and his responsibilities grew as he tried to help numerous family members who survived the war. He desperately tried to add new business ventures such as costume jewelry, but nothing seemed to work. Aunt Klara (Ehrlich) came from a well-to-do family and her parents, who now lived in New York, sent frequent food parcels. Ruth was a rather sullen and serious child, but Naomi was a ball of fire. Every meal became a power struggle over Naomi's eating.

My early childhood home was, of course religiously observant, but I was too young to have been directly influenced by it. From the time I left the monastery until we arrived in Newcastle, we had no religious life whatsoever. Religion never played an important role for Mother Tola, and the immediate postwar situation was not conducive to its development. I have often thought that this was fortunate. If I had come from the religious Christian life in the monastery into a strictly Orthodox Jewish life, I would undoubtedly have rebelled against it. I have seen this tragic state of affairs a number of times. The years of "neutrality" gave me breathing space and time to distance myself from my Christian religious life in the monastery. I brought two religious items from the monastery, my prayer book and my rosary. Shortly after I arrived at Mother Tola's house both of these disappeared. Although she denied it, I suspect that she threw them out. I have often wished that I still had them, but maybe it is best that I don't.

For the first time since my early childhood, I was now part of an Orthodox Jewish home. The only exception to this was Uncle Johni's love of twirling the radio dial, which he could not give up even for Shabbat, and this became a constant source of tension between him and Aunt Klara. The family belonged to the Jesmond Hebrew Congregation and uncle Johni, who had a pleasant though not powerful voice, sometimes led the *davening*. He was a good *baal tefilah*. I began going to *shul* every Friday evening

and Shabbat morning, often accompanying my grandfather who was very gruff in his demeanor and rarely spoke with me.

I was enrolled in the Hebrew school at the Jesmond Hebrew Congregation, in which both the educational content and the methodology were most rudimentary. Gradually, I learned how to read Hebrew haltingly and with many errors. On Shabbat, Uncle Johni would invariably ask me to lead the *benching*, (prayer after a meal) and each time I made a reading error, he would throw a glass of water in my face. I think he almost derived a sadistic pleasure from this practice, which I am sure he regarded as educational, while I was humiliated. When it came time for my bar mitzvah, poor Rev. E. Drukker (the Jesmond Congregation "Minister" or Rabbi), a yekke of the old school, gave up trying to teach me the *haftara*. Fortunately, Uncle Johni hired a young man, Walter Gerstle, to teach me. In later years, when I would chant the *haftara* without preparation to much acclaim and when I taught the chanting to

Exterior (above) and interior (right) of Jesmond Hebrew Congregation.

my children and my grandchildren, I would always say a quiet thank you to Walter. I had occasion in the 1990s to do so in person, when I walked into a shop selling religious articles in Haifa, and the proprietor looked up and said, "Shalom, mar Chameides." It was Walter.

We followed every scrap of news from Palestine and that, more than religion, developed within me a feeling of solidarity and love for my people. Since we couldn't buy a *magen David*, we ground down three pence coins ("thrupence"), which were 12 sided, into this symbol of the Jewish people. Those were exciting and anxious times: The King David Hotel explosion; the trial and hanging of Irgun and Hagana soldiers, the vote in the UN to partition Palestine; the electrifying announcement of the creation of the State of Israel by Ben Gurion; the War of Independence; and the Jewish victory against all odds. We collected and treasured New Year cards showing Jews with rifles fighting for their land. It is impossible to describe what these events, coming on the heels of so much loss, sorrow, and humiliation meant for us. It had been drummed into us for so long that we were 'untermenschen', worthless, and those of us who were too young to have a sense of balance and pride, internalized this propaganda. I remember, once during a spelling quiz at school I was given the word "synagogue" to spell. My face became crimson with shame and humiliation as I tried to spell the word. What was taking place in Palestine gave us pride and allowed us to stand up straight with our heads held high.

My cousin, Bernd (Dov), and I were about the same age, faced similar problems as "strangers in a strange land," and became very close friends. We worked on a number of projects, such as developing a lantern slide show, to raise money for "the liberation of Palestine." In those days, the phrase "liberation of Palestine" meant freedom for the Jewish people. It is interesting how words and phrases change their meaning over time. As Lewis Carroll had Humpty Dumpty say: 'When I use a word, it means just what I choose it to mean - neither more nor less.'

And then, one day in the spring of 1948, I was walking with Herbert when he said to me, "I will tell you a secret if you promise not to whisper a word to anyone."
"I promise"
"Guess where I am going tomorrow."
"London?"
"Much further"
"The continent?"
"Much further"
My eyes grew wide, "Asia Minor?" He nodded.
"Palestine?" I whispered, and when he nodded and said, "Shh! Don't tell any one!" I felt great pride and a little jealousy.

One of my first tasks after coming to Newcastle was to learn English since I didn't know a word. I have many painful memories of this process and

A photo Herbert sent me sometime after his arrival in Israel.

Report card from Northumberland County School, December 1946.

two amusing ones. When we were in Berlin, on the way to England, I needed to go to the bathroom. I looked around and saw a door marked "closed," which I assumed to be the right place since it bore an uncanny resemblance to the Polish word "kloset." I was frustrated and confused when I couldn't open the door. The other episode occurred when the young Princess (now Queen) Elizabeth paid a visit to Newcastle in 1946. This generated much excitement and I wanted to see her. As I walked downtown, I passed Fenwick's Department Store and stopped in front of a photographer's studio. In the window, there were photos of

the Princess and a distinguished gentleman in a red robe and a white wig. Curious, I read the inscription and saw that he was referred to as "Lord so-and-so." Now to me, a student at the Jesmond Hebrew Congregation, "Lord" referred to the one above and so I wondered how they ever got a photo of Him.

Shortly after arriving in Newcastle, I was taken to a doctor who determined that I needed exposure to ultra violet light in order to prevent rickets. The English were sensitized to the disease because England had a chronic lack of sunshine as a result of fog and the dreadful pollution brought on by the Industrial Revolution. And so, for the next several months, I was taken to Newcastle University Hospital every Thursday afternoon and, together with a group of English children, would sit for an hour in my underpants and goggles in front of a UV light.

I was enrolled in the Northumberland County School and was most fortunate that Mr. Ian Carr was my home room teacher. Mr. Carr would give the students an assignment, and ask me to sit by his desk. He then drew and wrote down the English word for everything he drew. I would take the drawings home and memorize the new vocabulary. With this help, and my interaction with my classmates, I soon learned to speak English. Since Mother Tola didn't want me to forget Polish, and her English skills were progressing at a much slower pace, she continued speaking to me in Polish. It is thanks to her insistence that I speak Polish with her, that I retained my Polish language skills.

Unfortunately, however, the remainder of my education was suffering. In order to understand why, I must explain the educational system in England in the 1940s. At that time, the class system was still very much alive and the division between social classes was a solid wall reinforced by the educational system. The upper social classes attended private, in England called "public" schools, which led to the university, civil service, and the professions. The lower social classes went to county schools, like Northumberland, where they obtained a rudimentary education that ended at the age of 14 and fed the factories. There was obviously some discomfort about the inequity of this system because, shortly before I arrived in England, a great innovation was introduced into the system. At age 11, children attending the county schools were given a comprehensive exam; those who passed this exam (called the "elevenses"), had their one and only opportunity to cross over into a school that led to a higher education. My eleventh birthday was in 1946 so I took the exam before I even learned English. I sat dumbfounded in front of examination questions, which I could not understand, and of course failed it. The English educational bureaucracy had decided that I should finish school at age 14, and enter the factory work force.

Mother Tola disagreed, and was very concerned about my future. Her dream was that I become a doctor, but Aunt Klara and Uncle Johni told her not to de-

lude herself, that I was no Herbert and didn't have the talent for such lofty goals. Mother Tola remained unconvinced, and agitated sufficiently that, in 1947, the Kayes had me transferred from the Northumberland County School to Skerry's College, a private vocational school, which trained its students to become secretaries, office managers, and bookkeepers. This was only a modest improvement. Mother Tola became quite discouraged, but was trapped because our British visa, which granted us permission to remain in England, had to be renewed every six months, and didn't allow her to work. In desperation, she wrote a letter to Rabbi Solomon Schoenfeld in London describing our predicament. She received a prompt reply that he would accept me at his school, the Hasmonean Grammar School, on a partial scholarship, and that he would obtain a position for her (sub rosa) as a housekeeper, which would enable her to pay the remainder of the tuition fees.

LONDON

In the fall of 1948, Mother Tola and I left Newcastle for London by steam train. I was enrolled at the Hasmonean Grammar School in Hendon with a dormitory on Hampstead Heath (12 East Heath Road), and Mother Tola started working for the Bodner-Schmidt family at 163 Golders Green Road. I spent the entire week at the dormitory, and took a public bus to school. I was often invited to the Bodners for weekends, and it was there that I had my first exposure to television.

The Bodners must have had one of the first sets in England. I was, of course, fascinated by this new contraption, which bore only a vague resemblance to today's sets. One had to view the tiny (probably not more then 8 inch) round screen in a completely dark room, and was rewarded with a snowy black and white picture, frequently interrupted by various lines and noises. We, however, thought it was marvelous, and never tired of the many cowboy movies and slapstick comedy routines broadcast.

Herbert had attended the Hasmonean Grammar School for two years, and had left for Israel just before I enrolled. He left a sterling reputation especially in the classics, (Greek and Latin) and even before I arrived, news spread that "little Chameides" was to be a student; expectations were very high. The school had two tracts, "Scientific" and "Classical," and I was automatically enrolled in the "Classical" tract based on Herbert's reputation. I began to study very hard in order to uphold the family reputation, and, much to my surprise, I succeeded. I had been an excellent student in the monastery, in Lwów, and in Bytom, but my experience in Newcastle made me lose self-confidence, and question my ability. The year at the Hasmonean helped rebuild it. My experience is consistent with the many studies in education that show that a student's performance is partly related to a teacher's expectations.

The Hasmonean Grammar School was part of the Jewish Secondary Schools of London founded by Rabbi Solomon Schoenfeld (1912-1984), whom we met in Bytom. At the time, it had two branches, the main branch in Hendon and an elementary school, Avigdor, named after Rabbi Schoenfeld's father. The Hasmonean Grammar School was quite small, and was administered with an iron fist by its principal, Mr. W. W. Stanton. The faculty was generally quite good, and consisted of both English and postwar refugee teachers from the continent. The student body was also a mix of natives and war refugees, but the Hampstead Heath dormitory was primarily for refugee children. The Jewish curriculum consisted of Hebrew language, Jewish history, Mishna, and Chumash while the general studies curriculum consisted of English grammar and literature, Latin, French, science, history, and math. The year at the Hasmonean was my introductory year to Jewish studies and during that year, which coincided with Israel's first, I resolved to switch to the Sepharadi Hebrew pronunciation. In Newcastle I had been taught the German (Yekke) pronunciation, but I felt that after the creation of Israel we should all adopt the Sepharadi pronunciation. It was also at the Hasmonean that I first became aware of the opposite sex, and developed my first crush. Hania, the object of my distant affection, was a survivor from Poland who, unable to adapt, committed suicide, tragically not an infrequent event among surviving children.

At the beginning of May (1949), I was notified that Uncle Johni was critically ill and that I should take the next train to

Newcastle. In fact, Uncle Johni, then 34 years old, was already dead, and I was coming to his funeral. The official cause was an asthma attack. My grandparents had celebrated their 50th wedding anniversary, and uncle Johni and Aunt Lotte had given them a gift of a trip to Israel to visit family members. Uncle Johni died while they were in Israel, but no one wanted to give them the sad news. When they returned, they looked around the train station and asked, "Where's Johni?" The silence told them the tragic news. They packed their bags and, as soon as possible, took Aunt Rosie, and immigrated to Israel. My grandmother died there in 1950 and was buried in a small temporary cemetery (Givath Ram) behind the Knesset because the War of Independence had made the other cemeteries inaccessible. My grandfather then moved to Haifa to be close to Aunt Gella. He died there the following year (1951) and is buried in Haifa. Aunt Rosie lived in an old age home in Tel Aviv until she died in 1992. Aunt Klara and her family also moved to Israel where she remarried. She died in 2006.

Uncle Johni had a lot of responsibilities on his young shoulders: aging parents without resources, a growing family, Aunt Rosie, Aunt Betty and Bernd (Dov), and Mother Tola and me at a time when his business was failing. I can see his faults but I also owe him a great debt.

Left-to-right: Naomi, David, Aunt Klara, and I in Israel, May, 1998.

Grandmother Martha Koenigshoefer's grave in Jerusalem.

XII

TO AMERICA

———— • ◆ • ————

At the beginning of May 1949, we were notified by the US Embassy that our quota number had come up, and our application to immigrate to the United States was approved. Mother Tola's half-sister (same father), Rose Pasternak, lived in Brooklyn and agreed to be her sponsor before the war. After the war, Mother Tola added my name to the application. Before departing for the United States, I went to Newcastle to say good bye and while I was there, I begged my cousin Felix, Dov's brother, to make a drawing of me. He was reluctant, but with sufficient pestering, he gave in and quickly sketched me.

We sailed from Southampton harbor aboard the HMS Queen Elizabeth (the original Queen Elizabeth) on June 7, and docked at the Cunard Line pier in mid-town Manhattan early on the morning of June 13, 1949. The ocean crossing was smooth and pleasant and we met some interesting people at our kosher dining table including the Chief Rabbi of Florence (his card read "Rabino Capo di Firenze," which I thought was very neat), who told me that he had known my father. On the day we were scheduled to dock, I awoke before dawn, and waited on deck in excited anticipation of catching a glimpse of the Statue of Liberty. Shortly after day-break, I was called to the chapel to make up a *minyan* for morning prayers. By the time we finished and I ran up to the deck, the Statue of Liberty was far behind us.

It took some time to pass through customs and immigration, but finally we were on dry land. We waited on the dock until it was almost completely empty and, since no one seemed to be waiting for us, we approached a HIAS (Hebrew Immigrant Aid Society) representative

Pencil drawing by Felix Glueck in 1949.

*On board
HMS Queen
Elizabeth on
the way to the
United States.
Mother Tola is
on my left.*

for help. The HIAS representative telephoned Mother Tola's sister, who suggested that we take a taxi. This representative was a very good looking gentleman who was unusually warm, and paid us a significant amount of attention. It took several meetings for me to realize that the attention was meant for Mother Tola and not for me. He disappeared rather suddenly from our lives. I suspect that he was married, and that Mother Tola must have told him to buzz off, but perhaps I am being unfair.

As we approached a taxi, a vendor selling little paper American flags for Flag Day approached us and pinned one on me. I gave him a penny, a considerable sum in England but, I gathered from the string of New York curses he unleashed on us, not in the United States. Welcome to America!

We took a taxi to 30 East 58th Street in Brooklyn and rang the doorbell. All our earthly belongings were in two suitcases. The door opened and mother's sister, Rose, looked at the suitcases and exclaimed, "So much baggage! Where am I going to put so much baggage?" We knew immediately this would not be easy. That evening, Aunt Rose took us to see the lights of Pitkin Avenue, and was disappointed that we were not impressed. She criticized my English pronunciation and claimed that her Brooklyn accent was the correct way to speak English. After a few days, it was clear to us that we would have to find other accommodations.

Mother Tola telephoned the only other person in New York whose name we knew. Phillip Gruss, whose wife we had met in Rabbi Kahane's apartment in Warsaw, had given us the name of his sister, Mrs. Clara Landa. She turned out to be a true friend. She encouraged us, showed us around New York, bought me a portable Emerson radio, helped us leave

Photo in Central Park shortly after our arrival in 1949.

The Broadway Central Hotel in its heyday.

Brooklyn and, under the auspices of HIAS, helped us move into a room at the Broadway Central Hotel on Broadway and Third Street.

When it was built in 1868, the Broadway Central Hotel (originally the Grand Central Hotel) was advertised as the grandest and largest hotel in the world. By 1949, it was neglected, run down, and used primarily by HIAS as a transient hotel for refugees. In later years, it would become a welfare hotel, and finally col-

lapsed in 1973, killing four people.

Conditions in the hotel were difficult. The rooms were small, dingy, and dirty; the residents were dejected and frightened, and the staff was less than helpful. I especially remember the communal meals. There was no variety and the food consisted almost exclusively of boiled potatoes and sour cream. Fortunately, we had Mrs. Landa who took us out almost daily, and often invited us to her apartment at 310 East 15 Street for a meal.

Her husband, Jonas, a family physician, was somewhat older than she, and was gruff and curt. Their only son, Walter, an ex-marine enjoyed telling me stories of his many real or imagined female conquests in much more detail than I wanted to know or was comfortable with.

A visit with Mr. and Mrs. Ehrlich, Aunt Klara's parents, proved to be extremely important for our future. After dinner, Mother Tola spoke with Mrs. Ehrlich, and I spent a little time with her husband. He asked me where I planned to go to school and I showed him a slip of paper on which one of my Hasmonean teachers, Rabbi Wahrhaftig, had written the name of Yeshivas Chaim Berlin. He looked at me and said, "You don't belong there." He suggested that I look into the Talmudical Academy (TA), High School of Yeshiva University. After he told me more about both schools, I had to agree.

Meanwhile, Mrs. Ehrlich told Mother Tola of a refugee pediatrician who gave classes on the care of newborns. After getting approval from HIAS, Mother Tola started a six-week course, which would prepare her to help new mothers care for their newborn babies after discharge from the hospital.

At last, we could have our own place. We rented a small furnished room at 240 West 102nd Street from a German Jewish refugee family, the Adlers. There was barely enough room for a bed for Mother Tola, a foldout cot for me, which, when unfolded, blocked the closet, and a small table. After finishing her 6-week training,

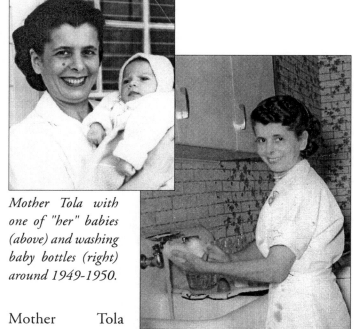

Mother Tola with one of "her" babies (above) and washing baby bottles (right) around 1949-1950.

Mother Tola worked in a variety of homes. Her work consisted of 20 hours on duty and four hours off, so there wasn't much opportunity for us to be together. I generally did a lot of the cooking by carefully following Mother Tola's directions. I became especially adept at preparing a corner steak, and baking chicken in a paper bag.

Mother Tola had some interesting experiences at work. Once, she was employed to care for the newborn grandson of one of New York's wealthiest families. The baby's grandfather was a prominent philanthropist, and a highly esteemed member of the Jewish community. His then newly born grandson, is today following in his footsteps. When Mother Tola finished, they thanked her profusely, sang her praises and, when she came home, she discovered an extra week's pay in her paycheck. We celebrated our good fortune, and a few days later Mother Tola

Mother Tola on Riverside Drive around 1950.

was described, he would have stood up and pledged many times the small amount the family requested Mother Tola to return. I guess philanthropy is philanthropy, and business is business.

Several weeks afterwards, I made my way to the office of the Talmudical Academy (TA) High School of Yeshiva University on Amsterdam Avenue and 185th Street. Mr. Norman B. Abrams, a short man with a funny Yiddish accent interviewed me. After listening to my background, he expressed sorrow, but indicated that my Jewish background was too weak for admission. When I begged him to give me a chance, he handed me three books to study: a Hebrew literature book, a Hebrew grammar book (Ivrith Haya), and a Chumash, and instructed me to return in September. That summer, an unusually hot one, even by New York standards, I sat hour after hour in the stifling heat of our little room and tried, without much success, to learn something in each book. When I returned to the school in September, I had to admit that I had not made much headway. Since I wouldn't take no for an answer, Mr. Abrams suggested that I speak with Dr. Hyman B. Grinstein, the Registrar of the Beth Midrash LeMorim (the Teacher's Institute or TI).

phoned to thank the family. There was a long pause after which she was informed that they had made an error and would Mother Tola be kind enough to send back the difference? I have no doubt that had this generous philanthropist been at a fund raising dinner at which our plight

The Beth Midrash LeMorim was a six-year school whose goal was to educate Hebrew teachers, with Hebrew as the only language of instruction. Its philosophy was religious Zionism of the Mizrachi variety. There was a great divide between TI and the Rabbinical School

(RIETS) whose faculty and students suspected that those who attended TI were not quite as kosher or religious. TI placed great emphasis on spoken Hebrew, Hebrew literature, Jewish history, and Tanach (Bible), with some Talmud, but less than in a traditional Yeshiva. I have often thought that my father would have approved and would have been very happy there. Dr. Grinstein proved to be understanding, and eventually became a good friend. He accepted me and I started in kita aleph itit (the lowest and slowest class) in September, and studied there six mornings a week. High school started at 1:00 PM and lasted until 6:00 PM. Because of my confusing educational background, I took some freshman and some higher level courses, and completed my high school requirements in two years (1951), just before my 16th birthday.

I had to study hard to advance in TI, but I earned a Teacher's Diploma at the end of six years (1955), concomitantly with a BA from Yeshiva College. When I started studying in TI, I had only the most rudimentary knowledge of Hebrew from my one year at the Hasmonean. I could read haltingly, but I could not speak or understand the language. I remember sitting in class not understanding a word until one day I heard one of my teachers, Rabbi Wind say the word "shulhan," and I

1951: High school graduation.

recognized that that meant "table".

I became fascinated with Hebrew literature, and gradually became familiar with the works of many of the classical Hebrew poets and authors. I loved Jewish history, and I especially fondly remember the lectures of Dr. Pinchas Churgin, later the first Chancellor of Bar Ilan University, and of Dr. Nahum Glatzer. A number of my teachers, such as Dr. Abraham Weiss and Dr. Joshua Finkel, were great scholars who were, unfortunately, not appreciated or respected by the students. Jewish History gave me an opportunity to see how I fit into the tapestry of the Jewish experience. I began to see a pattern; I liked to compare it to a moving train that got derailed in my lifetime. I concluded that in order for that train to move forward again, it would be up to my generation to put it back on track. This was a burden, but it also gave me a purpose. I tried to imagine how the generation after the flood, when everything on earth was destroyed, must have felt. They too bore a special burden as they rebuilt civilization.

I was inspired by the poetry of Chaim Nachman Bialik, but was disappointed that at Yeshiva they taught us only his so-called "religious" poetry (eg, "Im yesh et nafshcha ladaat"). That seemed to be a policy at YU - not to tackle anything that challenged Orthodoxy. For example, in all my years there, I never learned about the school of Biblical criticism. It would have been so much better to teach it and refute it, than to ignore it. I found that I had to study a great deal on my own in

Drs. Hyman B. Grinstein (right) and Pinchas Churgin (left) as they appeared in my yearbook.

order to round out my education. I became an intense Zionist, and saw the reestablishment of the State of Israel not so much as a response to the *shoah*, but rather as a natural process of modern nationalist history. I would have gone on *aliyah* in a heartbeat, but I could not fulfill this dream because I knew that it would have hurt Mother Tola very much, and that she would be left alone.

It is interesting that Yeshiva University closed the Teacher's Institute in the 1960s. The reason was surely not because the Modern Orthodox movement did not require Hebrew teachers. I think it was symptomatic of the gradual "haredization" of Judaism, as well as its cause. By "haredization" I mean insularity, an attempt to keep western civilization and everything considered not "authentically Jewish" out. The definition of "authentic" is made by an ever smaller circle of "authorities," and it has been further narrowed by the concept of "daas Torah," a catch phrase that extends rabbinical authority into every facet of life.

Our teachers at TI were erudite, with

a great love of the Hebrew language, literature, and history, but also with a deep understanding of the best of western civilization, and an urge to merge the best of both. They were deeply religious, but combined this with an equal love and respect for western knowledge and scholarly methodology.

This has, unfortunately, been lost and each generation since then has had a weaker appreciation for western culture as well as for Hebrew culture and language. The Mizrachi and Hapoel Hamizrachi movements have disappeared; the students' grasp of Hebrew has weakened, as can be appreciated by comparing the sparse amount of spoken Hebrew in the Jewish camps today compared with the "ivrith beivrith" policy prevailing in the Massad, and Yavneh camps of two generations ago. The closure of TI, Herzliyah, and the Jewish Theological Seminary's Teachers' Institute has meant that more of our children's teachers have been educated in Haredi Yeshivoth, and they have naturally transmitted that culture to them.

I found the high school subject matter quite easy, and I had an excellent record, but I had a great deal of difficulty socially. I simply didn't fit in. I found most of the students immature, not interested in learning, and without curiosity. All they seemed to want to talk about was baseball, a subject I did not understand or appreciate, and considered a waste of time. My life experiences were so different from theirs that the chasm between us was unbridgeable. The fact that most of my classmates were two years older than I also did not help. I was appalled at the behavior of most of the students and their lack of respect for their teachers. Many of the teachers had trouble controlling their classes. I had come from a system, which was, perhaps, too rigid. At the Hasmonean, teachers wore black gowns, students wore uniforms, and it would have been unthinkable for a student not to stand when a teacher entered a room. My friends now were primarily refugees from Europe, Israel, South and Central America. I can't think of a single American boy from this six-year experience, who has remained my friend. As a result, not once in six years was I invited for a Shabbat or Yom Tov meal in anyone's home. When I think back, I find it incredible that I would spend many a Shabbat at YU in the dormitory room eating tuna fish. I don't mean to put all of the blame for my social isolation on my classmates. Part of the fault was clearly mine because I resisted the "Americanization" process. As much as I admired the United States for its contribution to world politics and human dignity and freedom, I looked down on "pop" culture, and I did not want to be associated with it in any way.

Leon Schoenholtz was one of my European friends. He was orphaned during the war, spent some time in concentration camp, and was even uncertain about his exact age. He had studied Hebrew in one of the DP camps and was fluent.

Among other things, Leon taught me the beauty of the thirty-first chapter of Jeremiah and convinced me that we were seeing its fulfillment. When he graduated high school, Leon received a scholarship enabling him to visit Israel. On his return he didn't have 15 cents for the subway (that is what it cost then) but he brought me a small *siddur* as a present, and I was touched that he inscribed it "LeYudah, yedid neeman" (to Yehudah, a true friend – except that "yedid" is much closer than a friend). I was especially touched because I had never before had anyone consider me a friend. Tragically, Leon died under mysterious circumstances some years later (I heard that he committed suicide but am not sure). At their bar mitzvahs I asked Danny and David to read the 31st chapter of Jeremiah in Leon's memory, but I could not adequately explain to them why since their lives were, fortunately, so radically different from ours.

During my high school years, my roommate and closest friend was from Costa Rica. He came from a relatively well to do family and was one of the few boys to own a phonograph and some LP (long playing) vinyl records. This was of course before the days of CDs, and the big advance was the emergence of LP records, which turned at only 33 1/3 revolutions per minute, in contrast to the old 78 or 45 rpm, and so could play for a full 45 minutes. Chico, as we called him, and I began to educate ourselves musically with his records, and it was here that I first heard many of the classical pieces. We especially enjoyed listening to opera, and when Rudolph Bing became the General Manager of the Metropolitan Opera House, the *New York Times* published a number of articles that generated much excitement and anticipation about a new production of Faust for opening night. I was determined to see it and read that $2 standing-room tickets would be available for those hardy souls willing to wait in line. I stationed myself in line at the opera house on 39th street (this was the old house not the new one at Lincoln Center) the evening before armed with a blanket, a sandwich, and reading material. When the box office opened the following day I was still in line and happily bought my $2 ticket. That evening, unshaven and dressed in chinos and a sport shirt I entered together with the opening crowd dressed in tuxedos and evening gowns. The standing area was behind the orchestra section, and I stood next to the aisle. At intermission, Hedda Hopper (a society columnist for the *Daily News*) came down the aisle ready to file her report on who was seen with whom and who was wearing what and, as she passed me, she handed me her ticket and said, "Here, sonny, sit in my seat, I'm not coming back." I made my way to the first orchestra row, sat among the elegant crowd, and watched the magic of Gonoud's second act.

Despite my background, I don't recall any significant inner religious struggles during my years at YU. Fortunately, my understanding of Judaism did not require me to "believe" nor to abdicate my intellect. Judaism does make certain assump-

tions about the deity, but there is sufficient division of opinion even on this that it allows room for both "believers" and "skeptics." I have never resolved the question about the existence of God, and have not spent much time in what I consider to be an irresolvable issue. What is important to me is the effect that belief in God has on human behavior. I see faith in God as a way to give humans a healthy mixture of confidence and hope on one hand, and humility on the other. Confidence and hope in the order and predictability of the universe, and humility and a sense of wonder and awe, when trying to understand it. This is best summarized by the Hasidic teacher, Rabbi Simha Bunim (1765-1827), who stated that every person should always carry a slip of paper in each pocket. The one in his right pocket should state that "the entire world was created for me", and the one in his left pocket should state, "I am but dust and ashes."

In general, I followed religious traditions and tried to fulfill the mitzvoth, but I could never consider them as ends in themselves; for me they remained symbolic – important ways to transmit the heritage and to understand it. I didn't follow the minutiae (I fully realize that this term is relative) and new "*chumros.*" To believe that God wanted human beings to carry these out was for me tantamount to idol worship, and diminished the Devine concept. I developed the same attitude about prayer. I pray because I need prayer; not because I believe that God wants or needs it, nor for some wish to be granted. To believe this would be to insinuate that God can change his mind, and this would diminish the deity. For a long time, I was troubled by the ending of the "Untaneh Tokef" prayer recited on the High Holidays that ends with the phrase, "Ut'shuvah ut'filah, utz'daka mavirin et roa hagzera," but "repentance, prayer, and good deeds annul the severity of the decree," until I realized that the "severity" depends on us, on how an individual accepts it. The decree itself is not changed, but how we accept it, its "severity," can be because it is in our power to do so. In fact very few of our prayers ask for anything, and I have had difficulty with the few that do, such as the prayer for the ill, a much later addition to our prayer book. I have always looked upon this prayer as a means of informing the community who is ill and helping the relatives. I have not generally subscribed to Hasidic or kabalistic thought – I tend to the rational rather than the mystical, but I do like the kabalistic idea of zimzum. It suggests that God, by making a partnership with humans and giving us free will, has diminished his own power. By adhering to this philosophy, I don't need to ascribe to God either the good or the evil that human beings do to each other, including the Shoah. God is as helpless and as sad as I am when I see human inhumanity. This is, I believe, the overriding message of the book of Job, and the reason it was included in the cannon. Without this understanding, I could not, in all honesty, have participated in the traditions of Judaism or any other religion after the Shoah. I desperately needed to do so because I felt very keenly and consciously that I had a responsibility to continue our history and to live for the many who could not. I have, however, not been able to say the Kaddish prayer. I could find a philosophical justification that would allow me to feel sorry for God for not being able to intervene, but I could not praise him while remembering my parents' deaths.

I also stood somewhat apart religiously from my classmates and co-religionists because my life experiences have taught me that no single people, including my own, have a monopoly on the truth or have cornered the market on goodness or the capacity to do evil. The trick is to find the kernels of truth in all cultures, and integrate them into our religious experience. My study of Jewish history has taught me that previous generations have been more adept at this than ours.

Our finances remained precarious, and I could not have enjoyed the benefits of an education without the generous financial help of Yeshiva University. In addition to full tuition and free dormitory for six years (two in high school and four in college), I also received an $8/week food card, redeemable in the cafeteria and the dinette across the street. I am greatly indebted to YU for their generosity, which enabled me to get a Jewish and general education. Mother Tola gave me $2 (later increased to $5) a week "pocket" money. I knew how hard she worked and how much she denied herself and so, each time she wanted to increase my allowance, I declined. Despite my protests Mother Tola would go bargain shopping to Klein's on 14th Street, to Macy's, or to her favorite, Alexander's in Queens, and come back with shirts, suits for $15, etc. I spent almost no money. I once wanted to buy a set of Rambam's "Mishna Torah" from an itinerant bookseller who would come around every six months. The set cost $25, but when he saw how much I wanted it, he offered it to me for 25 cents a week. I eagerly accepted his offer and dutifully paid off my debt.

When it came time to apply to college I applied only to Yeshiva College. I did so primarily because it was convenient, but also because I didn't have enough money for application fees to other colleges. Once in college, I became a pre-med major mainly because it never occurred to me to do anything else. In truth, I had no idea what a doctor did since I had hardly ever been to one and had no role model, but I was impressed that refugee doctors almost always practiced their profession whereas refugee lawyers and other professionals were doormen, librarians, or janitors. I was not yet able to wrap my mind around the idea that I was no longer a transient; I needed a profession that was portable, just in case.

I did well in the first year of college, but my marks slipped considerably over the next three years. This was due to a combination of factors. The pre-med major re-

quired a commitment of a great deal of time and effort. I noticed that all of my classmates who were pre-med majors completely disregarded their Jewish studies, and if they came to class at all, either left immediately after roll call, or studied science during Judaica classes. In contrast, I took Jewish studies seriously and there wasn't enough time for both. We used to joke that YU's motto may have been "Torah Umada" (Torah and Science), but the students' actions suggested that it should have been Torah or Mada.

Secondly, I was becoming progressively more nearsighted, but I didn't realize it. When I entered medical school, I had a routine physical examination (probably my first) and, after my eye exam, the ophthalmologist said: "You are terribly nearsighted and have astigmatism. How did you ever see the board in college?" In fact, I don't remember seeing the board. I didn't know I was supposed to. When I subsequently got my first pair of glasses, I remember walking out of the optometrist's office in midtown Manhattan and being flabbergasted at what I saw. Previously, the world had looked to me like an impressionist painting – aesthetically pleasing, but not very practical.

And finally, there was Edward (known better by his nickname, Nunek) Stark who came into our lives during my freshman year in college. Mother Tola and Nunek were married on December 8, 1951. He was born Edward Schapira in Lwów on December 30, 1904 into a highly assimilated family, and studied law at Casimir University. He spent the war years as a Polish officer in a German prisoner-of-war camp, where he passed as a non-Jew under the name of Sapierski. After the war, he worked as a translator (German and Polish) for the US military in Germany. Friends of ours, Umek and Andzia Weinfeld, introduced him to Mother Tola. Mother Tola was lonely and liked him, but I had mixed emotions. I very much wanted Mother Tola to find some happiness and companionship, but no matter how much I tried, I could not warm up to Nunek. He had an extremely rigid, almost military personality, and he talked incessantly, the volume and speed directly related to his level of anxiety. He decided to pursue a master's degree in social work at Adelphi University, and I spent hours helping him with every paper, including his thesis. He would dwell over every word until I was ready to scream. From my observation, this union did not bring Mother Tola much happiness.

The nadir of my academic life came at the end of the first semester of my junior year, when Dr. Levine gave me an F in Organic Chemistry. This of course seriously jeopardized my chance of being accepted in medical school. In retrospect, I find my reaction to this calamity interesting and characteristic of the way I have handled adversity. I didn't go to Dr. Levine and argue about my grade, nor did I try to have it changed. In fact, I never spoke with Dr. Levine about it. My assumption was that this was his view of my ability, which he was entitled to have,

Mother Tola and Nunek in 1964.

and my job was to prove him wrong. I didn't feel sorry for myself, nor did I discuss this much with friends. In fact, I was disturbed to find that my graduating yearbook, Hamasmid, placed a quote next to my name: "Shall thy enemy blaspheme thee forever?" This was a view of the Levine "affair" that I did not share. Instead, I asked the YU Registrar, Dr. Silverman, for permission to take Organic Chemistry 2 in another college. I could only afford one of the city universities, and I found an evening course at Brooklyn College. The class met twice a week from 7 to 10 PM, and the trip lasted over an hour each way with a change of subways. So, after a full day of classes at YU, I would go to Brooklyn and return well after 11:00 PM. The most frightening part of the trip was the six block walk to the YU dormitory from the subway station on St. Nicholas Avenue and 181st Street. The neighborhood was not safe, especially for YU students who were periodically attacked. I felt vindicated when I received an A in the course. I then retook Organic Chemistry 1 during the summer at City College, and also obtained an A. My next, and last, encounter with Dr. Levine was on a visit to YU a number of years later, when he sought my opinion about a number of ailments from which he was suffering. I tried my best to give him appropriate advice.

I applied to about ten medical schools and was accepted only at Yeshiva's newly established Albert Einstein College of Medicine. Plans for establishing a medical school had been made public by Yeshiva's President, Dr. Samuel Belkin, in 1952. It would become the first new medical school established in the United States in about 50 years. American medical schools had rigid quotas for Jews and it was well known that it was almost impossible to get accepted directly from Yeshiva College. Most students had to go to graduate school, and then apply to medical school armed with a master's degree in one of the sciences from Columbia or NYU. We were thrilled with the idea of a medical school of our own, and I went to the groundbreaking in 1952 and wondered whether I would be lucky enough to be accepted there.

I suspect that I was accepted at Einstein on the basis of my interview, rather than on my scholastic record. The one courtesy that Einstein gave applicants from YU was an automatic interview. I was interviewed by several professors, but the one that stands out in my memory is

with Dr. Leo M. Davidoff. Dr Davidoff was a formidable neurosurgeon, a student of the great Cushing at Harvard, and one of the senior founding faculty members at Einstein. He spoke to me for about an hour about my experiences, religious ideas, and expectations. Although he had a reputation among the students for "ice flowing through his veins," my experiences may have reminded him of his own origins in Latvia, and early adaptation to this country.

Yeshiva College graduation 1955.

XIII

MEDICAL EDUCATION

— • ◆ • —

MEDICAL SCHOOL

I started my medical studies in September 1955 by meeting my 55 fellow students in a temporary hut on Morris Park Avenue in the Bronx. I lived with Mother Tola and Nunek at 610 West 145 Street during my first year, necessitating a one hour commute by bus each way. This became very difficult and so, in the second year, I rented a living room couch in an apartment near the school. So as not to interfere with the family's life, I agreed not to come "home" before midnight, and to leave by 6:00 AM. The couch was one of those Victorian couches intended for uncomfortable sitting, but definitely not for sleeping; it was not made for my height or the curvature of my back. I developed a routine of eating dinner in the school cafeteria, studying in the library until it closed at 11:00 PM, and then sitting with a cup of coffee and a book in Tepper's Drug Store until midnight, when I was allowed to go to my couch. The arrangement was neither comfortable nor convenient, but it was the only one I could afford. Since the campus was still unfinished and only a few floors were in use at Jacobi Hospital, one of the nurses suggested that I use the surgical recovery room, which was closed at night. So, about the middle of the school year, I moved my belongings to a locker in the surgical change room and slept in the comfort of an air conditioned recovery room until awakened by the morning shift of nurses with a hot cup of coffee. This worked out very well for the remainder of the second year, when several of my classmates, Sy Applebaum, Joe Mogilner, Shelly Eisenman, Cal Ackerman, and Mel Shay, suggested that we all rent and share a small house near the school for the last two years. They realized my financial situation and kindly charged me less than they were paying. This worked out quite well despite the fact that the house, located near railroad tracks, was overrun with rats and mice.

I spent the summer after my freshman year the way I had spent the previous several summers, as a counselor at Camp Massad. In the middle of August, I received a letter from Einstein Medical School informing me that I would not receive a full scholarship for the following year, and that I had to pay the tuition in advance. After factoring in the partial scholarship and all the money I had, I was

In anatomy class with Dr. Ernst Scharrer. I am in 5th row 7th from the right.

still $500 short. After agonizing over this, I called Dr. Grinstein at Yeshiva University. He was very kind and, without hesitation, assured me that the money would be forthcoming and that it would be a loan to be repaid at my convenience. I subsequently received a letter from him informing me that he had opened a special account with a donation of $375, and that he would get other donations towards the money I needed. When I joined the US Public Health Service in 1962 and received my first real paycheck, I wrote a letter of gratitude to Dr. Grinstein and enclosed a check. He assured me that the money would be saved in this fund to help others.

I survived the first two years of medical school although I did not enjoy

them. From time to time, I wondered whether I had made a mistake in the choice of my profession. I came into my own, however, during the clinical years, when my strong interpersonal skills, natural empathy, and good manners that Mother Tola taught me, engendered a sense of confidence in my patients. I truly enjoyed my patient interactions, and was stimulated to find solutions to their problems. I also found that my religious instruction helped me understand human frailty as well as my role as a physician. Some rabbinic texts that lay dormant in the inner recesses of my brain suddenly became clearer to me.

I gravitated towards pediatrics primarily because I found the pediatric faculty more genuinely interested in their

Albert Einstein College of Medicine
of YESHIVA UNIVERSITY

PROGRESS REPORT JANUARY 1959

First Commencement Year at College Enlists Coast-to-Coast Support

Dr. Detlev W. Bronk   Ralph J. Bunche   Gov. N. Rockefeller   Dr. S. A. Waksman   S. Sloan Colt

Harland C. Forbes   Gov. A. Ribicoff   Gen. Lucius D. Clay   Dr. L. Baumgartner   Sid Caesar

Over 200 nationally known figures in the United States and Canada are serving as members of the Commencement Year Committee of the College of Medicine.

Indicative of the mounting interest in this First Commencement, many top leaders in government, the arts, medicine, industry and community welfare are sponsoring the nation-wide observances to mark this major milestone in medical education. Some of the distinguished government figures on the Committee are: Hon. Abraham Ribicoff, Governor of Connecticut; Hon. Simon E. Sobeloff, Judge, U.S. Circuit Court; New York Senators Irving M. Ives and Jacob K. Javits.

(Continued on page 4)

National Leaders to Meet in Florida

Palm Beach, Miami Events Keyed To Graduation Year Observance

Members of the Board of Overseers of the College will take part in two Florida meetings which are expected to bring together community leaders from all parts of the United States and Canada.

Scheduled for Palm Beach on February 26, is a dinner at the Biltmore Hotel at which Charles Frost will be the host.

Senator Jacob K. Javits of New York will be the honored guest.

Hon. Jacob K. Javits

A Miami Beach reception will be held at the Fontainebleau Hotel on March 1, with George Frankel and Nathaniel L. Goldstein as hosts.

This marks the fifth year in which these national events have been held in Florida for the College of Medicine.

Research Assignments Give Students Glimpse Into "Medical Unknown"

Students at the College of Medicine are gaining valuable first-hand experience on a far-ranging research front, covering the major diseases, mental health, new drugs, advanced surgical techniques, radiology and other vital fields.

The aim of this program is to give students an insight into the complex process by which new medical knowledge is discovered. Working with the latest tools and techniques, students plan and follow through original research projects under the direction of the various departments.

This independent research work helps the students develop their critical judgment for evaluating the remarkable advances that have brought medicine to its present high level.

In the past, many gifted undergraduates had to spend summers as waiters or life

(Continued on page 4)

STUDENT WORKING on basic research project.

Business Outlook Bright for '59

1959 gives every promise of being a banner year for American business, according to leading government and industry economists.

There is every expectation that we will all benefit from the economic surge. This offers us an opportunity to advance medical education and science by giving tax dollars under the government's generous provisions for charitable deductions.

The Albert Einstein College of Medicine needs your help to raise $5,000,000 during this historic Commencement Year to complete the construction and equipment of essential training and research facilities.

You, your friends and associates can serve the nation's health and welfare by contributing generously to the College of Medicine.

Nathaniel L. Goldstein

Photo of me taken in microbiology laboratory in 1956 and published in an Einstein publicity bulletin in 1959.

Graduation from Albert Einstein 1959. I am sitting in 1st row on extreme left.

Graduation from medical school in 1959 with Mrs. Landa and Mother Tola (left) and with Zwi (right).

patients' well being. Many of the senior internists at Einstein in those days, it seemed to me, were more interested in the medical literature than in their patients. They reminded me of the pride with which Talmudic scholars could cite the exact page, and even the exact line, on which a particular law appeared and follow it punctiliously, while completely disregarding its underlying principle in their daily lives.

Medical school graduation finally arrived on a beautiful June day in 1959. In addition to being a milestone for my classmates and me, it was also a milestone for the school because we were the very first graduating class. What a joy that was for all of us, but especially for Mother Tola! Others who came to share my joy were Nunek, Mrs. Landa, whose husband had died some years before, Herbert, and Shosh.

Jean and I in 2009 on the 50th anniversary of medical school graduation.

I have previously mentioned that Herbert went to Israel from England in 1948. He went with a classmate from Hasmonean, Lillian Lieberman, who survived the war years hiding with non-Jewish families in Warsaw. Herbert (now known as Zwi) and Lillian (now known as Shosh) eventually married in Israel. After a number of jobs in education and kibbutz building, Zwi joined the Foreign Service

Herbert (Zwi) serving in the Israeli army (in the early 1950s).

and, in 1956, was sent to Vienna where one of his assignments was to help Jews flee Hungary during that country's brief uprising against Soviet control. Before going, he had to comply with a law initiated by Ben Gurion that all Israeli representatives abroad have Hebrew names, and he chose "Barnea." During his stint in Vienna, Zwi became disillusioned with politics and diplomacy and decided to study natural sciences. He attended mathematics and physics courses at the University of Vienna, and asked me to help him come to the US to finish his studies. I helped him apply to Brooklyn Polytechnic Institute, and helped Shosh to get accepted to the Jewish Institute of Religion, which enabled her to acquire a student visa. They came to the United States in 1958 and Zwi, in addition to taking a full course of studies, was able to support his family by translating nuclear physics articles from Russian into English. After finishing his studies, they went to Australia to join Shosh's mother who had immigrated there from Poland. Zwi has had a distinguished career at the University of Melbourne in x-ray crystallography and, after his retirement, in atomic physics.

PEDIATRIC RESIDENCY

I was extremely anxious to leave New York after medical school. My dream had always been to live in a small town "where people knew each other" and where I could develop a sense of belonging. While I was in college, I worked for several summers in Camp Massad, a Hebrew speaking camp in the Poconos. On my day off, I would go to Stroudsburg for a haircut and shopping. That became the ideal town of my imagination—with a Rockwell quality, where "everyone knows his neighbor, and no human malice exists."

On the New York Thruway on the way to intern at Strong Memorial Hospital in Rochester, NY.

Now, in our final year of medical school, a group of us set out for interviews for internships. We visited Syracuse, Rochester, Buffalo, and Cleveland. I found my ideal "small" town in Rochester, NY. I did not realize at the time that a book about the town was entitled "Smugtown, USA." As soon as I walked out of the YMHA in downtown Rochester, where I was staying overnight, and saw the clean streets, its "small" size, and the quaint lampposts, I fell in love with the town, and was deter-

mined to intern there, even before I visited the hospital. Like most love, it was blind. I didn't see the poverty, the slums, and the human misery, which were also present in abundance. The next day, I interviewed at Strong Memorial Hospital and I was thrilled when, a week later, Dr. William Bradford, Director of the Department of Pediatrics, called to tell me that they would list me on their first list on the match if I did the same. This was not strictly legal, but the match was still in its infancy and there was still a certain degree of flexibility in its enforcement.

A year earlier, my friend and roommate Joseph Mogilner ("Mogi") had given me a few driving lessons, and I made an appointment to take a driving test. He lent me his car, and I passed the test despite the fact that I misunderstood the examiner and made an illegal U-turn. Mother Tola offered to buy me a car before going off to Rochester, and I went car shopping. In a used car lot off the Whitestone Highway, I found a 1953 two toned green Chevrolet with power steering, and I fell in love. But when I got in to drive it home I realized that it had standard shift, and I had learned on a semi-automatic. I had to ask how to use a clutch, and drove out onto the Whitestone Expressway. It was a harrowing trip, more akin to riding a bucking bronco than a car, but by the time I came to Jackson Heights, where Mother Tola and Nunek now lived, I had the hang of it and driving became quite smooth. I grew very fond of that car and eventually had a new engine built for it rather than trade it in.

I started my pediatric training at Strong Memorial Hospital of the University of Rochester on July 1, 1959. By today's standards, the educational facilities were quite primitive, despite the fact that this was one of the country's most renowned medical centers. The Department of Pediatrics had only four full time teachers: Dr. William Bradford, Chief of the Department, who also maintained an active research laboratory in infectious disease and a private pediatric practice; Dr. Gilbert Forbes, a specialist in metabolism and endocrinology; Dr. Gerald Miller, hematologist; Dr. James Manning, cardiologist; and Dr. Christopher Katsampis, a generalist. None of these, with the exception of Dr. Manning did any significant bedside teaching or supervision of the interns; this job was left to the resident who was a year or sometimes only a few months ahead of the intern. My first rotation, on July 1, was in the emergency department and at 8:00 AM I was there all alone when a distraught mother brought in a 10-day old baby who promptly stopped breathing. I had no idea what to do. This was before the days of CPR education, resuscitation teams, etc., and I was expected to muddle through. Miraculously, I did and the baby, who turned out to have listeria monocytegenes meningitis, actually survived. I didn't know it then, but this frightening experience would stick with me and would determine the course of part of my professional life in the future.

We were overworked, on duty for 36 hours and off for 12, underpaid, at $1200 a year and a room, and yet life was exciting and we learned a great deal, especially from the nurses. God bless the nurses; they saved us many times. Strong friendships developed among the residents akin to the friendships one develops under siege or at war and so, despite the frustrations and hard work, or maybe because of them, I remember those days with great fondness. The patients and parents are vivid in my memory, especially the ones with terminal illnesses and those who, unfortunately, did not survive. I found, perhaps as a result of my experiences, that I was not afraid of dying patients and was able to find words, and sometimes silence, with which to comfort them and their parents.

I was once asked to write my recollections of residency training at Strong Memorial Hospital for a book on the history of pediatrics.[155] In part I wrote:

"My first rotation was in the emergency room where I would see a seemingly endless number of children. At appropriate seasons, it seems that most every febrile child had measles, and so a meticulous search for Koplik spots was always done. Another frequent diagnosis was impetigo, especially among the area's many migrant families. We had a small laboratory where we did our own blood counts and urinalyses. If we needed a chest x-Ray we had to wait until it was developed and then

[155] Jeffrey P. Baker and Howard A. Pearson (Eds), 75 Years of Caring (American Academy of Pediatrics Chicago 2005).

did a "wet reading" ourselves. Our therapeutic armamentaria were penicillin G, sulfadiazine, streptomycin, and chloramphenicol.

"There were three age-related wards. The infant ward was divided by wood and glass partitions to reduce infection. An ultraviolet light was on all the time and gave off an eerie glow at night. The many infants with diarrhea were treated with intravenous fluids. We had to mix the fluids ourselves in the treatment rooms. We carefully calculated the infant's extracellular volume and estimated the amount of electrolyte and fluid loss. From these we then determined the right amount of D_5W (dextrose 5% in water), normal saline, and lactated Ringer's solution, and mixed them together in a burette. The burette was attached to IV tubing, and a sterile piece of gauze was taped on top to ward off infection. We never used gloves while mixing these concoctions and there was no hand washing protocol. Needles were re-sterilized and used again and again, so they were often dull. It is a credit to the resiliency of the human species that so many infants not only survived, but also improved under our care."

During the two-year residency we only had a one month elective rotation so its choice was most important. I was interested in endocrinology, and I had carried out some research in 17-hydroxy steroids during my fourth year of medical school. I envisioned myself in the future spending two years at the NIH (National Institutes of Health) doing bench research, so I eliminated that as a possible elective. I decided that I should take an elective in a specialty I was afraid of, didn't know anything about, and would never encounter again. The obvious choice, once I phrased my choice in this manner, was cardiology. By the end of my elective month, Dr. Manning and cardiology had won me over. I was inspired by Dr. Manning's genuine interest in, and care of, his patients and the logic that led to a diagnosis. The diagnosis of congenital heart disease was not based on "hunches" as much as on logically combining clues derived from the history, physical examination, chest x-Ray, and electrocardiogram. In retrospect, it is amazing how often our diagnoses were correct despite our primitive tools. The specialty was still in its infancy; the first open heart operation had only been performed six years before and many of the diagnostic tools used today were still unimagined. It has been exciting to be involved at the beginning of this development. The greatest diagnostic advance in congenital heart disease that occurred during my career has been echocardiography. With this technology, we could actually "see" the abnormality rather than imagine what it looks like. When I saw the first primitive echocardiograms at a cardiology meeting in the early 70s, looking somewhat like the grainy flickering movies of the early days, I was excited by the future possibilities, but also somewhat saddened at the potential loss of the rigor of deductive reasoning using the tiniest of clues in arriving at a diagnosis.

It is interesting to look at the modern development of medicine. There was little science in medicine until the late 19th century when the marriage between medicine and chemistry began. At first, the results of this marriage were seen only diagnostically with the development of microbiology and the identification of the various disease-causing bacteria, but by the 1930s that marriage between medicine and chemistry produced sulfa, then the antibiotics, steroids, and the psychopharmacologic agents in the 1950s. The marriage of medicine with physics took place before and during my professional career. This expanded our diagnostic capabilities with the development of x-Rays, CAT scans, MRI, etc. The marriage of medicine and the ever more powerful computers has made ultrasound and the various other imaging techniques possible and practical.

In my second year of Pediatric Residency I had to decide on my future course. The University of Rochester encouraged its students to take a year "out", a tradition started by its first dean, Dr. Whipple. I liked the idea, and decided to take a year of pathology, during which I could devote myself to gaining a better understanding of disease processes. I thought that a year at Boston Children's Hospital, with its vast amount of clinical material, would offer me the best experience, an opinion supported by my Chief of Pediatrics, Dr. Bradford. When I interviewed with Dr. Sidney Farber, Chief of Pathology at the Children's, we discussed the year's experience, after which he asked

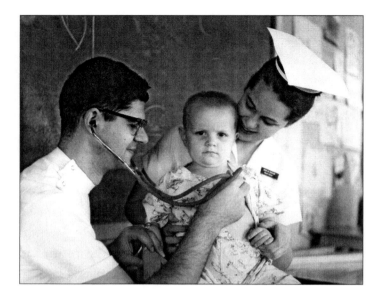

Examining a child as a resident at Strong Memorial Hospital.

whether I had any questions. "Yes," I hesitatingly asked, "what is my salary going to be?" There was a moment of silence as Dr. Farber stared at me and then, in measured tone, answered, "Young man, it is a privilege to study at the Children's Hospital of Harvard; there is no salary." When I returned to Rochester and reported to Dr. Bradford, I told him that I simply could not go without a salary. After a few phone calls Dr. Bradford informed me that he was able to get me a special fellowship that paid a stipend of $2,000 for the year and that I better take it.

Academically, the year at Children's proved to be excellent. Dr. Vaughter, a quiet and taciturn, but very intelligent man was our primary mentor. I met Dr. Farber twice – during my initial interview, and again during an exit interview. I took the year of pathology after my pediatric residency because I wanted to spend it reading and thinking about the disease processes I had seen. The year at Boston Children's gave me exactly what I sought

XIV

SUNRISE, SUNSET

—◆—

Two events, my marriage in 1961 and Mother Tola's death in 1965, marked the dawn of a new, and the end of an old era in my life.

I first noticed Jean Ann Easterbrook shortly after starting my internship at Strong Memorial Hospital in Rochester. She was the Department of Pediatrics Executive Secretary and extremely attractive. I took every opportunity to visit the office and after a while we started dating. The more I got to know her, the more I liked her. Despite our very different backgrounds, I found that our value systems and dreams for the future coincided. Our bond of love grew stronger; and we decided to build our future together. I was ready to settle down and longed for a home. It must not be forgotten that my last real home was when I was four years old. Since then, I had been a transient.

One Saturday morning, after we had announced our engagement, I was on duty and heard my name paged to Dr. Bradford's office. This was strange since Dr. Bradford, Chairman of Pediatrics at Strong Memorial Hospital, did not usually work on Saturdays. I answered my page and was asked to come to his office when I had a free moment. Since I wasn't especially busy, I went immediately and knocked on the door.

"Come in," came the reply in a female voice with a heavy southern accent. I entered and saw Mrs. Bradford sitting in a chair. She was a short, rather rotund lady, who was born and bred in Missouri, where her brother was then the governor.

"Leohhn, come in, sit down," she said in her thick southern accent. I was somewhat confused and I entered slowly, said good morning, and sat down wondering what on earth she wanted to speak to me about.

"Ah hear you're goin' to marry, Jeanie."

"Yes, Mrs. Bradford."

"Mahty fahne girl, that Jeanie."

"Yes, Mrs. Bradford, that's why I want to marry her."

"Ah want to tell you a story I never tol' anyone else. You know that Brad looves behsball."

"Yes Mrs. Bradford."

"An you know that every spring Brad an' ah go to Florida an' we stah in the same hotel, an' every day we go to a behsball game."

"Yes, Mrs. Bradford, I have heard about it."

"Ah sit there an' ah holler an' ah cheer an' the bench gits harder an' harder but ah holler an' ah yell an' ah sit with Brad. Ahm goin' to tell you somethin' ah've never tol' anyone before, ah haate baseball!"

That was the end of the conversation and I was dismissed. I have often thought about this story, and the fact that she felt a need to give me some motherly advice before my wedding. It was good advice; sometimes one does have to cheer no matter how hard the bench is, if the game is important enough to one's partner.

Because I didn't know much about the social norms of engagement and marriage and I didn't have any money, I didn't buy Jean a traditional engagement ring. I did go to the lower East side of New York (89 Canal Street) and ordered two wedding rings of white gold from Nisim Hizme, a Yemenite jeweler who made rings of beautiful design. Engraved within a circular crown were the words, וארשתיך לי לעולם – "And I will betroth you onto me forever." In the mid-1980s, Jean lost her ring in a snowstorm and, just before Debbie and David's wedding in 1988, I called information and asked for the telephone number of Hizme's. To my delight he answered, and after rummaging around in his "files," kept in shoeboxes, came up with the design and agreed to make a replica. "It's good you called today because I am retiring and about to close my shop," he told me. "Also," he continued, "don't forget that when you originally bought the ring, gold was $35 an ounce."

We were married by Rabbi Abraham Karp in the Chapel of Temple Beth El in Rochester, NY on June 25, 1961.

Every successful marriage requires compromises and sacrifices by both parties. In our case, Jean has made the greater sacrifices in order to assure our happiness, and I have loved her all the more for it. She normalized our family life, brought freshness to the Judaism we both practiced, and enriched it with her sense of honesty, decency and fairness. Jean has relied on me to define the boundaries of the Judaism we would practice, and sometimes that proved quite hard, but there is no question that the Jewish home we created is primarily Jean's contribution.

I have been incredibly fortunate in many of my life decisions. I went into medicine without knowing much about it, and have derived great satisfaction from my work and have had the opportunity to make some modest contributions. I went into marriage, as most of us do, not really sure how it would turn out. Fortunately, both of us are emotionally similar with the same values. We both have an even, steady temperament without hot flashes of emotion. We are both fairly cool under pressure, and we have enjoyed material possessions as a means to make life comfortable, but not as an end. As I write this, Jean and I have been married for more than 50 years, and they have been exceedingly happy years. We have never had a serious argument. Not that we haven't disagreed on issues, but we have been able to amicably resolve disagreements with the one to whom the issue was less important giving in. Both of us instinctively realized that it was more important to be happy together than to be "right." We have fortunately never played games with each other's emotions, and have truly striven to make each other happy. Jean assures me that that is the definition of love and I suppose it is.

Towards the end of 1964, Mother Tola didn't feel well. I prevailed on her to see a physician who found her to be slightly jaundiced and wondered whether she might have an inflamed gall bladder with obstruction. I was concerned about her and strongly urged her to come to Rochester for further diagnostic tests and surgery, if necessary. I asked Dr. Kingsley, one of the senior surgeons at Strong, to be her physician. The diagnostic studies showed that she did indeed have obstructive jaundice, but the cause was not clear and he advised exploratory surgery. I shall never forget the moment he told me that mother Tola had metastatic cancer involving the major organs and that little could be done. I was devastated and, for the first time in my memory, broke down. Unfortunately, in those days the word "cancer" was taboo and everything possible was done to keep the diagnosis from the patient.

After recovering from surgery, Mother Tola went back to New York, but it soon became evident that she could not manage. My dear wife, Jean suggested that she and our three month old son, Danny, stay in New York to care for her while I went back to work. Jean was used to small towns. The combination of living

in a New York apartment, caring for a baby, and caring for a sick person were overwhelming for her, but Jean never complained and accomplished it with her usual grace and cheerfulness. Danny's presence gave Mother Tola a great deal of pleasure. Towards the end of her life, she was hospitalized at Booth Memorial Hospital with intestinal obstruction. It is strange that the one physician who was kindest to her and spent a great deal of time with her, was a young trainee from Germany. I shall always be grateful to him, and I once told him that I considered it ironic that a member of the nation that caused her so much pain and loss, should be the one to now give her so much comfort.

The tenor of the times built a wall of silence around patients dying from cancer. I sat for hours at Mother Tola's bedside. I would have liked so much to review our life together and express my deep gratitude for her unconditional love, her many sacrifices, and the gift of a meaningful life. I wanted to reassure her that her life would continue in me and in many future generations. I am equally sure that she would have wanted to share her feelings with me, but social taboos were too powerful for us, and so we both sat in silence, each wrapped in our own thoughts, never sharing them.

When Mother Tola died on July 1, 1965, at the age of 56, I had to arrange the funeral.[156] Mother Tola never went to synagogue and didn't have a rabbi.

[156] Mother Tola and her husband are buried in the Cedar Park-Beth El Cemeteries in Westwood NJ. Their graves are in the Grothel Group Block 20 #57 and 58.

The funeral director at Riverside Chapel recommended a rabbi, but I declined and decided to lead the service myself. Despite all the death I had seen, I had never been to a funeral, and so I went to a Judaica bookstore and bought a *siddur* that contained the burial service. I don't think that I have ever done anything more difficult, but I am profoundly grateful that I could conduct the service. In my eulogy I described our first meeting, our long and loving relationship, the uniquely fine qualities of selflessness and devotion that this woman had, and the great debt that I owed her. She literally rescued me and gave me the foundation for everything that I have been able to accomplish. She was so thrilled to have been able to see Danny and shared our happiness when we told her that Jean was pregnant again. When Debbie was born we gave her the middle name of Tova in her memory, both because Mother Tola was such a good person and because that was her Hebrew name.

After Mother Tola's death, we went on with our busy lives and lost contact with Nunek. One day, I received a distraught phone call from him. I drove to New York, found his behavior bizarre, and convinced him to seek psychiatric help. The psychiatrist at Elmhurst Hospital advised me that he was suicidal and needed urgent admission, but that they had no space. He suggested several private psychiatric institutions. I started phoning the list and finally found one in Amityville, NY that had space for him.

After a short stay in the Amityville hospital, he was discharged, but his behavior became even more bizarre. On March 11, 1973 I received a phone call that he had died of a massive stroke. I went to his funeral and felt badly that I had never been able to develop a closer relationship with him.

Our engagement.

Left-to-right: Jean, I, Jean's mother.

Jean and I after the ceremony.

Left-to-right: Jean, I, Rabbi Abraham Karp, Nunek Stark, Tola Stark, Jean's mother.

Jean getting into our 1953 Chevy to drive to the wedding.

Jean with her parents.

XV

AFTER-WORD

———·◆·———

WW II had an enormous impact on our family tree. Some branches were cut off before they had an opportunity to blossom. We shall never know the potential experiences and stories of the unborn. How many children and grandchildren would Uncles Benu and Ajzyk have had? What would they have been like? What might have been their contributions?

Other branches were cut down before the blossoms fully matured and could bear fruit. What kind of people would cousins Mała and Benyomin have become? What would our relationship have been?

Descendants of the branches that managed to cheat the Angel of Death have been scattered across the globe on several continents, and are members of several nationalities and religions. A number have been displaced several times, and it is a tribute to the resiliency of the human spirit that, for the most part, we have rebuilt our lives, and have contributed to our communities.

Our relationship to the land in which our ancestors were born, lived, and sometimes died, is complicated. As far as I know, no one has returned. That alone is evidence of how unwanted we have felt, and those lands are all the poorer for it.

My own emotions in relationship to my native land are ambivalent. I love the Polish language, Polish food, and Polish music. Whenever I have visited Poland, I have felt, much to my surprise, very much at home. And then suddenly I see anti-Jewish graffiti or read in between the lines of a news story, and realize that the feeling is not mutual; that I am not really wanted there. The German language brings back memories of my early childhood and my mother's love. And yet, when we visited Germany I found that as much as I enjoyed hearing women speak, I found the sound of men's voices disturbing.

For those of us who survived, how are we changed? What kind of person would I have become if I had remained at home with my parents in Poland? We will never know, but I would most certainly not be writing this in English, I would never have met Jean, and my descendants would not have been the same.

My childhood war experiences have obviously influenced my personality and life-decisions, but it is not clear how because life is not a double blind controlled study, and we can never be sure that specific events are necessarily cause and effect. I am reminded of the wonderful story that Dr. Scharer, our late professor of anatomy, once told us. He was trying to teach us that two events occurring simultaneously are not necessarily related, and told of the man who ran out of his hotel after the great San Francisco earthquake and fire, looked around and said, "All I did was pull the toilet chain and look what happened!" In one of the essays that I translated, my father states that all of us carry heavy burdens but, because we carry them on our backs, others can see them quite clearly, while we can only feel the burden of their weight. In other words, we may not be the best judges of our own character or motivation.

I have always been told that I am relatively free of complexes, and I have attributed this to my innate nature, a wonderful warm and loving early home life, and Mother Tola's unconditional love and attention. And yet, the disruption I experienced during my mid-childhood years has definitely affected me. I don't believe that a day has passed that I have not thought about those days. But I have never used my experiences to gain advantage or feel that I was entitled to anything. I have never dwelt on the "why me" question. On the contrary, I consider myself extremely fortunate to have survived when 1.5 million children did not, and I have always been conscious that my experiences imposed a special duty on me to make my life meaningful and worthy and to live the lives of those who could not do so themselves. As our children were growing and developing I tried very hard, perhaps too hard, to

shield them from my childhood traumas. I have noted that I tend to avoid strife and confrontation. I have seen what these can lead to and I have found that most issues can be resolved amicably by compromise. I am told that I have special skills in mediation and I have used those skills to great effect in my various leadership positions. This need to compromise and live and let live has made me uncomfortable around people who think they know the truth – such people are found in every walk of life, but are especially numerous in religious circles. I have always tried to see the best in people and find it impossible to hate people as a group. For example, in our home we have never said the prayer, "Pour out Thy Wrath…" when the door is opened for Elijah at the Seder, and I feel uncomfortable with the Av Harahamim prayer on Shabbat morning. I understand why these prayers were written, but I think they ultimately have a negative effect on us. People are always amazed that I cannot hate the Germans or the Poles as a people. Ultimately, hatred and anger are destructive. When I came back from my first trip to Poland I was invited to several synagogues to speak about the visit. Invariably, a holocaust survivor would ask me how I could go to such an awful country. I answered that everyone has to make up his own mind what the minimal number of righteous people a community needs to contain before it is condemned as totally evil. Abraham, in discussing the issue with God, was willing to settle for 10. It is true that Poland had its share of anti-Semites, but it also had the largest number of Righteous Gentiles. Should we then condemn the entire society? The Ukrainians were even worse anti-Semites, but some of them saved my life at a risk to their own. Would I do this if the situation were reversed? I hope so, but I am not at all certain.

My childhood experiences have made me self-reliant, but have also isolated me to a degree. Except for Jean, I have never had a "best friend," and I am uncomfortable in asking for help or relying on someone else. The positive effect of this is that I have not been afraid to take chances and try new experiences. I believe that my life experiences have also made me somewhat fatalistic. Too much in life is not under our control. Whenever I have faced a difficult challenge I would remind myself that I have already survived the most difficult challenge; any subsequent challenge pales in comparison and I can easily overcome it.

When I began studying Jewish history I had the recurring feeling that we were a train moving in a certain direction that was derailed, and that it was up to our generation to get it back on its track. As I look at my children and grandchildren, their lifestyles and value systems, I am reassured that Jean and I have succeeded. They know who they are and what they represent. They are thoughtful about their people's past and comfortable with our people's traditions and writings.

As I mentioned in the Foreword, I deliberately left out much about our children or grandchildren in these memoirs because that is their story, which I hope, they will someday add. Jean and I are very proud of the type of people they have become. Each of them is different and we have always celebrated that difference, but each has integrity, honesty, and a devotion to their people and their past.

Before concluding this family history and memoir, I want to thank my immediate family, Jean, and our children; our son, Danny and his children, Nava and Noam; our daughter Debbie, her husband, Rabbi David Small, and their children, Gabrielle, Sharone, and Ilan; and our son David and his wife, Aliza, and their children, Maia and Tamar for having made it all worthwhile.

Remember the past, learn from it, add your unique perception, and continue the tradition into the future!

INTRODUCTION TO APPENDICES

———•◆•———

The following appendices contain our family's genealogic tables. These should be examined with reference to the text where they are cross-referenced.

They are organized as follows;

Appendix 1-9:   Descendants of the children of my maternal great-grandparents, Charlotte and Leopold Altmann.

Appendix 10-25:   Descendants of my great-great-grandparents, the Koenigshoefers, Feuchtwengers, Lufts and Chameides.

These genealogic tables are organized as follows: "1" identifies the primary person; the + sign refers to his/her spouse; "2" refers to their children; "3" to their grandchildren; "4" to their great-grandchildren, etc.

APPENDIX 1

Descendants of Joseph Georg Altmann
and Therese Hirsch

———— • ◆ • ————

1 Joseph Georg Altmann^A b: Abt. 1868 in Kattowitz d: 01 May 1934 in
Frankfurt/Main, Germany
  + Therese Hirsch^B b: 1868 in Frankfurt, Germany d: 1949 in London, England (see
  also ancestry tree below)
    2 Hans Siegfried Altmann^C b: 1895 in Kattowitz d: 1983 in London
    2 Manfred Altmann^D b: 25 May 1900 in Kattowitz d: 02 Sep 1954 in Vevey,
    Switzerland
    +Johanna (Hanna) Mayer b: 1898 in Ettlinger, Germany d: 02 Sep 1954 in
    Vevey, Switzerland
        3 Eva Dorothea Altmann^E b: 16 Aug 1929 in Germany
        +Kenneth Bernard Alberman b: 09 May 1926 in London
            4 Deborah Hannah Alberman b: 24 Aug 1957
              +Neville John Young
                5 Rebecca Alice Young b: 03 Aug 1985
                5 Charlotte April Young b: 09 Apr 1987
                5 Martha Alexandra Young b: 07 Sep 1990
            4 David Mark Alberman b: 27 Feb 1959
              +Martha Judith Prevezer
                5 Samuel Nathan Alberman b: 25 Dec 1994
                5 Hannah Beatrice Alberman b: 15 Jul 1996
            4 Daniel Steven Alberman b: 22 Oct 1961
            4 Catherine Rachel Alberman b: 13 Mar 1964
              +Richard Stoneman
                5 Joseph Michael Stoneman b: 01 Nov 1997
    2 Richard Altmann^F b: 05 Apr 1905 in Kattowitz d: 28 Mar 1983 in Cairo, Egypt
    +Fanny Lifshitz b: 1908 in Alexandria, Egypt d: 1991 in Cairo, Egypt
    2nd Wife of Richard Altmann:
    +Samia Zahran b: 25 Sep 1925 in Alexandria, Egypt d: 12 Feb 1989 in
      Cairo, Egypt
        3 Nihad Josef Altmann b: 08 Jun 1957 in Cairo, Egypt^G
        +Hadya el Minyawi b: 16 Dec 1958 in Cape Town, South Africa
            4 Omar Josef Altmann b: 10 Jun 1986 in Cairo, Egypt
            4 Joseph Richard (Joey) Altmann b: 18 Dec 1988 in Cairo, Egypt
            4 Hannah Hadya Altmann b: 16 Feb 1993 in Cairo, Egypt

      3 Hans Tamer Altmann b: 15 May 1963 d: 1983 in London
       +Siegrid Rudnik
         4 Miriam Altmann
         4 Sarah Altmann
      3 Taghrid Altmann b: 29 Apr 1956 in Cairo, Egypt d: 17 Sep 1987 in London[H]
      3 Nevin Altmann b: 16 Apr 1960 in Cairo, Egypt
       +Ali Saad El Din
         4 Tamara Altmann b: 28 Jan 1987
   2 Elizabeth Charlotte (Lieselotte) Altmann b: 05 May 1908 in Kattowitz d: 22 Feb 1942 in Petropolis, Brazil
    +Stefan Zweig b: 28 Nov 1881 in Vienna, Austria d: 22 Feb 1942 in Petropolis, Brazil

Joseph Georg Altmann with his favorite dog, Juliana about 1934.

[A]**Joseph Georg,** his wife Therese, and two of their children, Manfred and Charlotte (Lotte), moved to Frankfurt am Main in 1921 when Kattowitz became part of Poland; their other two children, Hans and Richard remained in Katowice. Joseph Georg is said to have suffered a heart attack when his son, Richard, informed him that he planned to marry a Jewish divorcee with two children. According to one story (from Aunt Lotte), Richard was urged to leave Germany in order to spare his father further grief.

[B]**Therese (Tirzah) Hirsch** was the granddaughter of Rabbi Shimshon Raphael Hirsch from Frankfurt/Main, the founder of Modern Orthodoxy. Her father, Rabbi Mendel Hirsch was Rabbi Shimshon Raphael Hirsch's eldest son. He was a pedagogue and Biblical commentator who succeeded his father as the Headmaster of the Realschule in Frankfurt.

Rabbi Dr. Mendel Hirsch, Therese's father.

Volume of humorous poems, 'Joseph and His Brothers' composed by his siblings on the occasion of the marriage of Josef Georg Altmann to Tirzah Hirsch on August 20, 1895.

Tirzah (Therese) and Georg Altmann probably around 1920.

Ancestors of Therese Hirsch

```
                                              ┌── Raphael
                                              │   HIRSCH
                                              │   b:1777
                                              │   d:1857
                               ┌── Samson (Shimshon) Raphael
                               │   HIRSCH
                               │   b:1808
                               │   d:1888
              ┌── Mendel ──────┤
              │   HIRSCH       │           ┌── Gella
              │                │           │   HERZ
 Therese ─────┤                └── Johanna ┤   b:1786
 HIRSCH       │                   JUEDEL   │   d:1860
 m:20 Aug 1895│                   b:1805 in Braunschweig
 in Frankfurt/Main                 d:1882
 d:1949       │
              └── Doris
                  BALLIN
```

^C**Hans (Jan) Siegfried Altmann** remained in Katowice and married a non-Jewish woman whom he subsequently divorced. On the eve of WWII, in 1938, he went to London on a business trip, remained there, and remarried. He died childless.

^D**Manfred Altmann** and his wife, Johanna, were both physicians. They came to London in 1933, where they completed their medical education. They were killed in an automobile crash while vacationing in Switzerland in 1954.

ᴱ**Eva Dorothea Altmann Alberman** grew up and studied medicine in London. Her specialty was Public Health and she went on to become Professor of Clinical Epidemiology at the University Of London School of Medicine. She has made original contributions on cerebral palsy and congenital developmental disorders. I met her and her husband in the 1990s and found her to be a charming lady. Her entire family was very musical and her son played in the London Philharmonic Orchestra. She was most gracious and generous with information about her family and those Altmanns whom she had known. Eva inherited the bulk of Stefan Zweig's literary estate. By agreement, this material, which includes letters, postcards, telegrams, etc. was transferred in the mid-1970s to the Stefan Zweig Collection at Reed Library, SUNY Fredonia.

Eva Alberman circa 1950 (above) and in her study in London in the 1990s (right).

[F]**Richard Altmann** moved to Egypt in March 1929, home of his first wife Fanny Lifshitz, and married a second wife (allowed according to Egyptian law), Samia Zahran, a Moslem. The two wives raised the children together. Richard prospered in Egypt and became a friend and poker partner of Gamal Abdul Nasser, President of Egypt. His children and grandchildren continue to live in Egypt. Aunt Lotte told me that shortly after the end of WW II, Richard brought his children for a visit to London, and while at a relative's house asked whether their home was *kasher*. "Why do you ask? Since when do you care whether it is *kasher*?" asked his host. "I don't", Richard is said to have replied, "but my children will only eat *hallal*."[157]

Richard Altmann (right) with President Gamal Abdul Nasser in Cairo, Egypt.

Therese Hirsch Altmann with her son, Richard in England about 1946 or 1948.

[G]**Nihad Josef Altmann** is a businessman in Cairo. One son, Omar is a champion tennis player studying international business at Pepperdine University in California; the other, Joey, is studying at the University of Toronto.

[H]**Taghrid Altmann** died of a brain tumor.

---

[157] Most of this information was obtained from Aunt Lotte (Holtzmann) and represents what she heard from her Altmann relatives. Undoubtedly, the story is much more complex and the facts as remembered by the other side of the family would be different. This should be kept in mind generally with third hand information.

[1]**Elizabeth Charlotte Altmann** was an extremely intelligent but somewhat introverted person. She became secretary to the great interwar Austrian author, Stefan Zweig, in 1933. She was most devoted to him and, as can be noted from her margin manuscript notes, had a great influence on his writings. Stefan Zweig divorced his wife Friderike in 1938, and married Charlotte in Bath, England the following year. Stefan Zweig suffered bouts of depression, especially after his books were burned in Germany and his Austrian citizenship was revoked because he was Jewish. As an icon of German literature and proud of his Austrian heritage, Stefan Zweig was devastated by these actions of his countrymen and his stateless status. He was convinced that the Germans would win the war and did not feel safe in England. Therefore, shortly after their marriage, Stefan and Charlotte left England for the USA and, in 1941, sailed for Brazil. He appears to have relaxed there and his final note was a thank you to Brazil. He and Charlotte committed suicide together in Petropolis, Brazil on February 22, 1942. Since his suicide note does not mention his wife, it is not clear whether he knew that she would join him in death. His final note states:

> "Before I depart from this life, of my own free will and with a clear mind, I want urgently to fulfill one last duty: I want to give heartfelt thanks to this wonderful country of Brazil which has been for me and my work so good and hospitable a resting place.
>
> Every day I have learned to love this country better and nowhere would I have more gladly rebuilt my life, now that the world of my native tongue has perished for me and Europe, my spiritual home, is destroying itself. But one would need special powers to begin completely afresh when one has passed one's sixtieth

Children of Josef Georg and Therese Altmann, probably around 1914. Left-to-right: Richard, Manfred, Lotte, and Hans Siegfried.   *Lotte Altmann in late 1920s or early 1930s.*

year and mine have been exhausted by long years of homeless wandering. It seems to me therefore better to put an end, in good time and without humiliation, to a life in which intellectual work has always been an unmixed joy and personal freedom earth's most precious possession.

I greet all my friends! May they live to see the dawn after the long night is over! I, too impatient, am going on alone."

Left-to-right: sitting: Therese (Tirzah), Joseph Georg; standing: Richard, Manfred, and Lotte Altmann circa 1918.

Lotte Altmann and Stefan Zweig probably around 1938.

APPENDIX 2

Descendants of Ismar Max Altmann and Mania Perlberger

———— • ◆ • ————

1 Ismar Max Altmann[A] b: Abt. 1869 in Kattowitz d: Abt. 1945 in London, England
  +Mania Perlberger
    2 Heinrich (Heini) Altmann[B] b: Oct 1899 in Kattowitz
    2 Irene Altmann[C] b: 18 Jan 1902 in Kattowitz
      +Rodeck Holzer b: in Krakow
        3 Susi Holzer d: Abt. 1990 in London
        3 Lollek Holzer
          +Marilyn ? d: Abt. 1984 in London
            4 David Holzer b: 1959 in London
            4 Sasha Holzer b: in London
    2 Margarite (Tamar Gretel) Altmann[C] b: 18 Jan 1902 in Kattowitz d: in Israel
      +Zeev Witzig
        3 Arie Manfred Witzig
        +Zila Oshna
          4 Daphna Witzig
          4 Ilan Witzig
          4 Ron Dvir Witzig
            +Nurith Gartler
            5 Tom Witzig

[A]**Ismar Max Altmann** moved to Berlin when Katowice became part of Poland in 1921. At some point he and his wife managed to get to London and lived off Finchley Road.

[B]**Heinrich Altmann** survived the war and was in Berlin immediately after the war.

[C]**Irene and Margarite** (also known as Tamar and Gretel) were twins, although not identical. Margarite immigrated to Israel.

APPENDIX 3

Descendants of Hermann Altmann
and Louise Totemian

———— • ◆ • ————

1 Hermann Altmann[A] b: Abt. 1870 in Kattowitz d: 09 Dec 1934
 +Louise Totemian d: 01 Mar 1921
   2 Julian Altmann[B] b: 27 Aug 1901 in Katowice d: 18 Nov 1987 in Sao Paulo, Brazil
     +Ilse Kergel b: 27 Jul 1909 d: 27 Jul 1992 in Sao Paulo, Brazil
       3 Monica Altmann b: 18 Jun 1946 in Sao Paulo, Brazil
         +Jose Fazio Filho b: 15 Oct 1944
           4 Luiz Alberto Altmann Fazio b: 02 May 1975 in Sao Paulo, Brazil
             +Giselly Diniz b: 01 May 1975
           4 Gabriela Fazio de Calvalho b: 19 May 1970 in Sao Paulo, Brazil
             +Marcelo Pereira de Carvalho b: 08 Mar 1970
               5 Isabel Fazio de Carvalho b: 25 Oct 2000
               5 Marina Fazio de Carvalho b: 23 Apr 2004
           4 Silvia Fazio b: 03 Mar 1972 in Sao Paulo, Brazil
       3 Odette Altmann b: 04 May 1940 in Sao Paulo, Brazil
         +Joaquim Theodoro de Souza Campos b: 29 Dec 1937
           4 Juliana Altman de Souza Campos b: 31 Jan 1970 in Sao Paulo, Brazil
           4 Henrique Altman de Souza Campos b: 22 Oct 1973 in Sao Paulo, Brazil
   2 Joseph George (Joerg) Altmann[C] b: 23 Mar 1904 in Kattowitz d: 24 Aug 1982
   in Sao Paulo, Brazil
     +Roselotte Altmann b: 02 May 1911 in Beuthen d: 22 May 1994 in Frankfurt
   2nd Wife of Joseph George (Joerg) Altmann
     +Katharina Angelika Rafeld b: 05 Aug 1929
       3 Tomas George Altmann b: 09 Mar 1954
         +Joyce Dessimoni Rodrgues
           4 Arthur Rodrigues Altmann b: 28 Mar 1991
           4 Yasmin Rodrigues Altmann b: 19 Mar 1994
       3 Dino Antonio Altmann b: 09 Nov 1955
         +Elisa Bento de Carvalho
           4 George Altmann b: 07 Dec 1986
           4 Kira Altmann b: 25 Jul 1989
   2 Theodore Altmann b: 01 Jul 1909 in Kattowitz
2nd Wife of Hermann Altmann
+ Rosa Brill[D] d: in Israel

[A]**Hermann Altmann** was said to have had an easy going personality. He remained in Katowice after it became part of Poland in 1921. Hermann's Hebrew name was Chaim and I suspect that I was named in his memory, since my mother was pregnant with me at the time of her uncle Hermann's death. Hermann's first wife, **Louise Totemian** died in 1921, and he then married **Rosa Brill**, a kindergarten teacher in the Katowice Jewish community, with whom he had no children. After his death, Rosa Brill Altmann moved to Israel and survived the war there.

[B]**Julian Altmann** studied astronomy in Heidelberg and had a life-long interest in this subject. He was a studious individual who amassed a significant library and was also interested in philosophy and Greek. His wife, Ilse, was Protestant, but they both converted to Catholicism after their move to Brazil in November 1934. He settled in Sao Paulo and established a successful business, which continues as Altmann S.A. Importação e Comércio Av. das Nações Unidas, 13.771-Bl. I -7 Andar 04794-000 - São Paulo - SP - Brasil. He did not speak about his past, and his daughter, Monica Altmann Fazio, told me that she did not discover her Jewish roots until long after his death.

Left-to-right: Georg Joseph, Louisa, Hermann, and Julian Altmann about 1911.

Hermann Altmann in late 1920s or early 1930s.

^C**Joseph George (Joerg) Altmann** married his first cousin, Roselotte Altmann, daughter of Gottfried and Frieda (see Appendix 8) and lived in Beuthen, later known as Bytom, which was only three miles from Katowice, but on the other side of the Polish-German border. They emigrated to Bath, England with Charlotte Altmann and Stefan Zweig just prior to WW II, and from there to Brazil. They divorced in Brazil and Roselotte, now known as Rosa remarried. Her daughter by this marriage, Gabriella Fallscheer, an actress, uses the stage name of Gabriella Scheer in performances in France and Germany. Joseph married Katharina Angelika in Brazil, and they had two children.

^D**Rosa Brill Altmann** was a teacher in the Katowice synagogue kindergarten and went to Palestine after her husband's death in 1934. She lived with her sister and brother-in-law, Mitwoch, in Tel Aviv. Her brother-in-law was the Middle East representative of NCR (National Cash Register Company), and the family continues to run that business.

APPENDIX 4

Descendants of Artur Altmann and Adelheid Goldschmidt

———•◆•———

1 Artur Altmann[A] b: 22 Mar 1871 in Kattowitz d: 26 Jun 1938 in Bytom
 +Adelheid Goldschmidt[B] b: 29 Jan 1883 in Nurnberg, Germany d: 1969 in Milwaukee, WI
  2 Charlotte Altmann b: 1905 in Bytom d: 1991 in US
   +Fritz Herlitz d: in USA
    3 Stephanie Herlitz b: 1929
     +Arnold Kranzler
      4 Michael Kranzler
      4 Lynn Kranzler
       +Peter Detrik
        5 Sara Detrik
  2 Meta Altmann[C] b: 13 Dec 1908 in Beuthen d: May 5, 2008 in Milwaukee, WI
   +Siegfried Baruch b: 1902 in Germany d: 1966 in Chicago, IL
    3 Steven Baruch[D] b: 14 Jun 1944
     +Judy Spivek
      4 Laura Baruch b: 09 Apr 1975 in Milwaukee, WI
      4 David Baruch b: 05 Jul 1979 in Milwaukee, WI

[A]**Artur Altmann** and his brother, Gottfried (see Appendix 8), left Kattowitz when it became part of Poland in 1921, and settled in Beuthen (later Bytom) only about 3 miles away, but across the then Polish-German border. The two brothers established an "L. Altmann" branch store selling hardware and mining equipment in the Rynek and lived above the store. Artur was said not to have been very religious and chafed under his parents' influence. As a young man, he wanted very much to move to the United States but did not want to disappoint his parents. After his brother's (Gottfried) death in March 1938 and, seeing no hope after the Nazi takeover, he committed suicide.

The Altmann store in Beuthen (Bytom) owned by Artur and Gottfried Altmann.

Left-to-right: Lotte (Herlitz), Adelheid, Meta (Baruch), Artur Altmann circa 1914.

Artur Altmann in Prussian army.

Left-to-right: Lotte (Herlitz), Georg Becker, Meta (Baruch), Artur Altmann.

Adelheid Altmann

[B]**Adelheid Goldschmidt,** Artur's wife, escaped to the United States before WW II with their children, Charlotte and Meta.

[C]**Meta Altmann Baruch** had been a bookkeeper in her father's store in Beuthen. Jean and I visited her in Milwaukee, WI in May 1988 when she was 90 years old. Even then she was a live wire. In her youth, she told us, she had been a flapper and loved to go dancing. She and her cousin Jonas, Bruno's son (see Appendix 6), were in love but the family was against the marriage. Meta would not go against her parent's wishes but even so, many years later, there was a wistful expression and twinkle in her eye at the mention of his name.

[D]**Steven Baruch** lives with his family in Milwaukee where he is an active member of the Orthodox Jewish community. He was an administrator in the Milwaukee public school system and, after retiring, became a consultant to the Jewish schools and community.

Left-to-right: Steven, Meta, and Judy Baruch, and I on my visit in 1998.

APPENDIX 5

Descendants of Gertrud Altmann

1 Gertrud Altmann[A] b: 13 Jun 1872 in Kattowitz d: 28 Feb 1938 in Marienbad,
Czechoslovakia
+Naftali Thalmann d: Abt. 1920 in Germany
   2 Gustav Thalmann b: 1895 in Karlsruhe, Germany d: Abt. 1942 in Auschwitz
    +Klaire Fleishmann
      3 Kurt Thalmann b: Abt. 1923
      3 Werner Thalmann b: 05 Sep 1929 in Katowice, Poland d: Abt. 1942 in Lódz
   2 Theodor Thalmann[B] b: 21 May 1907 in Beuthen d: Abt. 1942 in Auschwitz
    +Else Trudy Blandowski b: 03 Apr 1904 in Berlin
      3 Theodor Thalmann b: Abt. 1931 in Beuthen d: Abt. 1942 during the Shoah
   2 Hermann Thalmann[C] b: 11 Nov 1898 in Karlsruhe, Germany d: 24 Apr 1955
   in Israel
    +Hedwig Kochmann b: 04 Feb 1902 d: 17 Dec 1971 in Israel
      3 Naphtali Thalmann[D] b: 30 Apr 1926 in Danzig
        +Chana d: 1987
        2nd Wife of Naphtali Thalmann:
        +Eva
      3 Eva Thalmann b: 1932 in Danzig d: 1943 in Israel
2nd Husband of Getrud Altmann:
 +Max (Michael) Heinemann
   2 Emil Heinemann
   2 Charlotte Heinemann
   2 Rosi Heinemann
   2 Judith Heinemann
   2 Manfred Heinemann[E]

[A]**Gertrud Altmann** was said to have had a wonderful disposition and always had candy for the children. She lived in Karlsruhe and died of natural causes.

Gertrud and Naftali Thalmann.

[B]**Theodor Thalmann** worked in the Altmann store in Katowice.

[C]**Hermann Thalmann** survived the war and lived in Herzliyah, Israel.

[D]**Naphtali Thalmann** escaped to Palestine in 1939 from his native Danzig and became an agronomist in Hadera. His first wife, Chana, died in 1987. He married Eva and with her had five children and 14 grandchildren. He has a doctorate in Historical Geography and taught in a Teacher's Seminary for 37 years.

[E]**Manfred Heinemann** managed to flee to Montevideo, Uruguay prior to WW II. He married and had a daughter.

Manfred Heinemann.

APPENDIX 6

Descendants of Bruno Altmann

———— • ◆ • ————

1 Bruno Altmann b: 12 Jun 1874 in Kattowitz d: 1943 in Warsaw ghetto
  +Jette Koenigshoefer b: 20 Jun 1882 in Fuerth, Bavaria d: 12 Jan 1912 in Kattowitz
    2 Jonas Altmann[A] b: 01 Mar 1907 in Kattowitz d: Abt. 1943
    2 Charlotte Altmann[B] b: 03 Mar 1908 in Kattowitz d: 19 Jul 1983 in London,
    England
    +Adolph Felsenstein d: 1988 in London, England
      3 Kenneth (Kurt) Norbert Felsenstein[C] b: 1929 d: 2000 in Israel
      +Miriam Wiolf b: 1935
        4 Esther Felsenstein
          +Aaron Thee
            5 Eytan Thee
            5 Noa Sarah Thee
            5 Addi Thee
            5 Yael Zipporah Thee
        4 David Felsenstein
          +Sima Danino
            5 Moriah Felsenstein
            5 Natanel Avraham Felsenstein
            5 Avidan Arieh Felsenstein
        4 Rosalyn Felsenstein
          +Reuben Steiner
            5 Frumah Leah Steiner
            5 Sarah Steiner
            5 Yaacov Yisrael Steiner
            5 Avraham Yeshayahu Steiner
            5 Rivka Steiner
            5 Moshe Tuvia Steiner
        4 Ruth Felsenstein
          +Harel
      3 Ilsa Felsenstein b: 1932
      +Isaac Teitelbaum b: 1927
        4 Mendel Teitelbaum
          +Sara Malka Lev
            5 Yaacov Teitelbaum
      3 Gertrude Felsenstein b: 1936
      +Eli Jaswon b: 1932
        4 Jonathan Jaswon

+Iris Leibovitz
    5 Elchanan Jaswon
    5 Michal Zipora Jaswon
    5 Yisroel Meir Jaswon
    5 Moshe Jaswon
    5 Sarah Jaswon
    5 Bracha Jaswon
    5 Tuvia Jaswon
    5 Shulamit Jaswon
4 Malka Jaswon
  +Joel Weintraub
    5 Benyomin Tuvia Weintraub
    5 Tamar Jona Weintraub
    5 Shmuel Mordechai Weintraub
    5 Yair Weintraub
    5 Yehudah Eliezer Weintraub
    5 Zipporah Yehudith Weintraub
4 Michael Jaswon
  +Esther Witto
    5 Yael Miriam Jaswon
    5 Nechama Jaswon
    5 Avraham Jaswon
    5 Pinchas Jaswon
    5 Hadassa Jaswon
4 Hannah Jaswon
  +Amazia Levy
    5 Sara Levy
    5 Yefet Nadav Levy
    5 Naomi Levy
    5 Raaya Levy
    5 Hadas Levy
    5 Ayala Levy
4 Rina Jaswon
  +Joseph Berger
    5 Dvora Rivka Berger
    5 Yisroel Meir Berger
4 Sharona Jaswon
  +Avraham Weisrozen
    5 Yael Weisrozen
2nd Wife of Bruno Altmann:
+Hannah Koenigshoefer[D] b: 10 Jul 1890 in Fuerth, Bavaria d: Abt. 1943 in
  Concentration Camp
    2 Norbert Altmann b: 29 Jun 1916 in Kattowitz d: 07 Mar 1926 in Katowice
    2 Leopold Altmann b: 17 Mar 1918 in Katowice
    2 Manfred Josef Altmann[E] b: 06 Jun 1919 in Katowice

^A**Jonas Altmann** was very much in love with his cousin Meta, daughter of Artur (see Appendix 4). The family was opposed to the marriage and Meta would not disobey them. Jonas eventually married and had a child who is said to have lived in Israel. His brother, Manfred, wrote me that Jonas and eight friends escaped the Warsaw ghetto and managed to cross Europe into Russia on foot with the aim of getting to British controlled territory in India. While in Uzbekistan, they were shot by the Russians as spies, since they were overheard speaking German.

^B**Charlotte Altmann** married Adolph Felsenstein, moved to London in the mid 1930s, and lived on Finchley Road. I visited with them a number of times in 1948-1949. Two of their children, Kenneth and Ilse moved to Israel. See the text for photo of the wedding of Charlotte and Adolph Felsenstein.

^C**Kenneth Felsenstein** moved from London to Israel. Jean and I visited him in 1990 and found him to be a gentle, very religious person. Ken died of ALS. His sister, Gertrude remained in London. All the children and grandchildren of both are very observant.

^D**Hannah Koenigshoefer Altmann:** Following Jettchen's death in 1912, Bruno married her sister, Hannah, on Mar 26, 1913 in Ansbach. In 1942, Bruno and Hannah were taken from Katowice to the Warsaw ghetto and are said to have perished during the 1943 ghetto uprising.

^E**Manfred Altmann** was sent, just prior to the beginning of WW II, to London to study at the City of London College. I corresponded with him briefly, after which, my letters were unanswered.

APPENDIX 7

Descendants of Martha Altmann
and Izak Koenigshoefer

———•◆•———

1 Martha (Miriam) Altmann b: 12 Jan 1876 in Kattowitz d: 23 Oct 1950 in
  Tel Aviv, Israel
 +Izak Koenigshoefer b: 03 Aug 1870 in Fuerth, Bavaria d: 1951 in Haifa, Israel
    2 Gella Koenigshoefer b: 14 Jun 1900 in Fuerth, Bavaria d: 23 Apr 1982 in
       Tel Aviv, Israel
       +Raphael Seeberger b: 1890 in Gunzhausen, Germany d: 1940 in Haifa,
       Israel {See Appendix 18 for descendants of Gella Koenigshoefer and Raphael
       Seeberger}
    2 Rosie Koenigshoefer b: 20 Dec 1901 in Fuerth d: 1992 in Tel Aviv, Isreal
    2 Betty Koenigshoefer b: 28 Mar 1903 in Fuerth, Bavaria d: Jul 1978 in Israel
       +Villie (Wilhelm) Gluck b: 04 Aug 1887 in Hungary d: Dec 1944 in Hungary
       {See Appendix 20 for descendants of Betty Koenigshoefer and Villie Gluck}
    2 Gertrude Koenigshoefer b: 25 Sep 1904 in Fuert, Bavaria d: Abt. 1943 in ?
       in Shoah
       +Kalman Chameides b: 25 Apr 1902 in Szczerzec, d: 25 Dec 1942 in Lwow
       {See Appendix 22 for descendants of Gertrude Koenigshoefer and Kalman
       Chameides}
    2 Charlotte Koenigshoefer b: 27 Mar 1906 in Furth, Bavaria d: 03 Mar 2003
       in Jerusalem, Israel
       +Julius (Ulu) Bernet b: 31 Oct 1898 in Bamberg, Germany d: 27 Apr 1944 in
       Newcastle/Tyne, England {See Appendix 21 for descendants of
       Charlotte Koenigshoefer and Julius Bernet}
       2nd Husband of Charlotte Koenigshoefer:
       +Max Holtzmann b: in Mainz, Germany d: 1957 in England
    2 Johni Kaye b: Aug 31,1915 in Fuerth, Bavaria d: May 5, 1949 in
       Newcastle/Tyne, England
       +Klara Ehrlich b: 1918 in Czechoslovakia d: 13 Apr 2006 in Tel Aviv, Israel
       {See Appendix 24 for descendants of Johni Kaye and Klara Ehrlich}

APPENDIX 8

Descendants of Gottfried Altmann and Frieda Warschauer

———— • ◆ • ————

1 Gottfried Altmann[A] b: 1878 in Kattowitz d: 10 Mar 1938 in Beuthen
+Frieda Warschauer d: 1940
     2 Emil Altmann[B]
         3 Susana Altmann
     2 Roselotte Altmann[C] b: 02 May 1911 in Beuthen d: 22 May 1994 in Frankfurt
         +Joseph George (Joerg) Altmann[D] b: 23 Mar 1904 in Kattowitz d: 24 Aug
         1982 in Sao Paulo, Brazil
     2nd Husband of Roselotte Altmann:
         +Kurt Fallscheer b: 1906 d: 1981
         3 Gabriela Fallscheer[E]

[A]**Gottfried Altmann** and his brother, Artur, left Katowice when it became Polish in 1921 and established a similar store to their father's in nearby Beuthen (Bytom). The store was located in the center of town, the Rynek, on the ground floor with living quarters for the two families above (see Appendix 4). Gottfried died of an apparent heart attack in 1938. His granddaughter told me that he came home for lunch, didn't feel well, lay down on the living room couch, and died.

Roselotte Altmann.

[B]**Emil Altmann** died in Buenos Aires. He apparently had a daughter, Susanna, and three grandchildren. Susanna was involved in an automobile crash that left her brain injured.

[C]**Roselotte Altmann** married her first cousin, [D]**Joseph Georg (Joerg) Atmann** (see Appendix 3). They fled Beuthen (Bytom) in 1938 and went to Bath, England together with Charlotte Altmann and Stefan Zweig. They then went to Brazil where they divorced. Each remarried. Joerg's family, now Catholic, remained in Brazil, while Roselotte and her husband with their daughter went back to Europe after the war.

[E]**Gabriella Fallscheer** lives in France and performs on stage in France and in Germany under the stage name of Gabriella Scheer.

APPENDIX 9

Descendants of Robert Altmann

1 Robert Altmann[A] b: Mar 07, 1883 in Kattowitz d: 25 Nov 1938 in Buchenwald
   Concentration Camp
 +Elly Boehm
      2 Herbert Altmann[B] b: 20 Apr 1909 in Kattowitz
          3 Dusan Altmann
          3 Miriam Gal Altmann
      2 Suzanne Charlotte Altmann[C] b: 06 Oct 1912 in Kattowitz
      2 Marianne Altmann[D] b: 13 Oct 1916 in Kattowitz
          3 Ayeleth Altmann
          3 Idu Altmann
2nd Wife of Robert Altmann:
   +Ruth Valeria?[E] b: Abt. 1895 in Germany d: Abt. 1990 in Israel
      2 Leopold Jehudah Altmann[F]

[A]**Robert Altmann** moved to Breslau when Katowice became Polish in 1921, and started a business there. He was arrested during Kristallnacht in November 1938 and sent to Buchenwald Concentration Camp. According to his son, Jehudah, who was in an old age home in Israel when I spoke with him, his father's body was returned by the Gestapo in a sealed coffin with strict instructions that it not be opened. The Buchenwald Death Book gives his date of death as November 25, 1938.[158]

[B]**Herbert Altmann** was very musical and wanted to be a conductor. He was a communist, fought with Tito's partisan army in Yugoslavia during WW II, and married a fellow partisan (non-Jewish). Both Herbert and his wife were killed by Chetnick rebels. Dusan Altmann remained in Belgrade and Miriam Gal lived on Kibbutz Givath Haim in Israel.

[C]**Suzanne Charlotte Altmann** worked in the Jewish Hospital in Breslau. During WW II, she was sent to Theriesenstadt and then was transported to Auschwitz. The transport is said not to have reached Auschwitz because of a revolt on the way. She was, however, never heard from again. She was said to have had an unusually beautiful blonde son who was abducted.

^D**Marianne Altmann** was one of the founders of Kibbutz Givath Haim in Yihud, Israel. She was very religious and had three children (I only know the names of two) and 14 great grandchildren.

^E**Ruth Valeria Altmann** was a German convert to Judaism. After her husband's death, she was approached by the Nazis and told that she would not be harmed if she converted back to Christianity. She refused and managed to escape to England in 1939 with her son, Leopold Jehudah, and supported herself by cleaning houses. In 1955 she moved to Israel and became a member of the chevra kadisha of Haifa, helped the Rabbinate of Haifa to prepare women for conversion, and, after learning Braille, translated 15 books into Braille. When she was almost 90 years old, she wrote a book on Judaism.[159] In the introduction she wrote: "I was born a child of Christian parents. In time I realized that the Christian religion was entirely based on the Jewish religion and that the alteration which the founders of the Christian religion made was unacceptable to me...I also realized that the practice of the Christian religion gave me no fulfillment and that I had to return to the original religion, our Jewish religion. I had good friends who were Jewish, from whom I borrowed the books I needed and they often took me along when they went to the synagogue. I felt very comfortable in the company of Jewish women and liked the system of divine worship and the atmosphere of unity. Above everything else I was enthusiastic about the ethical level and the high morality upon which God sealed his covenant with Noah. I understood that these commandments were given as the last testament of Noah to his descendants and thereby to all mankind. At last I was ready to convert. At that time I lived in Hamburg with my married sister. I understood that for a proper conversion I could only consider Dr. Salomon Shpitzer, the Orthodox Rabbi. During my first visit to him he was very restrained since he was generally against accepting converts. After a lengthy interview however he gave me a small volume with the title "Hebrew Reader" by Michael Abraham and he said, "with this book you will learn Hebrew by yourself and when you are able to read the first chapter of the shema you will return." The Rabbi added, "also read the five books of Moses in German translation." I studied day and night for four weeks and I was able to read. When I returned to Rabbi Shpitzer after such a relatively short time, he asked me with surprise, "you already know how to read?" When I read the first chapter of the shema to him he said, "now I know that you want to be Jewish out of conviction and I will therefore help you." The Rabbi instructed the Principal of the Hamburg Talmud Torah, Dr. Yitzhak Hineman to give me instruction. I converted in 1925 and in 1926 I married a very religious man who was killed in Buchenwald on November 25, 1938."

[159] V. Altmann, *The Jewish Way of Life-Shaarei Yahaduth: Moreh Derech Lechayei Yom Yom Yehudim* (Nezer David, Jerusalem 5745-1986).

In the 1960s, she was contacted by her brother, a former Nazi who became a Priest after WW II, and who wanted to reconcile with her. She finally agreed to meet him, but only in Israel, and only in a coffee shop. She then wanted no further contact with him.

^F**Leopold Jehudah Altmann** was a member of the Jewish Brigade. He never married and when I contacted him in the 1990s he was living in an old age home in Israel and didn't remember much.

APPENDIX 10

Descendants of Emanuel Loeb Koenigshoefer

———— • ◆ • ————

1 Emanuel Mendel Loeb Koenigshoefer b: 06 Jun 1806 in Ermreuth, Germany d:
   13 Jan 1878 in Fuerth, Bavaria
  +Merle Miriam Suggenheimer b: in Theilheim, Bavaria d: 25 Jul 1847 in
   Welbhausen, Germany
      2 Babette (Bella) Koenigshoefer b: 09 Dec 1836
        +Emanuel Bodenheimer b: in Hamburg, Germany
      2 Fratel Koenigshoefer b: 18 Jan 1839 in Welbhausen d: Sep 1840 in Welbhausen
      2 Moses Jonas Koenigshoefer b: 10 Apr 1840 in Welbhausen, d: 28 Jun 1894 in
        Fuerth, Bavaria
        +Rebecca Ottenheimer b: 26 May 1844 in Kleinerdlingen, Germany
        d: 08 Mar 1868 in Fuerth, Bavaria
          3 Unknown Koenigshoefer b: 04 Mar 1868 in Fuerth, Bavaria
            d: 04 Mar 1868
        2nd Wife of Moses Jonas Koenigshoefer:
          + Lea Feuchtwanger b: 22 Sep 1850 in Schwabach, d: 15 Mar 1919 in
            Fuerth, Bavaria
          3 Unknown Koenigshoefer b: 28 Mar 1869 in Fuerth, Bavaria
            d: 28 Mar 1869 in Feurth, Bavaria
          3 Izak Koenigshoefer b: 03 Aug 1870 in Fuerth, Bavaria
            d: 1951 in Haifa, Israel
            +Martha (Miriam) Altmann b: 12 Jan 1876 in Kattowitz d: 23 Oct 1950 in
              Tel Aviv, Israel {See Appendix 7 Descendants of Martha Altmann and Izak
              Koenigshoefer}
          3 Meir Loeb Koenigshoefer b: 27 Feb 1872 in Fuerth, Bavaria d: 1962 in
            Jerusalem, Israel
            +Bertha Kahn b: 12 Dec 1880 d: 1970 in Jerusalem, Israel {See Appendix 12
            Descendants of Meir Loeb Koenigshoefer and Bertha Kahn}
          3 Samuel Gedaliah Koenigshoefer b: 24 Nov 1873 in Fuerth, Bavaria
            d: in Israel
            +Rosa Freundlich b: in Nürnberg, Germany {See Appendix 13
            Descendants of Samuel Gedalia and Rosa Freunlich}
          3 Merle Miriam Koenigshoefer b: 06 Feb 1875 in Fuerth, d: 05 Jul 1942 in
            Sobibor Concentration Camp
            +Salomon Bamberger b: 1860 d: 1920 in Hanau, Germany {see Appendix
            14 Descendants of Merle Koenigshoefer and Salomon Bamberger}

3 Fannie Koenigshoefer b: 22 Aug 1876 in Fuerth, Bavaria d: in Israel
  +Laiser (Eliezer) Wolff d: in Israel {See Appendix 15 Descendants of Fannie
    Koenigshoefer and Laiser (Eliezer) Wolff}

3 Bella Koenigshoefer b: 04 Mar 1878 in Fuerth, Bavaria d: 17 Jul 1968 in
  Kibbutz Hafetz Haim, Israel
  +Aaron Arnold Cohn b: 1873 in Hamburg, Germany d: 03 Mar 1966 in
  Kibbutz Hafetz Haim, Israel {See Appendix 19 Descendants of Bella
  Koenigshoefer and Aaron Arnold Cohn}

3 Emanuel Loeb Koenigshoefer b: 27 Sep 1879 in Fuerth, Bavaria d: 01 Nov
  1905 in Berlin, Germany

3 Unknown Koenigshoefer b: 18 Jun 1881 in Fuerth, Bavaria
  d: 18 Jun 1881 in Fuerth, Bavaria

3 Jette Koenigshoefer b: 20 Jun 1882 in Fuerth, Bavaria d: 12 Jan 1912
  in Kattowitz
  +Bruno Altmann b: 12 Jun 1874 in Kattowitz d: 1943 in Warsaw ghetto
  {See Appendix 6 Descendants of Bruno Altmann}

3 Betty Koenigshoefer b: 30 Dec 1883 in Fuerth, Bavaria d: in Breslau, Germany
  +Heinrich Siechel b: in Germany
   4 Fanny Siechel

3 Gelche Karoline Koenigshoefer b: 30 Jan 1885 in Fuerth, Bavaria
  d: 06 May 1886

3 Leopold Wolf Koenigshoefer b: 13 Apr 1886 in Fuerth, Bavaria
  d: in Aushwitz
  +Else Loewenstein b: in Fulda, Germany {See Appendix 17 Descendants
  of Leopold Koenigshoefer}

3 Frieda Koenigshoefer b: 29 Jul 1887 in Fuerth Bavaria d: 26 May 1889 in
  Fuerth, Germany

3 Joseph Koenigshoefer b: 14 Nov 1888 in Fuerth, Bavaria d: 23 Aug 1916
  (or 3 Feb 1916) in Kirlibaba, Stry, Romania

3 Hannah Koenigshoefer b: 10 Jul 1890 in Fuerth, Bavaria d: Abt. 1943 in
  Concentration Camp
  +Bruno Altmann 1943 b: 12 Jun 1874 in Kattowitz d: 1943 in Warsaw
  ghetto {See Appendix 6 Descendants of Bruno Altmann}

2 Samuel Koenigshoefer b: 06 Aug 1843 in Welbhausen d: 25 Jun 1915 in
Frankfurt/Main, Germany
+Helena Flamm (Schoenfeld) b: 16 Mar 1842 in Dornheim bei Helmitzheim,
Bavaria d: 09 Feb 1929 in Frankfurt/Main, Germany {See Appendix 16
Descendants of Samuel Koenigshoefer and Helena Flamm (Schoenfeld)}

2 Jettchen Koenigshoefer[A] b: 1847 in Welbhausen, Germany d: Feb 1, 1928 in Koeln,
Germany
+Rabbi Salomon Shalom Wolf b: 1830 in Crutenburg, Germany d: 17 Aug
1892 in Koeln

3 Joseph Wolf b: 1875 in Crtutenburg, Germany d: 1944 in Theresienstadt
  +Malchen Marianne Koenigshoefer {See Appendix 16 Descendants of
  Samuel Koenigshoefer and Helena Flamm (Schoenfeld)}

3 Jonas Wolf

+? Bodenheimer
    4 Menachem Arieh Wolf
    4 Shalom Wolf
2nd Wife of Emanuel Mendel Loeb Koenigshoefer:
+Jeanette Mork b: 01 Jun 1811 in Euerbach, Germany d: 19 May 1905 in
  Fuerth, Bavaria

[A]**Jettchen Koenigshoefer** was left with the task of raising 11 small children when her husband died in 1892 at the age of 62. She appears to have done a remarkable job as described in a glowing obituary in Der Israelit. Her mother, Merle Miriam Sugger-heimer, died when giving birth to her in 1847 and, as a result she was said to have had an unusually close relationship with her stepmother, Jeanette Mork.

Betty and Heinrich Siechel with their daughter, Fanny.

Betty and Heinrich Siechel with their daughter Fanny and friends probably around 1910.

APPENDIX 11

Descendants of Meir Feuchtwanger
and Fradel ?

————•◆•————

1 Meir Feuchtwanger b: 1759; d: before Sep 1839
 +Fradel d: before 1844
   2 Nathan Feuchtwanger b: 21 Apr 1809 in Schwabach, Bavaria d: Apr 1899 in
     Schwabach, Bavaria
    +Gelche Bechhofer
      3 Mayer Feuchtwanger b: 22 Jun 1840 in Schwabach, Bavaria
      3 Low Wolf Feuchtwanger b: 22 Sep 1841 in Schwabach, Bavaria
      3 Joseph Feuchtwanger b: 26 Nov 1842 in Schwabach, Bavaria
      3 Fradel Feuchtwanger b: 23 Jan 1844 in Schwabach, Bavaria
      3 Bayla Feuchtwanger b: 08 Sep 1845 in Schwabach, Bavaria
      3 Juttel Feuchtwanger b: 19 Oct 1847 in Schwabach, Bavaria
      3 Perla Feuchtwanger b: 18 Jan 1849 in Schwabach, Bavaria
      3 Leah Feuchtwanger b: 22 Sep 1850 in Schwabach, Bavaria d: 15 Mar 1919
        in Fuerth, Bavaria
        +Moses Jonas Koenigshoefer b: 10 Apr 1840 in Welbhausen, Lower
          Franconia d: 28 Jun 1894 in Fuerth, Bavaria m: 1877 {See Appendix 10
          Descendants of Emanuel Loeb Koenigshoefer}
      3 Jacob Feuchtwanger b: 28 Apr 1853 in Schwabach, Bavaria
      3 Regine Rethel Feuchtwanger b: 23 Aug 1854 in Schwabach, Bavaria
      3 Hanne Feuchtwanger b: 12 Jun 1856 in Schwabach, Bavaria
      3 Unknown Feuchtwanger b: 05 Jul 1858 in Schwabach, Bavaria d: 05 Jul
        1858 in Schwabach, Bavaria
      3 Unknown Feuchtwanger b: 22 Sep 1859 in Schwabach, Bavaria d: 22 Sep
        1859 in Schwabach, Bavaria
      3 Salomon Feuchtwanger b: 26 Feb 1862 in Schwabach, Bavaria
   2 Salomon Feuchtwanger b: 08 Mar 1812 in Schwabach, Bavaria
    +Ester Simonsfeld
      3 Mayer Feuchtwanger b: 24 Sep 1839 in Schwabach, Bavaria
      3 Fradel Feuchtwanger b: 03 Sep 1840 in Schwabach, Bavaria
      3 Fanny Feuchtwanger b: 16 Oct 1841 in Schwabach, Bavaria
      3 Simon Feuchtwanger b: 22 Nov 1843 in Schwabach, Bavaria
      3 Nathan Feuchtwanger b: 15 Sep 1845 in Schwabach, Bavaria
      3 Heyum Feuchtwanger b: 17 Dec 1846 in Schwabach, Bavaria
      3 Jette Feuchtwanger b: 05 Nov 1848 in Schwabach, Bavaria

3 Vogel Feuchtwanger b: 05 Dec 1850 in Schwabach, Bavaria

3 Joseph Bar Feuchtwanger b: 06 Sep 1852 in Schwabach, Bavaria

3 Sophie Feuchtwanger b: 13 Mar 1856 in Schwabach, Bavaria

2 Hanna Feuchtwanger b: 17 Sep 1813 in Schwabach, Germany

2 Rosetta (Rosalie) Feuchtwanger b: 18 Oct 1817 in Schwabach, Germany

APPENDIX 12

Descendants of Meir Loeb Koenigshoefer and Bertha Kahn

—— • ◆ • ——

1 Meir Loeb Koenigshoefer[A] b: 27 Feb 1872 in Fuerth, Bavaria d: 1962 in Jerusalem, Israel
+Bertha Kahn b: 12 Dec 1880 d: 1970 in Jerusalem, Israel
    2 Martha Koenigshoefer[B] b: 24 Aug 1903 in Fuerth, Bavaria d: Mar 1932 in London, England
    +Leo Yehudah Pinhas Kohn[C] b: 1894 in Frankfort/Main, Germany d: 03 Jun 1961 in Israel
        3 Mordechai Kohn[D] b: 22 Feb 1932 in London, England
        +Gloria Caroline Stollard b: in London, England
    2 Klarchen (Clara) Koenigshoefer[E] b: 02 Nov 1904 in Fuerth, Bavaria d: 1945 in Israel

[A]**Meir Loeb Koenigshoefer** immigrated to Palestine via London in 1939. When he was 90 years of age, he wrote his memoirs, which I have translated into English and which I quote in the text. His memoirs have not been published but are available at the Leo Beck Institute in New York.

A drawing of Meir Loeb Koenigshoefer from the cover of his memoirs.

Meir (3rd row center) and Berta (2nd row on right) Koenigshoefer with their two daughters, Clairchen and Martha.

Wedding of Martha Koenigshoefer and Leo (Yehuda Pinchas) Kohn in March 1931. Next to the groom is Klarchen K. (sister of the bride); front row, third from left is Meir Koenigshoefer, and his wife, Bertha (4th from left); Samuel Gedalia Koenigshefer is in front row (7th from left) and on his right is his wife, Rosa; to Samuel's left is Malchen (Merle Miriam) Koenigshoefer and next to her (extreme right front) is Bella K. Cohn.

[B]**Martha Koenigshoefer** was a teacher in the Jewish school of Stuttgart. She married **Leo (Yehudah Pinchas) Kohn** who was then the Political Advisor to the Jewish Agency in London. Shortly after her son's *brit mila* (circumcision) in 1932, she was not feeling well and went to lie down. When her attendant went to check on her, she found her dead.

[C]**Leo Kohn** [From Encyclopedia Judaica]: "Israel scholar and diplomat. Kohn settled in Palestine in 1921. For 27 years he was at the center of Israel and Zionist diplomatic activity. In 1932 he went to Dublin where he wrote a study of the constitution of the Irish Free State. From 1934 he was Political Secretary of the Jewish Agency and from 1948 to 1952 he was Political Adviser to Chaim Weitzmann. From the establishment of the State (1948) until his death, Kohn served as Political Adviser to the Ministry of Foreign Affairs. In recognition of his services he was given the personal rank of Ambassador in 1958. From 1953 he also held the Chair of International Relations at the Hebrew University. His draft constitution for Israel was adopted as the basis for deliberations of the Constitution Commission of the State Council in 1948. Kohn's draft constitution stipulated Israel's historical claim to Eretz Yisrael, followed Jewish teachings on the sanctity of Jewish life and the dignity of man, and rejected the death penalty and all forms of degrading punishment. However the Knesset decided to legislate a series of Basic Laws that would eventually be consolidated into a written constitution." Israel has still not adopted a constitution.

ᴰ**Mordechai Kohn's** mother died after his *brit mila* (circumcision) and he lived with his grandparents in Germany. In 1939, when his grandparents went to Israel, he was returned to his father in England. He now lives in Germany.

ᴱ**Klarchen (Clara) Koenigshoefer** was a graduate of a Jewish Teacher's college and taught in the Israelitische Volkschule in Würzburg. She immigrated to Palestine in December 1935 and taught in the Maaleh School. She developed severe pneumonia in 1945, was hospitalized, and died suddenly of a pulmonary embolus.

APPENDIX 13

Descendants of Samuel Gedalia Koenigshoefer and Rosa Freundlich

———— • ◆ • ————

1 Samuel Gedaliah Koenigshoefer b: 24 Nov 1873 in Fuerth, Bavaria
  d: 1962 in Jerusalem, Israel
 +Rosa Freundlich b: in Nurnberg, Germany
    2 Moshe Jona Koenigshoefer[A]
    2 Leo Koenigshoefer[B] d: Abt. 1989 in Israel

[A]**Moshe Jona Koenigshoefer** was a physician who lived in Tel Aviv. Menachem Begin used his passport as a cover while hiding from the British in 1947. In his book, *The Revolt,* Begin writes: "Quite by chance a passport had been found in one of the public libraries in the name of Dr. Yonah Koenigshoefer. It was a rather long name but it had the advantage of being purely 'Germanic.' It was a name reeking of royalty and the preservation of law and order. So it was decided to suit me to the passport, or rather to adapt my new photograph to it."

[B]**Leo Koenigshoefer** lived in Israel; his daughter lives in Marseille, France.

Leo Koenigshoefer.

APPENDIX 14

Descendants of Merle Miriam Koenigshoefer and Salomon Bamberger

———•◆•———

1 Merle Miriam Koenigshoefer[A] b: 06 Feb 1875 in Fuerth, Bavaria d: 05 Jul 1942 in Sobibor Concentration Camp
+Salomon Menachem Bamberger[B] b: 1860 d: 1920 in Hanau, Germany
    2 Isaac Bamberger d: in Tel Aviv, Israel
    2 Jonas Moshe Bamberger d: in Concentration Camp
    2 Julie (Julchen) Bamberger[C] d: in USA
      +? Katz
    2 Gella Bamberger d: in Israel
      +? Heckscher
    2 Benno Yitzhak Dov Bamberger d: Abt. 1943 in Concentration Camp

[A]**Merle Miriam Koenigshoefer** was also known as Amale and Malchen. She was deported from Frankfurt/Main to Westbrook and killed in the Sobibor Extermination Camp on Tammuz 20.

Greetings from the wedding of Malshen (Konigshofer) and Rabbi Slomo Bamberger. 28 June 1898.

[B]**Salomon Bamberger** was a rabbi in Bingen, Burgepreppach, and Hanau. He was a member of a famous German rabbinic family and a descendant of the Wurzburger Rav. He gave a D'var Torah at the wedding of my grandparents, Izak Koenigshoefer and Miriam Altmann, and gave my grandmother an engagement gift of an inscribed Tzena U'rena, which I have.

[C]**Julie Bamberger** lived in an orphanage in Switzerland, then in Israel, and finally in the United States.

APPENDIX 15

Descendants of Fannie Koenigshoefer
and Laiser Wolff

———— • ◆ • ————

1 Fannie Koenigshoefer b: 22 Aug 1876 in Fuerth, Bavaria d: in Israel
  +Laiser (Eliezer) Wolff d: in Israel
    2 ? Wolff[A]
    2 Theo Wolff[B] d: 1948 in Israel
    2 Moshe Yona Wolff b: Abt. 1910 d: Abt. 1991 in Jerusalem, Israel
      +Else Hecht
        3 Eliezer Wolf[C] b:1938
    3 Ruth Wolff

[A][?] **Wolff** (first name unknown) was mentally ill and was killed by the Nazis as part of their effort to kill all "non-useful" members of society.

[B]**Theo Wolff** was killed in Israel's War of Independence.

[C]**Eliezer Wolf** is a well-known lawyer, businessman, and university lecturer in Jerusalem. He earned a Masters and Doctorate in Law from the Hebrew University

APPENDIX 16

Descendants of Samuel Koenigshoefer and Helena Flamm (Schoenfeld)

———•◆•———

1 Samuel Koenigshoefer[A] b: 06 Aug 1843 in Welbhausen, Middle Franconia
  d: 25 Jun 1915 in Frankfurt/Main, Germany. Married May 19, 1870
 +Helena Flamm (Schoenfeld) b: 16 Mar 1842 in Dornheim bei Helmitzheim,
  Bavaria d: 09 Feb 1929 in Frankfurt/Main, Germany
    2 Jonas Koenigshoefer[B] b: 17 Sep 1873 in Frankfurt/M, Germany
      d: 06 Aug 1946 in Copenhagen, Denmark
     +Rachel Recha Bamberger[C] b: 24 Apr 1885 in Würzburg, Bavaria
      d: 01 Jan 1981 in Jerusalem, Israel
      3 Nathan Koenigshoefer[D] b: 05 Nov 1920 in Frankfurt/Main, Germany
       +Inger Cohn b: 1928 in Copenhagen, Denmark
         4 Joergen Koenigshoefer b: 15 Aug 1949 in Copenhagen, Denmark
          +Elaine Trizant
            5 Michael Koenigshoefer
            5 Judith Koenigshoefer
         4 Lilian Koenigshoefer[E] b: 16 Dec 1952 in Copenhagen, Denmark
          +Dan Arbel b: 1937
            5 Jonathan Arbel
            5 Adam Arbel
            5 Sarah Arbel
         4 Annette Koenigshoefer b: 05 Mar 1962 in Copenhagen, Denmark
          +Michell Donath b: 1959
            5 Jeremi Donath b: 1996
      3 Martha Martel Koenigshoefer[F] b: 15 Aug 1915 in Frankfurt/Main, Germany
       +Max Koplowitz b: 29 Mar 1907 in Strassburg, Alsace d: 1982 in Kfar
       Haroeh, Israel
       2nd Husband of Martha Martel Koenigshoefer:
       +Ephraim (Gustav) Gruenbaum[G] b: 05 Jul 1914 in Würzburg, Bavaria
       d: 1969 in Jerusalem, Israel
         4 Judith Gruenbaum b: 09 Mar 1940 in Israel
          +? Kadmon
         4 Uri Gruenbaum b: 07 May 1942 in Israel
         4 Raphi Gruenbaum b: 04 Apr 1945 in Israel
         4 Chanah Gruenbaum b: 11 Jan 1947 in Israel
          +? Weiner

4 Arie Gruenbaum b: 06 Feb 1951 in Israel
4 Ruthi Gruenbaum b: 12 Jul 1955
+? Berger b: 12 Jul 1955 in Israel
3 Kela Koenigshoefer b: 31 Jan 1917 in Würzburg, Bavaria
d: 09 Mar 1918 in Würzburg, Bavaria
2 Jakob Loeb Koenigshoefer b: 03 Jul 1872 in Frankfurt, Germany
d: 27 Dec 1943 in Theresienstadt
+Helene Tarlowski 1945 b: 11 Aug 1885 in Halberstadt, Magdeburg
d: 08 May 1945 in Auschwitz
3 Emanuel Koenigshoefer[H]
3 Siegfried Koenigshoefer
3 Miriam Koenigshoefer
+? Schauli
2 Josef Heimann Koenigshoefer[I] b: 09 May 1879 in Frankfurt/Main, Germany
d: 1941
+Annie Nelken b: 10 Sep 1892 in Lodz, Poland
3 Leo Ganiel
3 Erich Arie Ganiel
2 Naftali Koenigshoefer b: 08 Sep 1875 in Frankfurt/Main, Germany
d: 25 Mar 1943 in Concentration Camp
+Esther Jacobson b: 17 Mar 1885 in Hamburg, Germany
d: 03 Feb 1943 in Aushwitz
3 Manfred Kingshoff[J] b: 1909 in Hamburg, Germany
3 Lore Kingshoff[K] b: 22 Sep 1922
+Roger Bryan
3 Senta Kingshoff
2 Simoni Koenigshoefer
+? Eismann
3 Blanka Eismann
3 Else Eismann
3 Sigi Eismann
2 Emanuel Koenigshoefer b: 05 Jan 1881 d: Abt. 1917 (WW I)
2 Flora Koenigshoefer b: 07 May 1885 in Frankfurt/Main, Germany d: 1942
2 Malchen Marianne Koenigshoefer b: 02 May 1871 in Frankfurt/Main,
Germany d: in Theresienstadt
+Joseph Wolf b: 1875 in Koeln d: 1944 in Theresienstadt
3 Willy Wolf[L]
+Jaine Wechsler
3 Emanuel Wolf d: in Israel
+Else Friedmann
4 Helga Wolf Wolf
3 Salomon Wolf
2 Jettchen Koenigshoefer b: 05 Mar 1877 in Frankfurt/Main, Germany
+Leopold Flamm
3 Lilly Flamm b: 1908

3 Martha Martel Flamm b: 1909
  +Kurt Kellerman
     4 Uri Kellerman Kellerman
     4 Kurt Kellerman Kellerman
     4 Ernst Kellerman Kellerman
3 Kurt Flamm b: 1910
3 Ernst Flamm b: 1914

[A]**Samuel Koenigshefer**, also known as Shmuel Gedalia, was a ritual slaughterer (shohet) for the community of Rabbi Shimshon Raphael Hirsch. His wife, Helena (born Schoenfeld) was a widow of Flamm.

[B]**Jonas Koenigshoefer** was a businessman who grew up in Frankfurt and attended the Jüdische Realschule, but had to withdraw because of illness. He was subsequently employed for 8 years by the haberdashery store of Gutman and Marx in Frankfurt. He was drafted into the German army in 1916 and spent eight months at the front. He moved his family to Würzburg in 1927 and opened a kosher dairy produce business (Buettnerstr. 10). He was arrested during the November 1938 pogrom (Kristallnacht), but was released after 3 days. He had a large library in his home, which had once been the Rabbis's home with a prayer hall, and during the pogrom, all his books were thrown into the street. He was denounced to the Gestapo on November 30, 1938 because he had supposedly insulted a co-worker and he was imprisoned for another 6 days. He immigrated to Copenhagen in September 1939 with his wife (a Danish citizen) and his mother-in-law. As part of the mass evacuation, he fled to Sweden in 1943 and, at the end of the war, returned to Copenhagen.[160] His wife immigrated to Israel after her husband's death.

[C]**Rachel Bamberger Koenigshoefer** was the granddaughter of Yitzhak Dov Halevi Bamberger also known as the Würzburger Rav who opposed Rabbi Shimshon Raphael Hirsch's drive for the Orthodox community to secede from the general organized Jewish community.

[D]**Nathan Koenigshoefer** came to Würzburg with his parents. He attended the Jüdische Volkschule, the New Gymnasium and, beginning in 1933, the Israelitische Lehrerbildungsanstalt (Jewish Teacher's Institute). He belonged to the gymnastic and sports organization of the Jewish religious youth organization, Noar Agudati. In 1935, he went to the Yeshiva of Frankfurt in the hopes of getting a certificate for Youth Aliyah but when this did not succeed he came home after a year. He left Würzburg in June 1938 with a child visa valid for Denmark and Palestine, but was turned away at the border. He lived

[160] This information is summarized from the Würzburg Memorbuch.

illegally in Hamburg for two months until he was able to get a travel permit to work as an unpaid agricultural worker in Denmark. He fled to Sweden in 1943, and, after the war, spent a year in Sweden in a home for children who survived concentration camps. After further study, he passed exams in economics and bookkeeping and from 1946 to 1966 he worked as chief accountant for an export firm in Copenhagen. In 1973 he re-settled in Switzerland to become Director of Sanitorium Dewania in Davos. I had an interesting and productive correspondence with him, which stopped rather abruptly.

ᴱ**Lilian Koenigshoefer Arbel** lives in Mevasereth Zion, Israel.

ᶠ**Martha Koenigshoefer Gruenbaum Koplowitz** lived in Kfar Haroeh near Hadera. She came to Würzburg with her parents in 1927 and attended Jüdische Volkschule until 1930 and then studied for two years at a state business school. She immigrated to Palestine in 1939.

ᴳ**Ephraim (Gustav) Gruenbaum** was a business man and civil servant who was arrested in November 1938 and spent 2 months in Buchenwald, after which he immigrated to Palestine.

ᴴ**Emanuel Koenigshoefer** was a rabbi at Rechov Baal Shem Tov 22 in Jerusalem.

ᴵ**Josef Heimann Koenigshoefer** was head of an orphanage in Breslau.

ᴶ**Manfred Kingshoff** changed his name from Koenigshoefer and was in the US Army Intelligence. When I was in touch with him, he lived in Florida.

ᴷ**Lore Kingshoff** lived in Wynnewood, PA when I spoke with her in 1997. She was on a ship ?Donna that the British sent to Australia at the beginning of World War II.

ᴸ**Willy Wolf** lived in Baltimore, MD.

APPENDIX 17

Descendants of Leopold Wolf Koenigshoefer

———•◆•———

1 Leopold Wolf Koenigshoefer[A] b: 13 Apr 1886 in Fuerth, Bavaria d: 1942 in
  Auschwitz
 +Else Loewenstein b: Aug 21,1897 in Fulda, Hesse-Nassau d: in Auschwitz
    2 Samuel Koenigshoefer b: 1928
       + Debbie
        3 Esther Koenigshoefer b: 1951
    2 Joseph Koenigshoefer b: 1931 d: 1992 in Kibbutz Kfar Hanasi, Israel
       + Estelle
        3 Three daughters
2nd Wife of Leopold Wolf Koenigshoefer:
  +Flora Ettinger b: in Mannheim, Germany d: 1922
    2 Moshe Jona Hazor[B] b: 20 Dec 1920
       +Alice Hirsch b: in Essen, Germany d: in Israel in 2009
    2 Ludwig (Arie) Koenigshoefer b: 1922 d: 1992 in Israel
    2 Lea Koenigshoefer[C] b: 1922 d: 1988 in Kibbutz Degania B

[A]**Leopold Wolf Koenigshoefer** moved to Hamburg in 1919 and, according to the
archive I found in Fürth, officials of the Nazi Justice Department were looking for him
in 1932. His residence in Köln was given as 2 Julienstrasse. He escaped from Köln to
Belgium, which he knew well from pre-war business activities, but the Nazis caught up
with him and, according to the Fürth Gedenkbuch, he and his wife were deported on
Nov 9, 1942 to Drancy and then on transport 31 to Auschwitz, where they were killed
in 1943.

[B]**Moshe Jonah Hazor** changed his name from Koenigshoefer. He told me that he chose
Hazor because the literal translation of "hazor" is courtyard (hoef) and ancient kings
(koenig) were buried there. He joined the Palestine Division (Jewish Brigade) of the
British Army in May 1941, was assigned to a transport unit and, as lieutenant, fought
with Montgomery in Libya, Egypt, and Italy. Promoted to captain towards the end of
the war, he helped house and feed Jewish refugees and, with his connections in transport, helped with illegal immigration to Palestine through the Bricha. After his demobilization from the British Army, he returned to Palestine and the following year joined
the infantry of the newly formed Hagana as major and fought as a battalion commander

in the War of Independence. After the war he became chef de cabinet for Israel's first President, Chaim Weizmann, and from 1953 to 1960 he was in charge of security for the Knesset. He warned Prime Minister David Ben Gurion that he could not guarantee his safety if he allowed visitors free access but Ben Gurion refused to change this part of a free society. After a bomb was thrown into the Knesset that almost killed Ben Gurion, Hazor resigned his position. He was thereafter appointed to a government position that regulates diamond exports and subsequently became the Israel representative of the DeBeers diamond merchants. This was an important position inasmuch as Israel at that time was the largest diamond exporter in the world.

[c]**Samuel Koenigshoefer** immigrated to Palestine and, together with his brother, Joseph, was among the founders of Kibbutz Kfar Hanasi in which both held important leadership positions.

APPENDIX 18

Descendants of Gella Koenigshoefer and Raphael Seeberger

———•◆•———

1 Martha (Miriam) Altmann b: 12 Jan 1876 in Kattowitz d: 23 Oct 1950 in
Tel Aviv, Israel
+Izak Koenigshoefer b: 03 Aug 1870 in Fuerth, Bavaria d: 1951 in Haifa, Israel
   2 Gella Koenigshoefer[A] b: 14 Jun 1900 in Fuerth, Bavaria d: 23 Apr 1982 in Tel
   Aviv, Israel
   +Raphael Seeberger b: 17 Aug 1890 in Gunzenhausen, Germany d: 1940 in
   Haifa, Israel
      3 Rudolph Seeberger[B] b: 10 Jul 1923 in Gunzenhausen, Germany
      d: 1996 in Haifa, Israel
      +Alisa (Lisl) Krieger[C] b: 1926 in Vienna, Austria
         4 Raphael Seeberger b: 1954 in Haifa, Israel
         +Nava Noi b: 1958 in Petach Tikva, Israel
            5 Gal Seeberger b: 1990 in Haifa, Israel
         4 Ron Seeberger b: 1957 in Haifa, Israel
         +Avital Kasler b: 1960 in Kfar Saba
            5 Shachar Seeberger b: 1984 in Haifa
            5 Alon Seeberger b: 1987 in Haifa, Israel
            5 Dekel Seeberger b: 1992 in Haifa, Israel
      3 Sara (Charlotte) Seeberger b: 13 Nov 1929 in Gunzenhausen, Germany
      d: December 2007 in Israel
      +Shimon Stein b: 1919 in Kolo, Poland d: in Israel
         4 Anat Stein b: 1959 in Haifa, Israel
         +Shimon Sagi b: 1958 in Kiryat Shemone, Israel
            5 Gilat Sagi b: 1982 in Haifa, Israel
            5 Moran Sagi b: 1986 in Haifa, Israel
            5 Lital Sagi b: 1986 in Haifa, Israel
         4 Moshe Stein b: 1952 in Haifa, Israel
         +Michal ? b: 1954 in Haifa, Israel
            5 Tomer Stein b: 1980 in Haifa, Israel
            5 Roi Stein b: 1985 in Haifa, Israel
         4 Benyamin Stein b: 1955 in Haifa, Israel
         +Alisa? b: 1957 in Beer Sheva, Israel
            5 Liron Stein b: 1981 in Haifa, Israel
            5 Nir Stein b: 1985 in Haifa, Israel

3 Johanna (Hannah) Seeberger b: 3 Mar 1921 in Gunzenhausen, Germany
+Bernd AltmannD b: 1921 in Berlin, Germany
4 Miriam Altmann b: 1954 in Haifa, Israel
+Yitschak Yaniv b: 1937 in Tel Aviv, Israel
5 Jonathan Yaniv b: 1986 in Vancouver, Canada
4 Ilana Altmann b: 1957

AGella Koenigshoefer Seeberger was a nurse. She fled Germany together with her husband and son, Rudolph, who celebrated his Bar Mitzvah on board the ship taking them to Palestine in 1936. Her marriage was arranged by my grandfather Izak and was said to have been most unhappy. The story is that my grandfather picked the groom and then arranged a meeting with the prearranged sign that if she approved, she would tell a joke. Gella became very uncomfortable and did not like the prospective groom and, to pass the time, she told a joke and my grandfather said "mazal tov" and they were engaged.

BRudolph Seeberger was a baker and lived in Haifa.

CAlisa Krieger Seeberger is a short and slim lady, probably less than 5 feet tall, but a bundle of energy and a lot of fun to be around. She never took herself too seriously and refused to discuss politics or religion. Hobbies include painting and reading. My last contact with her was in 2007.

DBernd Altmann and Hanna moved to Vancouver, Canada. No relation to the Katowice Altmanns.

Left-to-right: Jean, Lisl Seeberger, Rudolph Seeberger, Moshe Stein, Sara Stein.

APPENDIX 19

Descendants of Bella Koenigshoefer
and Aaron Cohn

———•◆•———

1 Bella Koenigshoefer[A] b: 04 Mar 1878 in Fuerth, Bavaria d: 17 Jul 1968 in
  Kibbutz Hafetz Haim, Israel
 +Aaron Arnold Cohn b: 1873 in Hamburg, Germany d: 03 Mar 1966 in
  Kibbutz Hafetz Haim, Israel
　　2 Hannah Cohn
　　+Jacob Kahan
　　2 Rosie Cohn d: Abt. 1946 in Copenhagen
　　+Joseph Kahan
　　　3 Lea Kahan
　　　+Salomon Katzenstein
　　　　4 Suzanne Katzenstein
　　　　4 Deborah Katzenstein
　　　　4 Zipporah Katzenstein
　　　　4 Jacob Katzenstein
　　　3 Moses Kahan
　　　+Shulamit Kurzweil
　　2 Miriam Cohn[B] b: 01 Jul 1917 in Hamburg, Germany
　　+Kalman Adler Nesher b: 30 Aug 1912 in Kissingen, Germany
　　　3 Varda Nesher b: 13 Oct 1943 in Israel
　　　+Klonimus Godlevsky b: 25 Apr 1942
　　　　4 Ahron Godlevsky b: 29 May 1966 in Israel
　　　　+Nechama Druck b: 05 Aug 1968
　　　　　5 Ester Rivka Godlevsky b: 17 Nov 1988 in Israel
　　　　　5 Jehuda Godlevsky b: 08 Jan 1990 in Israel
　　　　　5 Tirza Godlevsky b: 16 Oct 1991 in Israel
　　　　　5 Ruchama Godlevsky b: 23 Jul 1993 in Israel
　　　　　5 Schlomo Godlevsky b: 18 Nov 1995 in Israel
　　　　4 Elijahu Godlevsky b: 13 Aug 1967 in Israel
　　　　+Tali Dudenfeld b: 07 Jun 1972
　　　　　5 Sara Godlevsky b: 14 Mar 1990
　　　　　5 Avraham Menachem Godlevsky b: 09 Jul 1991
　　　　　5 Shulamit Godlevsky b: 16 Aug 1994
　　　　　5 Moshe Zwi Godlevsky b: 31 Mar 1996
　　　　　5 Joel Godlevsky b: 26 Jan 1995

                5 Jael Godlevsky b: 22 Jul 1998
            4 Shifra Godlevsky b: 04 Nov 1968 in Israel
            +Moshe Lifschiz
                5 Israel Meir Lifschiz b: 14 Jan 1991
                5 Ruth Lifschiz b: 16 Jun 1992
                5 Elazar Lifschiz b: 13 Mar 1994
                5 Lea Lifschiz b: 15 Apr 1996
            4 Bezalel Godlevsky b: 11 Mar 1971 in Israel
            +Fruma Karlinsky b: 31 Dec 1972
                5 Michal Godlevsky b: 15 Aug 1994
                5 Tamar Godlevsky b: 04 Oct 1995
            4 Elazar Godlevsky b: 16 Jul 1972 in Israel
            +Hurda Wolf
                5 Josef Avraham Godlevsky b: 27 Aug 1997
            4 Rachel Godlevsky b: 23 Sep 1974 in Israel
            +Meshulam Kassel
                5 Chaja Kassel b: 17 May 1997
                5 Moshe Elchanan Kassel b: 18 Jun 1998
            4 Israel Godlevsky b: 16 Jul 1977 in Israel
            +Pnina Weiss b: 29 Oct 1976
            4 Lea Godlevsky b: 25 Apr 1979
            4 Itamar Godlevsky b: 03 Jun 1981
            4 David Godlevsky b: 22 May 1985
    3 Tirzah Nesher b: 09 Apr 1947 in Israel
    +Arnon Mordechaj b: 23 Apr 1941
        4 Lea Mordechaj b: 05 Sep 1979
        4 Jehuda Leib Mordechaj b: 19 Jan 1983
        4 Nechama Mordechaj b: 21 Aug 1986
        4 Shalom Jakob Mordechaj b: 08 Jan 1987
    3 Naftali Arje Nesher b: 06 Jan 1949 in Israel
    +Zerna Polack b: 06 Mar 1953
        4 Tamar Nesher b: 13 Oct 1976
        4 Jael Nesher b: 10 Dec 1978
        4 Dafna Nesher b: 12 Feb 1982
        4 Awichaj Nesher b: 27 Aug 1987
    3 Leah Nesher b: 27 May 1951 in Israel
    +Simcha Fruchter b: 16 Aug 1951
        4 Elijahu Fruchter b: 31 May 1976 in Israel
        +Ronit Moskowitz b: 13 May 1976
        4 Jakob Moshe Fruchter b: 16 Jan 1979
        4 Michal Fruchter b: 01 Jun 1980
        4 Jehudit Fruchter b: 25 Dec 1982
        4 Gershon Fruchter b: 28 Jul 1984
        4 Josef Fruchter b: 14 Oct 1986
        4 Avraham Jeshiah Fruchter b: 19 Oct 1988

  4 Rivka Fruchter b: 02 Oct 1990
 3 Emanuel Menachem Nesher b: 17 May 1957 in Israel
  +Tova Silbert b: 20 Dec 1958
   4 Shifra Jehudit Nesher b: 23 Mar 1979 in Israel
    +Zeev Pfenfer b: 13 Mar 1979
   4 Nechemia Nesher b: 20 Mar 1980
   4 Avraham Nesher b: 25 Sep 1981
   4 Sara Nesher b: 14 Dec 1982
   4 Jakov Elijahu Nesher b: 04 Oct 1985
   4 Esther Nesher b: 06 Mar 1984
   4 Rchael Nesher b: 22 Feb 1987
   4 Moshe Yitzchak Nesher b: 11 Oct 1988
   4 Ahron Nesher b: 12 Jul 1990
   4 Elisheva Nesher b: 29 May 1992
   4 David Nesher b: 26 Jan 1994
   4 Shmuel Nesher b: 21 Jan 1996
   4 Debora Nesher b: 28 Nov 1997
2 Yona Cohn
 +Shteffi Bodenheimer b: in Frankfurt, Germany
  3 Ruth Cohn Cohn
  3 Rafael Cohn

^A**Bella Koenigshoefer** and **Aaron Cohn**: Their daughter, Miriam Adler Nesher, wrote in 1998 that her parents, Bella Koenigshoefer and Aaron Cohn, escaped from Denmark to Sweden during World War II. After the war, they returned to Copenhagen where their daughter, Rozi, died after which they immigrated to Israel. After living for 6 months in Jerusalem with their son, they joined Miriam and her family in Kibbutz Chafetz Chaim, a religious kibbutz founded by Poalei Agudath Yisrael. By that time they were elderly but despite the difficult conditions, they adapted well. Aaron died in 1966 at the age of 93 and Bella died in 1968 at the age of 90. Both were buried in Jerusalem.

Aaron and Bella Cohen. The man in the front row is incorrectly labeled as Bruno Altman (Katovitz).

R' Ahron & Bella Cohen   21.VI.20

Bella and Aaron Cohen (front row, 5th and 6th from left) in June 1920.

Bella Koenigshoefer Cohn (1878-1968).

Bella and Aaron Cohn in early 1960s.

[B]**Miriam Cohn** arrived in Palestine on January 1, 1940 as a companion on an Aliyat Hanoar transport. She had left Germany in 1936 for Copenhagen to join her two sisters, Hannah and Rozi, who were married to two brothers (Kahan). Because she was unable to obtain a passport to remain in Copenhagen, she lived for over a year in Rotterdam, Holland working as a nursemaid. In Israel she lived with her brother, Yona and his wife, Stefi Bodenheimer who had established the "Horev" school in Jerusalem. She then joined kibbutz Chafetz Chaim when she married a member of the kibbutz, Kalman Adler Nesher and established a kindergarten. Her husband was born in Kissingen, studied at the Teacher's Seminary in Würzburg, and then worked as a shohet, cantor, and teacher in a small town in the south of Germany. He was a teacher in Kibbutz Hofetz Haim. Her children and grandchildren, all extremely religious, left the Kibbutz to "learn." We visited her in the kibbutz in the 1990s and found her to be a delightful and very gracious lady. Already in her 80s, she arrived on a large tricycle. As she served us tea she wore a shaitel and bemoaned the fact that none of her children or grandchildren remained on the kibbutz.

Miriam Nesher as she appeared in the early 1990s.

APPENDIX 20

Descendants of Betty Koenigshoefer and Villie Gluck

———— • ◆ • ————

1 Martha (Miriam) Altmann b: 12 Jan 1876 in Kattowitz d: 23 Oct 1950 in
Tel Aviv, Israel
+Izak Koenigshoefer b: 03 Aug 1870 in Fuerth, Bavaria d: 1951 in Haifa, Israel
  2 Betty Koenigshoefer[A] b: 29 Mar 1903 in Fuerth, Germany d: Jul 1978 in Israel
    +Villie (Wilhelm) Gluck b: 04 Oct 1887 in Hungary d: Dec 1944 in Hungary
      3 Felix Gluck[B] b: 13 May 1923 in Fuerth, Germany d: 1981 in London,
      England
        +Michelle Yellinek b: 07 Oct 1932 in England d: 1994 in London, England
          4 Tim Gluck b: Apr 1964 in England
            +Nicole ?
              5 Ilana Michelle b: 21 Jun 1994 in London, England
          4 Sybil Gluck
      3 Bernd (Dov) Joseph[C] Gilon b: Apr 7 1935 in Darmstadt, Germany
        +Shirley Perkoff b: 25 Dec 1934 in London, England
          4 Gadi Gilon b: 17 Oct 1958 in Israel
            +Nofia Haviv b: 19 Nov 1961 in Jerusalem, Israel
              5 Mor Gilon b: 16 Mar 1983 in Israel
              5 Adi Gilon b: 18 Nov 1984 in Israel
              5 Shani Gilon b: 28 Feb 1986 in Israel
          4 Yoram Gilon b: 17 Dec 1959 in Israel
            +Yonat Zonnenfeld b: 21 Dec 1962 in Israel
              5 Boaz Gilon b: 18 Dec 1983 in Israel
                +Liron Asher
              5 Sivan Gilon b: 31 Jan 1987 in Israel
          4 Naor Gilon b: 17 Feb 1964 in Israel
            +Orly Gliner b: 02 May 1964 in Israel
              5 Noam Gilon b: 04 Aug 1988 in Israel
                +Liat Brandel
              5 Oren Gilon b: 24 Aug 1991 in Israel
              5 Dana Gilon b: 20 Jul 1994 in Israel
              5 Rony Gilon b: 22 Mar 2004 in Israel

[A]**Betty Gluck** was a kind and very sweet person and I was very fond of her. Betty, her husband and two children lived with grandparents in Germany but were expelled in 1939 because Villie was a Hungarian citizen and Germany considered the entire family's citizenship according to the husband's citizenship. When they came to the Hungarian border, the Hungarians regarded the citizenship of each family member separately and were willing to allow Willie in but not Betty and her children. It took a fair amount of bribing to reverse that. Betty and Dov survived the war in Hungary and towards the end were under the diplomatic protection of the Swiss in a so-called safe house but Willie did not survive. Aunt Betty came to England with her youngest son, Dov, in 1946 and then immigrated to Israel in 1949.

[B]**Felix Gluck** was an extremely talented artist in painting, charcoal, and woodcuts. He studied painting at the Budapest Free Academy of Art. During the war, he was in Mauthausen Concentration Camp, and was denied entry into England after the war, because he was exposed to tuberculosis in concentration camp and had evidence of infection. Between 1946 and 1948 he was hospitalized in a sanatorium in Davos, Switzerland. While in the sanatorium he continued to pursue his artistic interests and developed a special interest in linocuts. Many of his art works from that period express his longing and love for a girl he left in Hungary. Felix came to England in 1948 and studied at the University of Durham. He returned to Hungary in 1950. After he arrived in Hungary, he found that his "girl friend" was married and that it had all been a trick to lure him back. He worked as an illustrator and art editor for the State until the 1956 Hungarian uprising, when Aunt Betty went to Vienna and helped him escape. He returned to England, resumed his artistic career, and founded a fine publishing house in Twickenham that published classics. He died of bladder cancer. His wife, Michelle, died of liver cancer shortly after the birth of their first grandchild. I met Felix in England in 1949 and pestered him sufficiently to draw a likeness of me that he finally gave in. Jean and I visited with his family in the 1970s.

A linocut by Felix Gluck from the time he was in Davos.

[C]**Dov Gilon** is the cousin with whom I have had the closest and special relationship. We arrived in Newcastle within a few months of each other. Both of us struggled with the language and with a sense of alienation, of being "fish out of water." After I left Newcastle for London and then the United States, our grandfather decided that Dov needed a deeper religious education and therefore enrolled him in the Yeshiva of Gateshead, an extremely right wing institution, which had the opposite of the intended effect. Dov became increasingly Zionist and, in May 1949, at the age of 14, he made Aliyah under the auspices of the Youth *Aliyah* organization. After living in a number of youth settlements and working in the city, Dov was conscripted into the army in 1953. His mother, my Aunt Betty, decided at this time to move to Israel also. After demobilization in 1956, he joined Moshav Kfar Mordechai, where he met his future wife, Shirley, and became a farmer. He left agriculture to train as a tour guide in 1963 and ended his career by arranging all the Israel tour experiences for the Reform Movement's youth organization, NFTY.

Matzah cover sown by Betty Gluck with a linocut by Felix Gluck.

Betty and Villie Gluck shortly after their marriage.

APPENDIX 21

Descendants of Charlotte Koenigshoefer and Julius Bernet

———•◆•———

1 Martha (Miriam) Altmann b: 12 Jan 1876 in Kattowitz d: 23 Oct 1950
  in Jerusalem, Israel
 +Izak Koenigshoefer b: 03 Aug 1870 in Fuerth, Bavaria d: 1951 in Haifa, Israel
   2 Charlotte Koenigshoefer b: 27 Mar 1906 in Fuerth, Bavaria
     d: 03 Mar 2003 in Jerusalem, Israel
     +Julius (Ulu) Bernet b: 31 Oct 1898 in Bamberg, Germany d: 27 Apr 1944 in
     Newcastle/Tyne, England
       3 Manfred (Michael) Bernet[A] b: 19 Jul 1930 in Nurnberg, Germany
         d: 30 Mar 2010 in New Rochelle, NY
         +Veda Rachel Saul[B] b: 01 Apr 1928 in Mandalay, Burma
           4 Miriam Bernet b: 12 Aug 1954 in Newport Pagnel, England
             +Joseph (Yoji) Arie b: 23 Jul 1951 in Haifa, Israel
               5 Matan Arie b: 02 Jan 1984 in New Haven, CT
           4 Ilan Bernet b: 07 Oct 1955 in Haifa, Israel
             +Elite Prag b: 23 Feb 1954
               5 Adam Bernet b: 07 Oct 1986 in Tel Aviv, Israel
               5 Avigail Bernet b: 20 May 1988 in Tel Aviv, Israel
               5 Avinoam Bernet b: 10 Jun 1992 in Tel Aviv, Israel
       2nd Wife of Manfred (Michael) Bernet:
         +Rena Rickler[C] b: 24 Jul 1930 in London, England d: 11 Oct 1997 in New
         Haven, CT
           4 Yoram Bernet b: 31 May 1961 in Eilat, Israel
             +Maya Kanzler b: 23 Nov 1970 in Hawaii
               5 Zakai Bernet b: 21 Jun 2006 in Seattle, WA
               5 Malachi Bernet b: 27 Jul 2008 in Seattle, WA
           4 Eytan Bernet b: 14 Aug 1965 in Englewood, NJ
       3rd Wife of Manfred (Michael) Bernet:
         +Sheila (Siegel) Tanenbaum b: 5 Jul 1939 in Brooklyn, NY
       3 Erna Bernet b: 18 Jun 1929 in Nurnberg, Germany d: 17 Dec 1995
         in Rehovoth, Israel
         +Herbert Kahn b: 11 February 1928 in Frankfurt/Main, Germany
         d: Jan 2003 in Israel
           4 Shoshana Kahn b:1950 in Israel
           4 Yael Kahn b: 1953 in Israel
           4 Aliza Kahn b: 1960 in Israel

[A]**Michael Bernet** grew up in England and attended the Hasmonean Grammar School. He emigrated to Israel in 1948 and volunteered for the army serving in the maps and photography division of its Intelligence Corps during the War of Independence. He then became a journalist writing in both English and Hebrew for a number of British and Israeli papers including Haaretz and the Jerusalem Post. From 1959 to 1960, he edited and published Hashavua Beilat, Israel's first independent small town newspaper. He came to the United States in 1962 and worked as a writer and translator. His book, *The Time of the Burning Sun*, a report on the 1967 war as seen by ordinary soldiers from a variety of viewpoints was reprinted three times (1967, 1968, 2004). He also wrote *The Longest Six Days: The Psychology of War and Peace in the Middle East*, about the 1967 war. After moving to the United States, he studied psychology in which he received a masters and doctorate. Michael was a brilliant, but complex individual. He had a most difficult relationship with his mother, which I know caused her much pain.

Michael Bernet.

Left-to-right: Erna, Julius, Charlotte, and Michael Bernet in England about 1942.

Left-to-right: Miriam, Eytan, and Rena Bernet in 1987.

Left-to-right: Front: Michael Bernet, Rena Bernet, David Chameides, Jean Chameides, Miriam Ari, Jogi Arie. Back: Yoram Bernet, Eytan Bernet, Leon Chameides, Debbie Chameides, Danny Chameides."

[B]**Veda Saul** was married to Michael Bernet but after their divorce and Erna's divorce from Herbert Kahn, Veda married Herbert. All, including their children once attended our seder.

[C]**Rena Rickler** was an extremely fine, sensitive woman. She was a social worker by training and somewhat unconventional in her thinking. We got to know her quite well and were extremely fond of her.

Aunt Lotte and I on a visit to Newcastle in 1978.

APPENDIX 22

Descendants of Gertrude Koenigshoefer
and Kalman Chameides

———— •◆• ————

1 Martha (Miriam) Altmann b: 12 Jan 1876 in Kattowitz d: 23 Oct 1950
  in Tel Aviv, Israel
+Izak Koenigshoefer b: 03 Aug 1870 in Fuerth, Bavaria d: 1951 in Haifa, Israel
    2 Gertrude Koenigshoefer b: 25 Sep 1904 in Fuerth, Bavaria d: Abt. 1943 in ?
    +Kalman Chameides b: 25 Apr 1902 in Szczerzec, Austrian Galicia
    d: 25 Dec 1942 in Lwów
        3 Leon Chameides b: 24 Jun 1935 in Katowice, Poland
        +Jean Ann Easterbrook b: 10 Jul 1939 in Elmira, NY
            4 Daniel Adar Stark Chameides b: 13 Feb 1964 in Columbus, OH
            +Laurie Weissman b: 23 May 1960 in New York
                5 Nava Hana Chameides b: 09 Oct 1998 in New York, NY
                5 Noam Chameides b: 29 Sep 2005 in Keraganda, Kazakhstan
                (adopted July 2006)
            4 Deborah Tova Chameides b: 15 Dec 1965 in Rochester, NY
            +David Jay Small b: 10 Jun 1960 in Kansas City, MO
                5 Gabrielle Trudi Small b: 29 Jun 1990 in Spring Valley, NY
                5 Sharone Michal Small b: 12 Nov 1992 in New York, NY
                5 Ilan Kalman Small b: 21 Mar 1998 in Pittsfield, MA
            4 David Alon Chameides b: 11 Apr 1969 in Hartford, CT
            +Aliza Corson b: 19 Oct 1965
                5 Maia Hana Chameides b: 03 Jan 2002 in Los Angeles, CA
                5 Tamar Gail Chameides b: 05 Aug 2004 in Los Angeles, CA
        3 Zwi Barnea b: 16 Sep 1932 in Katowice, Poland
        +Lilian Shoshana Liberman b: 12 May 1932 in Warsaw, Poland
            4 Michele (Miki) Barnea b: 26 Sep 1963 in New York, NY

APPENDIX 23

Descendants of Moshe Jonas (Johni) Kaye and Klara Ehrlich

———•◆•———

1 Martha (Miriam) Altmann b: 12 Jan 1876 in Kattowitz d: 23 Oct 1950
  in Jerusalem, Israel
 +Izak Koenigshoefer b: 03 Aug 1870 in Fuerth, Bavaria d: 1951 in Haifa, Israel
    2 Moshe Jonas (Johnie) Kaye b:1915 Fuerth, Bavaria d: 5 May 1949 in
       Newcastle/Tyne, England
       +Klara Ehrlich b: 1918 in Czechoslovakia d: 13 Apr 2006 in Tel Aviv, Israel
        3 Ruth Leviatan b: 26 Aug 1941 in Newcastle/Tyne, England
           +Yacov Zvi Buchalter - d: 1994 in Israel
        3 Naomi Leviatan b: 25 Mar 1943 in Newcastle/Tyne, England
           +Ran Stern
              4 Roi Stern b: 25 Aug 1974 in Israel
                 + Avia Pelzer b: 12 May 1973 in Haifa, Israel
                    5 Ido Stern b: 7 Aug 2002 in Ramat Gan, Israel
                    5 Dvir Stern b: 24 Feb 2006 in Montreau, France
                    5 Ofri Stern b: 13 Dec 2008 in Hadera, Israel
              4 Nir Stern b: 26 Mar 1978 in Israel
                 + Ifat Musseri b: 25 Jul 1982 in Tel Aviv, Israel
        3 David Leviatan b: 14 Feb 1946 in Newcastle/Tyne, England
           +Shoshi Malka
              4 Yoni Shai Leviatan b: 10 Mar 1978
              4 Keren Leviatan b: 25 May 1975
                 +Mark Drits
                    5 Lily Rose Drits b: 05 May 2009 in Atlanta, GA

APPENDIX 24

Descendants of Kalman Chameides and Beile Lanes

1 Kalman Chameides b: 1836 d: 02 Dec 1896 in Szczerzec, Poland
 +Beile Lanes
    2 Shulim Chameides d: 07 Dec 1942 in Szczerzec, Poland
       +Miriam Luft b: in Jaworów, Poland d: 07 Dec 1942 in Szczerzec, Poland
          3 Kalman Chameides b: 25 Apr 1902 in Szczerzec, Austrian Galicia
             d: 25 Dec 1942 in Lwów ghetto
             +Gertrude Koenigshoefer b: 25 Sep 1904 in Fuerth Barvaria d: Abt. 1943
             in ? {See Apendix 22 for descendants of Gertrude Koenigshoefer and
             Kalman Chameides}
          3 Benjamin Chameides
          3 Yitzchak (Ajzak) Chameides b: 1911 d: Abt. 1943 in ?Szczerzec, Poland
             +Zipporah Betersfeld b: 1913 in Górlice d:Abt 1943
          3 Hirsh Chameides b: 1904 in Szczerzec, Austrian Galicia d: Abt. 1928
          3 Rivka Chameides d: Abt. 1942 in ? Belżec
             +Elias Karl
                4 Binyomin Karl b: Abt. 1934 d: about 1942
                4 ? Mala Karl b: Abt. 1927 d : about 1942
          3 Dresel Chane Chameides b: 13 Jun 1898 in Szczerzec, Austrian Galicia
          3 Chaje Chameides b: 29 Jun 1899
    2 Reisel Chameides b: 1871
       +Josef Hersh Koch b: 21 Nov 1859 in Rudki, Poland
    2 Ester Chameides b: 1869
       +Nathan Jungmann b: 1870 in Stryj, Poland
          3 Rachel Blime Chameides b: 1896
          3 Czarna Chameides b: 1898 in Stryj
    2 Ruchel Lea Chameides
       +Schmelke Billig
          3 Mindel Cipre Chameides b: 19 Jan 1892 in Grodek, Poland
          3 Mendel Chameides b: 1894 in Grodek, Poland
          3 Feige Sprinze Chameides b: 1897 in Grodek
          3 Kalmen Chameides b: 1900 in Grodek
    2 Mayer Chameides b: 1860[A]
       +Chaja Ruchel Schiff b: 1862
          3 Machle Chameides b: 1901 in Borysław
          3 Juda Schiff Chamajdes[B] b: 27 Aug 1880 in Borysław, Austrian Galicia

d: before 1942 in Belgium
+Chana Lustig-Koppel b: 20 Sep 1884 d: 1943
    4 Isaac Chamajdes[C] b: 1905 in Drohobycz, Austrian Galicia d: 1943
    4 Adele Chamajdes[D] b: 1906 d: 1943
     + Abraham Abraham
       5 Artur Abraham b: 1942 d: 1943
    4 Sarah Chamajdes b: 1923 d: 1943
3 Miriam Schiff 1883 b: 1882 in Borysław, Austrian Galicia d: 1883
3 Dobre Ester Schiff b: 1884 in Borysław
3 Moses Schiff b: 1885 in Borysław, Austrian Galicia d: Abt. 1941
    4 Salka Chameides b: Abt. 1916 in Borysław, Austrian Galicia
      d: 1941 in Borysław, Poland
    4 Bela Chameides d:17 Feb 1943 in Borysław, Poland
3 Schewe Schiff b: 1888 in Borysław, Austrian Galicia
3 Isak Schiff b: 1894 in Borysław, Austrian Galicia
3 Rifka Miriam Schiff b: 1894 in Borysław d: 1896
3 Chaje Ciwje Schiff b: 1896 in Borysław, Austrian Galicia
3 Kalman Chameides[E] b: 1904 in Borysław, Austrian Galicia d: 1971 in Israel
 +Tova ? b: 1919 in Radom, Poland
    4 Meir Chameides[F] b: 1948 in Israel
    4 Aryeh Chaim Chameides[G] b: 1948 in Israel
     +Nurit ? b: 1951
       5 Shai Chameides b: 1970 in Israel
       5 Inbal Chameides b: 1975 in Israel
       5 Hadar Chameides b: 1977 in Israel
        +Eli ?
3 Leib (Leon) Chameides b: in Borysław, Austrian Galicia
2 Fayvush Chameides[H] d: 1942 in Borysław, Poland
 +Leah Schiff
   3 Avraham Chameides[I] b: 1898 in Borysław, Austrian Galicia d: 1984 in Israel
   +Freide (Fryda) Roth b: 1900 in Borysław, Poland d: 17 Feb 1943
   in Borysław, Poland
      4 Meir Chameides[J] b: 1928 in Borysław, Poland
       +Edith Yehudith Davidovich b: 13 Sep 1930 in Tokai, Hungary
        5 Michael Chameides[K] b: 14 Feb 1959 in Israel
         +Yonat Rapaport b: 10 Oct 1959 in Israel
        5 Mira Chameides b: 27 Jun 1962 in Israel
         +Yaron Standel b: 29 Sep 1959
        5 Uri Chameides[L] b: 15 Dec 1953 in Israel
         +Nofi De Medina
      4 Adela Chameides b: 06 May 1924 in Borysław, Poland
       +Yerucham Leiner b: in Sambor d: 1985 in Israel
        5 Fryda Leiner b: 15 May 1945 in Krakow, Poland
         +Mike Joffe b: in South Africa
          6 Judith Joffe b: 01 Dec 1959 in Israel

3 Mechel Chameides b: 1897 in Borysław, Austrian Galicia d: 1942 in
   Janowska Camp, Lwów, Poland
     4 Milek Chameides b: 1922 d: 1942 in Janowska Camp, Lwów, Poland
3 Hersh Chameides b: 1896 in Borysław, Austrian Galicia d: 1896 in
   Borysław, Austrian Galicia
3 Sheindl Chameides b: in Borysław d: 1942 in Borysław, Poland
    4 ? Chameides b: 1940 in Borysław, Poland
3 Tema Chameides d: 1942
    4 ? Chameides
3 Reisel Chameides d: 1942 in Belrżec
  +Bernard ? d: 1942
    4 Leah Chameides b: 1932 d: 1942 in Belrżec
    4 Mundzio (Moshe) Chameides b: 1934 in Borysław d: 1942 in Belżec
    4 Yankele Chameides b: 1937 in Borysław d: 1942 in Borysław, Poland
3 Izak (Itzie) Chameides b: in Borysław d: 1943 in Plaszow extermination camp
  +? d: 1943 in Borysław, Poland
    4 Mundek Chameides d: 1943 in Plaszow extermination camp
2 Frimet Gittel Chameides
 + Hersch Tanne
   3 Moses Leib Tanne b: 1894 in Komarno
   3 Freide Jachet Tanne b: 1898 in Komarno
2 Braindel Chameides b: in Szczerzec
 + Pinchas Zwass
   3 Rachel Lea Chameides[M] b: 1887 in Szczerzec d: 1942
    + Jakov Ollech b: 1882 in Dobromil d: 1942
     4 Hinde Ollech b: 1909 in Baligrod d: 1973 in Israel
      + Chaskel Wolf/Jechurun b: 1906 in Wisnicz d: 1986 in Israel
       5 Elimelech Jechurun b: 1935 in Belgium
       5 Chaya Jechurun
       5 Pinchas Jechurun
   3 Berel Zwass
    + Miraim Bider
     4 Frieda Zwass
      + Alex Berendt
       5 Eli Berendt d: 2004
        + Janine
     4 Bruno Zwass
   3 Kalman Zwass b: 1897 d: 1987 in USA
    + Laura Bider
     4 Bruno Zwass[N] b: 1923 in Breslau
     4 Joseph Zwass b: 1921 d: 1942
   3 Israel Zwass lived in Tarnow
    + Dora Konigsberg
     4 Ruchel Zwass b: 1915
      + Naftali Bogen
       5 Gershon

```
        5 Chaya
      4 Josel Zwass b: 1918 d: 1942
      4 Chaya Zwass b: 1921 d: 1942
      4 Ida Zwass b: 1924
      4 Itche Zwass d: 1942
    3 David Zwass b: 1907
     +Frieda
      4 Beverely
      4 Sam
      4 Anna
    3 Roza Zwass
    3 Sourche
```

[A]**Mayer Chameides** and **Chaja Ruchel Schiff** did not have their religious wedding registered with the state until 1900. Their children born before were given the mother's last name whereas the two born after 1900 were given the father's last name.

[B]**Juda Schiff** came to Antwerp with his wife and two children on Feb 1, 1907, according to the State Archives of that city, and left in August 1914 (on the eve of WW I) to come back again through Germany in 1926. As noted above, he was given his mother's last name at birth because his parents' religious marriage was not recognized by the State. When he arrived in Antwerp, he gave his name as Chamajdes (the Polish phonetic spelling of the name) and his three children bore this name.

Judah Schiff Chamajdes 1880-1942 from identity card with his signature.

[C]**Isaac Chamajdes** is listed in the Deportation List (Service for War Victims image #75) as having been a bookbinder. He was confined in the Mechelen assembly camp on September 12, 1942. Mechelen, in Flanders, Belgium, was the collection point from which Jews were transported to Auschwitz; between 1942 and 1944, 24,916 Jews were transported from Mechelen. Two thirds were gassed on arrival and at the time of liberation only 1,221 survived. Isaac Chamajdes was deported to Auschwitz on September 15 in the Tenth train as prisoner #849 and arrived in Auschwitz on September

17, 1942. ᴰ**Adele Chamajdes**, Isaac's sister, married Abraham Abraham. Together with a one year old son, Artur, they were taken on Transport XX to Auschwitz. This was the only train convoy of Jewish deportees in Europe to be attacked by the Resistance in order to rescue prisoners. This took place on April 19, 1943 in Boortmeerbeek. Some prisoners were able to escape. We know that Adele and Artur arrived and perished in Auschwitz but I have not been able to find out what happened to Abraham.

Identity card photo in 1940s of Adele also known as Zipre Chamajdes.

Sarah Chamajdes 1923-1943.

ᴱ**Kalman Chameides** came to Palestine in 1936 and became a prominent comedian and actor.

ᶠ**Meir Chameides** was involved in a severe motor vehicle crash and is incapacitated. He lives in Haifa with his family.

ᴳ**Aryeh Chameides** is Meir's twin brother. He is an electrician and lives in Kibbutz Kfar Aza, very close to the Gaza strip.

ᴴ**Fayvush Chameides** was a *shochet* in Borysław. There is a Nazi list from 1942 noting that Fayvush Chameides of Gomicza 3 was wanted for not paying his water bill. According to his grandson, Meir, he died in the ghetto from disease and starvation.

Fayvush or Faivel Chameides.

Avraham Chameides.

[1]**Avraham Chameides** and his wife owned a well known fabric store in Borysław. His wife, Fryda, was killed during a roundup of Jews in Borysław in 1943. Avraham together with his son, [J]Meir, managed to hide in a number of places including a stable loft.[161] They made aliyah in 1947. Meir went on to become chief engineer for Kol Yisrael Broadcasting Authority and lives in Ramat Gan with his wife, Yehudith.

Left-to-right: Meir, Leon, Aryeh, Yehudit Chameides, and granddaughters of Meir and Yehudith.

Rachel Lea Chameides (1887-1942) identity card in 1940s.

[K]**Michael Chameides** is director of software development and lives with his family in Ramat Gan.

[L]**Uri Chameides** is a musician and choral conductor in Milan, Italy.

[M]**Rachel Lea Chameides** lived in Dobromil and arrived in Belgium with her husband on April 6, 1924.

[N]**Bruno Zwass** survived a number of concentration camps and, together with his father, came to the United States and settled in Los Angeles where I met him in 2009. He became a physician, never married, but was very close to his many nieces and nephews whom he called his children. A very humorous gentleman, he is totally irreligious.

[161] Meir Chameides, *The War and Me* (Hebrew Edition 2000, English Edition 2001)

APPENDIX 25

Descendants of Zwi Yosef Luft
and Zipporah Zwiebel

———•◆•———

1 Zwi Yosef (Hersh Yosel) Luft[A]
  +Zipporah Zwiebel d: 1902
    2 Mayer Luft
      +Dresel Singer d: Bef. 1898
        3 Miriam Luft b: in Jaworów, Austrian Galicia d: 07 Dec 1942 in
          Szczerzec, Poland
          +Shulim Chameides d: 07 Dec 1942 in Szczerzec, Poland
            4 Kalman Chameides b: 25 Apr 1902 in Szczerzec, Austrian Galicia,
              d: 25 Dec 1942 in Lwów
              +Gertrude Koenigshoefer b: 25 Sep 1904 in Fuerth, Bavaria d: Abt.
              1943 {See Appendix 22 for descendants of Gertude Koenigshoefer and
              Kalman Chameides}
            4 Benjamin Chameides
            4 Yitzchak (Ajzak) Chameides b: 1911 d: Abt. 1943 in ?Szczerzec, Poland
              +Zipporah Betersfeld b: in Gorlice
            4 Hirsh Chameides d: Abt. 1928
            4 Rivka Chameides d: Abt. 1942 in ? Belzec
              +Elias Karl
                5 Binyomin Karl b: Abt. 1934 d: Abt. 1942
                5 Mala Karl b: Abt. 1927 d: Abt. 1942
            4 Dresel Chane Chameides b: 13 Jun 1898
            4 Chaje Chameides b: 29 Jun 1899
        3 Feige Luft
          +Samuel Mendel Harsztark
            4 Moses Harsztark b: 01 Feb 1891 in Grodek, Austrian Galicia
            4 Chaje Sprinze Harsztark b: 10 Feb 1892 in Grodek, Austrian Galicia
        3 Samuel Luft
          +Erna Toder
            4 Max Luft
                5 Raul Luft
                5 Robert Luft
            4 Frieda Luft
              +Henry Wilner
                5 Phil Wilner

            5 Martin Wilner
            5 Arthur Wilner
      3 Isak Eisig Luft b: 1875 d: 1902 in Szczerzec, Austrian Galicia
2nd Wife of Mayer Luft:
 +Ester Gelernter
      3 Naftaly Kasyl Luft b: 1873
        +Beile Schwartz b: 1880 in Sadowa Wisznia
2 Samuel (Shmelke) Luft b: 1839 d: 1913
   +Fradl Glass
      3 Abraham Luft
        +Zilly Schiff
      3 Shlomo Luft
      3 Meir Luft
        +Elzbieta Schache
      3 Netty Neczie Luft
        +Asher Hensel Rubel
      3 Miriam Rachel Luft b: 1858 d: 1897 in Przemyślany
        +Manes Pinkas Wickler b: 1857 in Przemyślany
           4 Osias Wickler b: 1885 in Szczerzec, Austrian Galicia
      3 Leah Luft
        +Iziu Koch
      3 Chavzie Eva Luft
        +Isaac Diller
      3 Naftuly Luft b: 1875 in Szczerzec, Austrian Galicia d: 1878 in Szczerzec
2nd Wife of Samuel (Shmelke) Luft:
 +Lea Taubes b: 1850 in Botischan, Moldavia
      3 Levy Chaim Luft b: 1878 in Szczerzec, Austrian Galicia
        +Nelly Hoffman
      3 Shulim Luft
        +Anna Ochs
      3 Elias Feivel Luft b: 09 Feb 1892 in Szczerzec, Austrian Galicia
        +Rose Rubel
           4 Tutty (Neddy) Luft
             +Salo Widner
           4 Freddy Siegfried Luft d: 2002
             +Dora ?
                5 Ana K. Luft
                   6 Corey Luft b: 1973
                5 Jacob Benshalom Luft
      3 Gizella (Gitel) Luft b: 1877
        +Bernard Mayberg b: 1873 in Lwow
           4 Friedrich Salem Mayberg b: 1899
      3 Ruzia Luft
        +David Muhlstein
      3 Faiga Luft

+Michael Phillip
3 Dresel Luft b: 1882
2 Mindel (Mincia) Luft b: 1855 in Lwow
+Michael Klinghoffer b: 1852
3 Gabriel Klinghoffer b: 1878 d: 1878 in Szczerzec
3 Lea Klinghoffer b: 1882 in Szczerzec
3 Gitel Rivka Klinghoffer b: 1885
3 Chawa Klinghoffer
+? Zwiebel
4 Clara Zwiebel
+? Crest
4 Rachel Zwiebel
+? Krolik
5 Tamar Krolik
4 Szymek Zwiebel
3 Adela Klinghoffer
+Yehoshua Koch
4 Yitzhak Koch
+Havazelet ?
5 Tamar Koch
5 Ofra Koch
5 Karen Koch
4 Zila Koch
3 Josef Klinghoffer
+Clara Menschel
4 David Dolik Klinghoffer
5 Miriam Klinghoffer
5 Michael Klinghoffer
5 Yosef Klinghoffer
5 Batya Klinghoffer
4 Leon Klinghoffer
5 Tamar Klinghoffer
4 Bathia Klinghoffer
+? Blum
3 David Klinghoffer
+? Landau
3 Leib Leon Klinghoffer
4 Rosa Klinghoffer
4 David Klinghoffer
2 Abraham Luft b: 1861
+Taube Hirsch b: 1861 in Kolomyja
3 Yula Eva Luft b: 1882 in Kolomyja
+Yoel Hersas
4 Anna Hersas
+Otto Weiss

```
        5 Josephine Antoinette Weiss
          +Steven Guss
              6 July Guss b: 16 Dec 1968
              6 Jennifer Guss b: 13 May 1970
        5 Suzanne Weiss
          +Phil Schneider
              6 Laura Schneider
              6 Craig Schneider
    3 Naftali Herz Luft b: 1893 in Szczerzec
      +Erna Wallach
        4 Yoram Luft
          +Nily Kanarer
            5 Gal Luft
            5 Tal Luft
            5 Hai Luft
        4 Nurit Luft
          +Chaim Cohen
    3 Norbert Luft
    3 Eisig Hersch Luft b: 1879 in Kolomyja
```

^A**Zwi Yosef Luft** was the great-grandson of the famous *zaddik* and author, Rabbi Zwi Ashkenazi (b: 1658 in Moravia; d: 1718 in Lemberg) who was known as the "Chacham Zwi Torah Zahav," after his book of Torah commentaries. Both his father, Jacob Sak, a famous scholar and his maternal grandfather, Ephraim ben Jacob haCohen, escaped from Vilna to Moravia during the Cossack uprising of 1655. He studied with his father and grandfather in Moravia before being sent (in 1676) to the Yeshiva of Elijah Covo in Salonika to learn the Sephardic method of scholarly study. Here, he adopted Sephardi customs and the name "Ashkenazi." He also was given the title of Haham, the Sephardi title of Rabbi. He returned to Ofen (later Buda as in Budapest) in 1680 and continued his studies. His wife and daughter were killed during the siege of Ofen by the Imperial Army of Leopold I (the Holy Roman Emperor) and Zwi Ashkenazi fled to Sarajevo where he became the Haham of the Sephardi community. His parents were imprisoned by a Brandnburg regiment during the siege and were ransomed by the Jews of Berlin. He went to Berlin in 1689 via Venice and Prague and married the daughter of Meshullam Zalman Neumark-Mirels, the *av bet din* of the "Three Communities" of Hamburg, Altona, and Wandsbeck. He moved to Altona and, for the next 18 years, he taught in the *Klaus* founded for him by members of the community. On the death of his father-in-law in 1707, he was appointed Rabbi of Hamburg and Wandsbeck. He resigned his position in 1709 over a violent controversy about a chicken said to have had no heart, which he ruled as being kasher. In 1710 he was invited to serve the Ashkenazi community of Amsterdam. Relations with the local Portuguese community deteriorated and

became embittered when Ashkenazi ruled to excommunicate Nehemiah Hayon, an emissary of Shabbetai Zwi (the false messiah who eventually converted to Islam) and led to Ashkenazi's resignation in 1714. After brief stays in London, Opatow (Poland), and Hamburg, he was appointed as Chief Rabbi in Lemberg in 1718 where he died after a few months. He was considered by his contemporaries to be a true scholar, fiercely independent, opposed to the pilpul method of study, and vigorously against the movement of Shabetai Zwi. He was a linguist and learned in general as well as religious subjects. His sons included Jacob Emden, Abraham Meshullam Zalman (*Av Beth Din* of Ostrog), and Zewi Hirsh.[162]

Zwi Yosef Luft was said to have bought an estate in 1848, named "Hrusno" in which he raised his family.

---

[162] Information gleaned from Encyclopedia Judaica and the Jewish Encyclopedia.

CPSIA information can be obtained at www.ICGtesting.com
Printed in the USA
LVOW091054100413

328519LV00006B/12/P